CAMBRIDGE

UNLOCK

BASIC SKILLS

Sabina Ostrowska

CAMBRIDGE
UNIVERSITY PRESS

Shaftesbury Road, Cambridge CB2 8EA, United Kingdom

One Liberty Plaza, 20th Floor, New York, NY 10006, USA

477 Williamstown Road, Port Melbourne, VIC 3207, Australia

314–321, 3rd Floor, Plot 3, Splendor Forum, Jasola District Centre, New Delhi – 110025, India

103 Penang Road, #05–06/07, Visioncrest Commercial, Singapore 238467

Cambridge University Press & Assessment is a department of the University of Cambridge.

We share the University's mission to contribute to society through the pursuit of education, learning and research at the highest international levels of excellence.

www.cambridge.org
Information on this title: www.cambridge.org/9781316636459

First published 2017

20 19 18 17 16 15 14 13 12 11 10 9 8 7 6 5 4 3 2

Printed in Italy by Rotolito S.p.A.

A catalogue record for this publication is available from the British Library

ISBN 978-1-316-63645-9 Unlock Basic Skills Student's Book with Downloadable Audio and Video
ISBN 978-1-316-63646-6 Unlock Basic Literacy Student's Book with Downloadable Audio
ISBN 978-1-316-63648-0 Unlock Basic Skills Teacher's Book with Downloadable Audio and Video
ISBN 978-1-316-63649-7 Unlock Basic Literacy Teacher's Book with Downloadable Audio

CONTENTS

MAP OF THE BOOK

UNIT	LISTENING	SPEAKING	READING	WRITING
STARTER	Greetings, numbers, the alphabet, classroom instructions, consonant sounds and vowel sounds, singular and plural nouns, day and time			
1 MEETING PEOPLE Communication studies Listening and reading: 1 Introductions 2 ID cards 3 Personal details	*Key listening skill*: Listening for key information Listening for detail Listening for main ideas	*Language focus*: Study objects (e.g. *book, library card, pen*) *Speaking task*: Ask and answer personal questions.	*Key reading skill*: Reading for general understanding Reading for detail Scanning for key information Reading for main ideas	*Writing task type*: Complete descriptive sentences. *Writing task*: Write about your partner. *ACADEMIC WRITING SKILLS*: Punctuation: capital letters and full stops Vowels
2 PEOPLE AND THINGS Sociology Listening and reading: 1 Family 2 Relationships 3 My things	*Key listening skill*: Listening for detail Listening for key information	*Language focus*: Numbers 11–100 *Speaking task*: Ask and answer questions about people and things.	*Key reading skill*: Reading for detail Reading for key information Reading for numbers	*Writing task type*: Complete sentences with *and*. *Writing task*: Write about your family. *ACADEMIC WRITING SKILLS*: Sentences with *and* Spelling
3 UNIVERSITY LIFE Cultural studies Listening and reading: 1 University subjects 2 When and where 3 What's it like?	*Key listening skill*: Listening for key information Listening for detail Listening for main ideas	*Language focus*: Time *Speaking task*: Ask and answer questions about university classes and time.	*Key reading skill*: Reading for key information Reading for main ideas Scanning for key information	*Writing task type*: Complete sentences with time. *Writing task*: Write about your timetable. *ACADEMIC WRITING SKILLS*: Punctuation: capital letters and commas Using *and* to link sentences Spelling
4 DIFFERENT COUNTRIES Urban geography Listening and reading: 1 What's your country like? 2 Where is it from? 3 Describing cities	*Key listening skill*: Listening for key information	*Language focus*: *Wh-* questions *Speaking task*: Ask and answer questions about your country or a city.	*Key reading skill*: Reading for key information Reading for detail Scanning for key information	*Writing task type*: Complete sentences with *and*. *Writing task*: Write about a country. *ACADEMIC WRITING SKILLS*: Punctuation: capital letters Spelling Using pronouns to link sentences
5 WORK Careers guidance Listening and reading: 1 Is she a nurse? 2 My day 3 He works in the city.	*Key listening skill*: Listening for detail Listening for key information	*Language focus*: Months *Speaking task*: Ask and answer questions about jobs.	*Key reading skill*: Reading for key information Reading for main ideas Reading for detail	*Writing task type*: Complete descriptive sentences. *Writing task*: Write about your studies. *ACADEMIC WRITING SKILLS*: Punctuation: capital letters, full stops and question marks Spelling Using *and* to link sentences

VIDEO	LANGUAGE	PRONUNCIATION	INTRODUCTION TO CRITICAL THINKING
A video about people and countries ***More vocabulary***: City names	***Vocabulary***: ID (e.g. *email address, phone number*) Countries (e.g. *Saudi Arabia, Mexico*) ***Grammar***: Possessive adjectives The verb *be*	***Sound and spelling***: *e* ***Pronunciation for listening***: Word stress ***Pronunciation for speaking***: Main stress	***Understand and apply***: Complete an application form.
A video about families and things ***More vocabulary***: Family	***Vocabulary***: Family (e.g. *grandfather, grandmother*) My things (e.g. *car, computer*) ***Grammar***: The verb *be*: *we* and *they* *our* and *their*	***Sound and spelling***: *th* ***Pronunciation for listening***: Word stress ***Pronunciation for speaking***: Main stress	***Understand, remember and create***: Complete fact files.
A video about students and objects ***More vocabulary***: What floor is it on?	***Vocabulary***: Subjects (e.g. *Maths, Chemistry*) Days of the week (e.g. *Sunday, Monday*) Adjectives (e.g. *boring, interesting*) ***Grammar***: *When/where* and *in/on* The verb *be*: *it*	***Sound and spelling***: *sh, ch, s* ***Pronunciation for listening and speaking***: Main stress	***Understand, evaluate and analyze***: Complete a timetable.
A video about old and new places ***More vocabulary***: Places	***Vocabulary***: Describing countries (e.g. *big, small*) Describing cities (e.g. *new, old*) ***Grammar***: The verb *be*: negative The verb *be*: questions	***Sound and spelling***: *w, v* ***Pronunciation for listening***: Sentence stress ***Pronunciation for speaking***: Corrective intonation stress Target language Word stress	***Understand, create and remember***: Complete fact files.
A video about jobs and holidays ***More vocabulary***: Jobs	***Vocabulary***: Jobs (e.g. *police officer, pilot*) My day (e.g. *go to work, go to university*) Work (e.g. *take photographs, read emails*) ***Grammar***: Present simple affirmative Present simple affirmative: *he* and *she*	***Sound and spelling***: *ph, f, o* Vowels with two letters ***Pronunciation for speaking***: Word stress Target language	***Remember, analyze, understand and create***: Complete mind-maps.

6 FOOD AND HEALTH Food and health studies Listening and reading: 1 I eat bread and cheese. 2 My daily routine 3 Healthy people	*Key listening skill*: Listening for detail Listening for key information	*Language focus*: Feelings ***Speaking task***: Talk about what you eat.	*Key reading skill*: Reading for detail Scanning for key information	*Writing task type*: Complete affirmative and negative sentences. *Writing task*: Write about what you eat. *ACADEMIC WRITING SKILLS*: Spelling
7 PLACES Tourism geography Listening and reading: 1 I live near a train station. 2 There are two universities. 3 It's a beautiful city.	*Key listening skill*: Listening for key information Listening for detail	*Language focus*: Location ***Speaking task***: Give a short presentation about an interesting place in your city.	*Key reading skill*: Reading for detail Scanning for key information	*Writing task type*: Complete descriptive sentences with *There is* and *There are*. *Writing task*: Write about places at a university. *ACADEMIC WRITING SKILLS*: Spelling
8 SPENDING Economics Listening and reading: 1 How many tablets do you have? 2 What's on your shopping list? 3 How often do you buy new clothes?	*Key listening skill*: Listening for general understanding Listening for detail Listening for key information Listening for main ideas	*Language focus*: Money ***Speaking task***: Talk about things you have and buy.	*Key reading skill*: Reading for general understanding Reading for detail Reading for key information	*Writing task type*: Complete and write descriptive sentences. *Writing task*: Write about how you spend your money. *ACADEMIC WRITING SKILLS*: Word order Spelling
9 TECHNOLOGY Information technology Listening and reading: 1 I usually learn English online. 2 It can go online. 3 There are 2 million new website names every month.	*Key listening skill*: Listening for main ideas Listening for key information Listening for detail	*Language focus*: Asking for and giving opinions ***Speaking task***: Talk about things and what they can and can't do.	*Key reading skill*: Reading for detail Scanning for key information Reading for main ideas	*Writing task type*: Complete and write sentences with *can* and *can't*. *Writing task*: Write about what you can and can't do in English. *ACADEMIC WRITING SKILLS*: Punctuation: capital letters Spelling Using *and* and *but* to link sentences
10 FREE TIME AND FASHION Fashion studies 1 What do you do in your free time? 2 I like going shopping. 3 These are trousers from Thailand.	*Key listening skill*: Listening for detail Listening for main ideas Listening for key information	*Language focus*: Colours ***Speaking task***: Ask and answer questions about free time, clothes and colours.	*Key reading skill*: Reading for key information Reading for detail	*Writing task type*: Complete and write sentences with *-ing*. *Writing task*: Write an email about a student club. *ACADEMIC WRITING SKILLS*: Sentences with prepositions Spelling

	A video about food and drink ***More vocabulary*:** Food	***Vocabulary*:** Food (e.g. *bread, cheese*) Daily routine (e.g. *get up, go to bed*) Health (e.g. *get up early, go to bed late*) ***Grammar*:** *don't* and *doesn't* *A lot of, some, not a lot of*	***Sound and spelling*: *ea*** ***Pronunciation for listening*:** Sentence stress Target language ***Pronunciation for speaking*:** Sentence stress	***Understand, apply and create*:** Completing a survey and a food pyramid.
	A video about places in a city ***More vocabulary*:** Places	***Vocabulary*:** Places in a city 1 (e.g. *hospital, beach*) Places in a city 2 (e.g. *restaurant, factory*) Famous places (e.g. *old street, interesting market*) ***Grammar*:** *There is / There are* Adjectives	***Sound and spelling*: *r*** ***Pronunciation for listening*:** Sentence stress ***Pronunciation for speaking*:** Target language	***Remember, apply, analyze and evaluate*:** Working with a map.
	A video about money and things people buy ***More vocabulary*:** Food	***Vocabulary*:** Things we buy (e.g. *smartphone, video game*) Calendar time (e.g. *a day, a week*) Shopping (e.g. *go shopping, buy clothes*) ***Grammar*:** Frequency expressions Present simple questions	***Sound and spelling*: *a, th, o, w*** ***Pronunciation for listening*:** Target language ***Pronunciation for speaking*:** Sentence stress	***Understand and apply*:** Working with a graph.
	A video about technology and what it can do ***More vocabulary*:** Technology	***Vocabulary*:** Computers and the internet (e.g. *blog, app*) Things we use (e.g. *smartwatch, fridge*) People (e.g. *person, people*) ***Grammar*:** *Can* and *can't* (for possibility) Frequency expressions 2	***Sound and spelling*: *p, b*** ***Pronunciation for listening*:** Sentence stress ***Pronunciation for speaking*:** Target language Main stress	***Understand and analyze*:** Working with a questionnaire.
	A video about free time and clothes ***More vocabulary*:** Food and clothes	***Vocabulary*:** Free time 1 (e.g. *go for a walk, bake cakes*) Free time review (e.g. *go shopping, watch TV*) Clothes (e.g. *coat, jacket*) ***Grammar*:** Order of adjectives *Like + -ing* *This is / These are* Possessive *'s*	***Sound and spelling*: *o, a, i, -ing, s, sh*** ***Pronunciation for listening*:** Main stress ***Pronunciation for speaking*:** Sentence stress	***Understand and create*:** Taking notes.

UNLOCK BASIC SKILLS UNIT STRUCTURE

The units in *Unlock Basic Skills* are carefully scaffolded so that students build the skills and language they need throughout the unit in order to produce a successful Speaking and Writing task.

UNLOCK YOUR KNOWLEDGE	Introduces Learning Objectives for the unit and encourages discussion around the theme of the unit with inspiration from striking visuals.
LISTENING AND READING 1 LISTENING AND READING 2 LISTENING AND READING 3	Provides information about the topic, introduces new vocabulary and grammar in context and practises listening and reading skills. Where relevant, this section also includes a focus on sound and spelling or a pronunciation feature which will further enhance listening and speaking comprehension.
WATCH AND REMEMBER	Features engaging and motivating video which generates interest in the topic, recycles the language taught in Listening and Reading 1–3 and extends vocabulary.
LANGUAGE FOCUS	Practises the vocabulary and grammar from Listening and Reading 1–3, focuses on functional language for speaking and pre-teaches the vocabulary and grammar needed for the final Speaking and Writing tasks.
ACADEMIC LISTENING AND SPEAKING	Features an academic listening text that practises listening skills and acts as a model for the final interactional speaking task that uses the skills and language learnt over the course of the unit. It includes a Critical Thinking section that prepares students for speaking.
ACADEMIC READING AND WRITING	Features an academic reading text, practises reading skills and acts as a model for the final writing task that uses the skills and language learnt over the course of the unit. It includes Academic Writing Skills and a Critical Thinking section that prepares students for writing.
OBJECTIVES REVIEW	Allows learners to assess how well they have mastered the skills covered in the unit.
WORDLIST	Includes the key vocabulary from the unit.

These lessons give learners the opportunity to use all the language and skills they have learnt in the unit. Students practise the unit's main learning objectives.

UNLOCK RESEARCH

Expert research ensures the course meets your pre-A1 student's academic and language needs.

BLOOM'S TAXONOMY

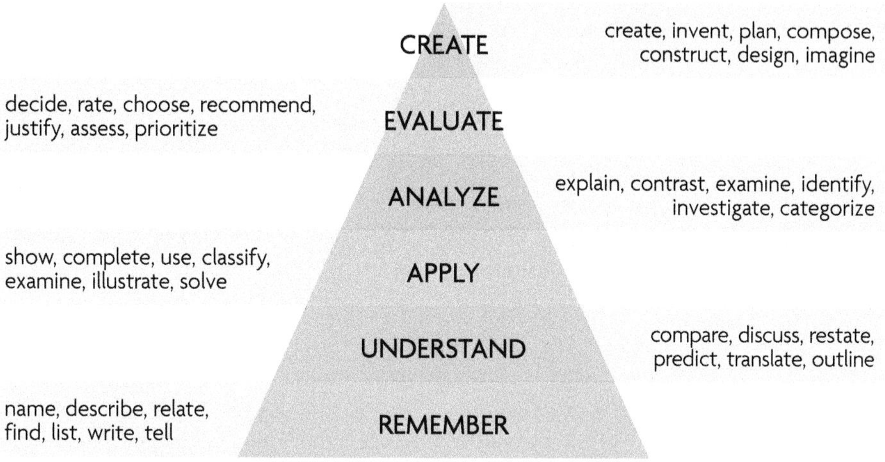

- **CREATE** – create, invent, plan, compose, construct, design, imagine
- **EVALUATE** – decide, rate, choose, recommend, justify, assess, prioritize
- **ANALYZE** – explain, contrast, examine, identify, investigate, categorize
- **APPLY** – show, complete, use, classify, examine, illustrate, solve
- **UNDERSTAND** – compare, discuss, restate, predict, translate, outline
- **REMEMBER** – name, describe, relate, find, list, write, tell

CRITICAL THINKING

The critical thinking exercises in *Unlock Basic Skills* are informed by Benjamin Bloom's research into the classification of learning objectives, **Bloom's Taxonomy**. These introduce students to **lower-** and **higher-order thinking skills**, and **prepare them for academic study**. The margin headings highlight the exercises which develop Bloom's concepts.

THE CAMBRIDGE CORPUS

Unique research using the **Cambridge English Corpus, the Cambridge Learner Corpus and English Profile** has been carried out to ensure the language provided is the right level and relevant to learners' studies. Our exclusive insights into official Cambridge English exam papers enable us to identify the most common errors that learners make and provide focussed practice material to give them support where they need it most. In addition, we know what academic language students use and need, and this has been integrated into the *Unlock Basic* syllabus.

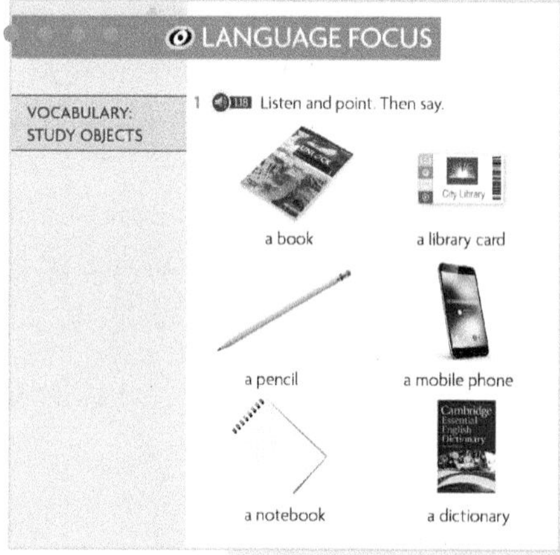

LANGUAGE FOCUS

VOCABULARY: STUDY OBJECTS

1 Listen and point. Then say.

a book · a library card · a pencil · a mobile phone · a notebook · a dictionary

UNLOCK BASIC ADVISORY PANEL

Unlock Basic has been developed in collaboration with the *Unlock Basic* Advisory Panel, expert teachers experienced in teaching pre-A1 level EAP students, so we can be sure the course meets your students' needs.

UNLOCK SKILLS

Listening, Speaking, Reading and Writing skills are integrated within academic contexts to provide students with an effective and manageable learning experience.

> *The small bite-sized sections make it easy for the learner to build step-by-step competence in the language.*
>
> Dr Wafa Aws, Dar Al-Uloom University, Saudi Arabia

READING FOR GENERAL UNDERSTANDING
2 1.1 Read and listen. Then say.
What's your name?
I'm Murat.
How do you spell that?
M – u – r – a – t

COMBINED SKILLS PRACTICE

Combined skills practice to support students as they learn the correspondence between the spoken and written forms of English.

UNLOCK CRITICAL THINKING

An introduction to critical thinking supports students as they take their first steps towards academic success.

CRITICAL THINKING: CREATE

6 Write about a country.

Country: ______________ –
______________, not ______________
City: ______________ –
______________, ______________, not ______________
Place: ______________ –
______________, ______________, not ______________

LEARN TO THINK

Learners engage in **critical thinking activities** that are designed to ensure they do all of the thinking and information-gathering required to prepare them for the speaking and writing task.

UNLOCK VIDEO

Watch and remember lessons in every unit include video and motivate students to recycle and extend the language they've learned.

UNLOCK BASIC

COURSE COMPONENTS

- *Unlock Basic* consists of two Student's Books: *Unlock Basic Skills & Unlock Basic Literacy* and an accompanying Teacher's Book for each.
- Complete course audio and video are available to download from esource.cambridge.org using the activation codes inside the front cover of the Student's book.
- The *Unlock* Teacher's Books contain step-by-step lesson plans, additional activities, common student errors and teaching tips.
- Unit Review Tests, mid-level and end-of-level tests are available to download from esource.cambridge.org using the activation codes inside the front cover of the Teacher's Books.
- *Presentation Plus* software for interactive whiteboards is available for both Student's Books.

LISTENING AND SPEAKING
LEVELS 1–4

READING AND WRITING
LEVELS 1–4

STARTER UNIT THE BASICS

GREETINGS

1 0.1 Listen and read.

Hello.
Hi.
I'm Manal.
I'm Lucy. Nice to meet you.
Nice to meet you, too.
Bye.
Goodbye.
NOTICE
I
you

2 Say.

Hello.	Hi.
I'm ...	I'm ...
Nice to meet you.	Nice to meet you, too.
Bye.	Goodbye.

NUMBERS

3 0.2 Listen. Then say.

0	1	2	3	4	5	6	7	8	9	10
zero	one	two	three	four	five	six	seven	eight	nine	ten

4 0.3 Listen and circle.

3 5 | 2 7 | 8 9
0 8 | 0 10 | 2 5
1 4 | 6 7

5 Say.

●●●●●	●	●●●	●●●●●●	●●●●●●●●●	●●●●	●●●●●●●●●●	●●●●●●●●●	●●		●●●●●●●
five	one	three	six	nine	four	ten	nine	two	zero	seven

THE ALPHABET

6 0.4 Listen. Then say.

→ a b c d e f g
→ h i j k l m n o p
→ q r s t u v w x y z

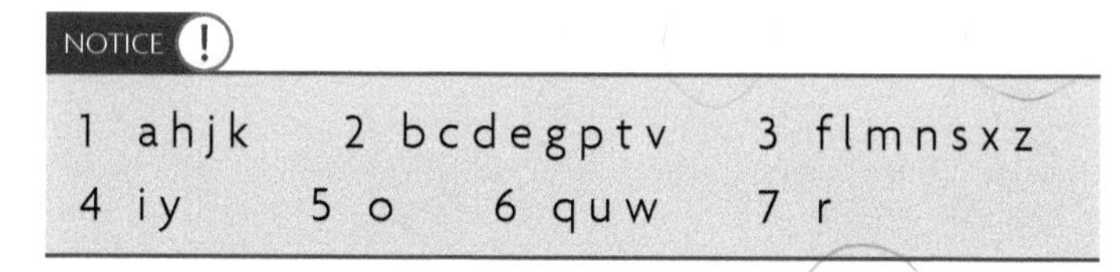

NOTICE !

1 ahjk 2 bcdegptv 3 flmnsxz
4 iy 5 o 6 quw 7 r

7 0.5 Listen and circle. Then say.

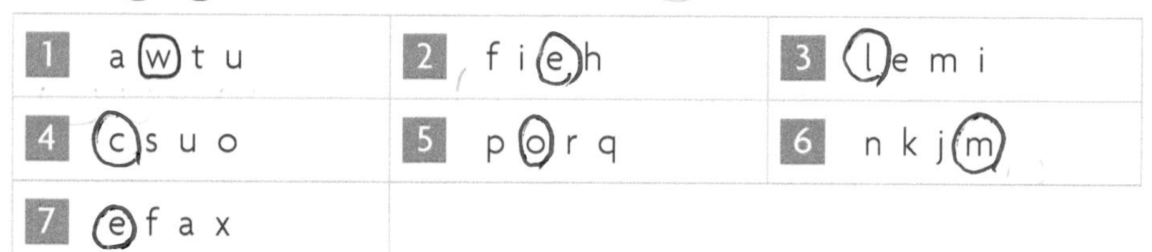

1 a w t u	2 f i e h	3 l e m i
4 c s u o	5 p o r q	6 n k j m
7 e f a x		

CLASSROOM INSTRUCTIONS

8 0.6 Listen. Then say.

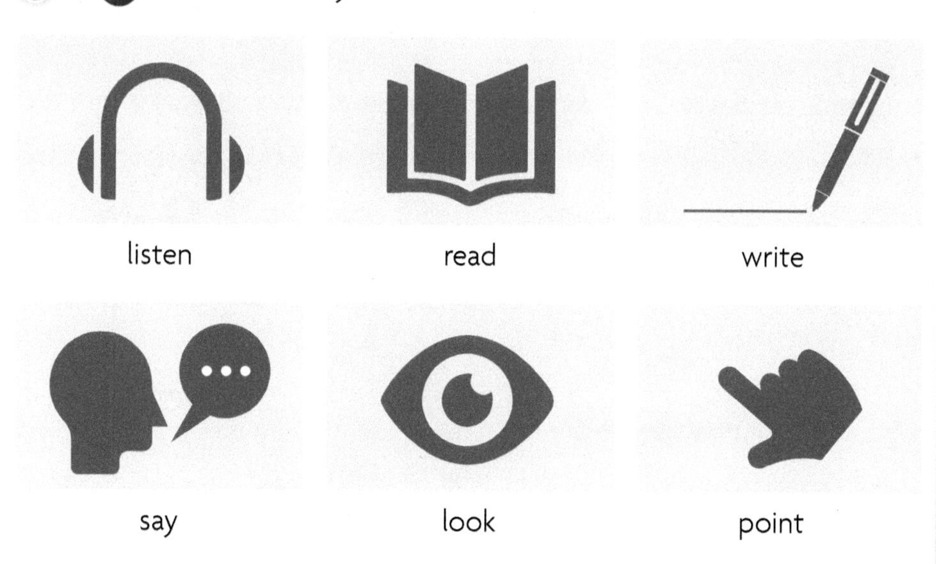

listen read write

say look point

THE ALPHABET

9 0.7 Listen and read. Match. Then say.

1 Read and listen. [b]
2 Point and say. [c]
3 Look and write. [b]

a

b

c

10 0.8 Listen and point. Then say.

→ Aa Bb Cc Dd
→ Ee Ff Gg
→ Hh Ii Jj Kk
→ Ll Mm Nn Oo Pp
→ Qq Rr Ss
→ Tt Uu Vv
→ Ww Xx Yy Zz

11 0.9 Listen and circle. Say.

1 A H B P K D
2 B R C U E Z
3 F O M P Z N
4 E P Y T V I
5 Z Q U W F M

12 0.10 Listen and say.

1 VIP

2 USB

3 OK

4 VW

5 HDMI

6 MBA

7 PC

NUMBERS

13 0.11 Listen and say.

1	2	3	4	5
one	two	three	four	five
6	7	8	9	10
six	seven	eight	nine	ten
11	12	13	14	15
eleven	twelve	thirteen	fourteen	fifteen
16	17	18	19	20
sixteen	seventeen	eighteen	nineteen	twenty

14 0.12 Listen and circle.

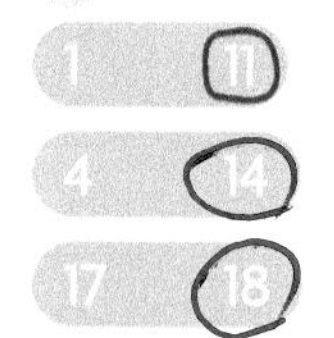

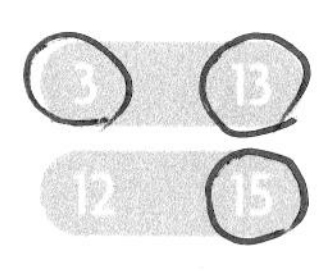

15 0.13 Listen and read. Then say.

8
He is eight.

18
He is eighteen.

4
She is four.

14
She is fourteen.

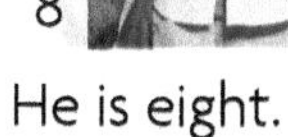

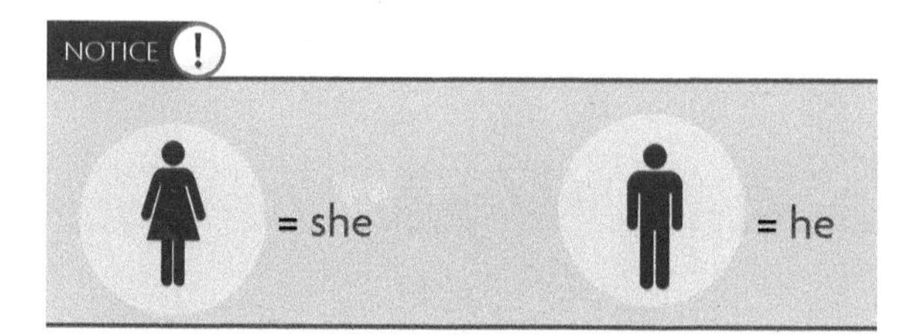

16 0.14 Listen. Then say.

He is sixleen 2- sheis ninhteen

SOUND AND SPELLING: CONSONANT SOUNDS

17 0.15 Listen. Then say.

bus | coffee | doctor | four
gas | hello | jeans | karate
lemon | message | nine | palm
queen | radio | salad | ten
video | Wi-Fi | taxi
yacht | zero

18 0.16 Listen and point in 17.

19 0.17 Listen and (circle). Then write.

1 _v_ ideo f (v) w	2 ___ us b d p	3 ___ alad c s z
4 ___ eans g l j	5 ___ octor d g p	6 ___ emon i k l
7 ___ as g j k	8 ___ essage l m n	

SINGULAR AND PLURAL NOUNS

20 0.18 Listen and read.

a doctor

two doctors

a salad

three salads

a coffee

four coffees

a lemon

ten lemons

21 Read and circle.

1  two *taxis* / *taxi*

2  *a coffee* / *coffees*

3  a *yacht* / *yachts*

4  three *doctor* / *doctors*

> NOTICE !
>
> a salad = one salad

22 0.19 Listen and read.

23 0.20 Look and listen. Then say.

1 

2 

> REMEMBER !
>
> Please. Thank you. I'm sorry.

24 0.21 Listen and read. Then say.

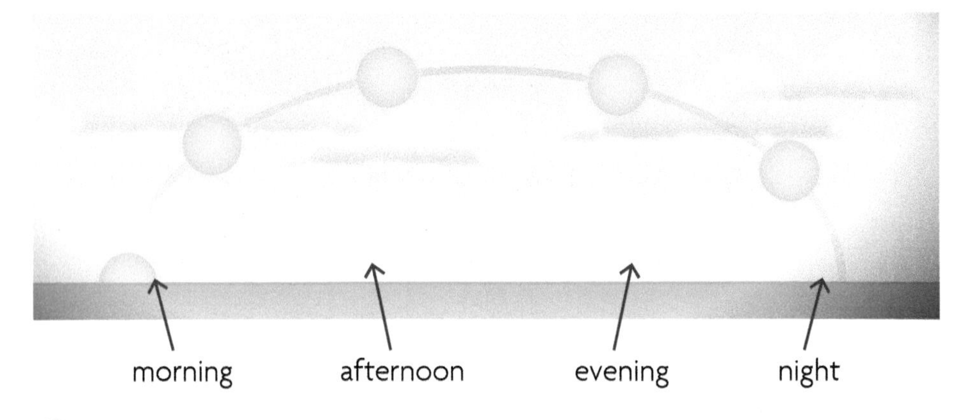

25 0.22 Listen and read. Then say.

26 Look. Then say.

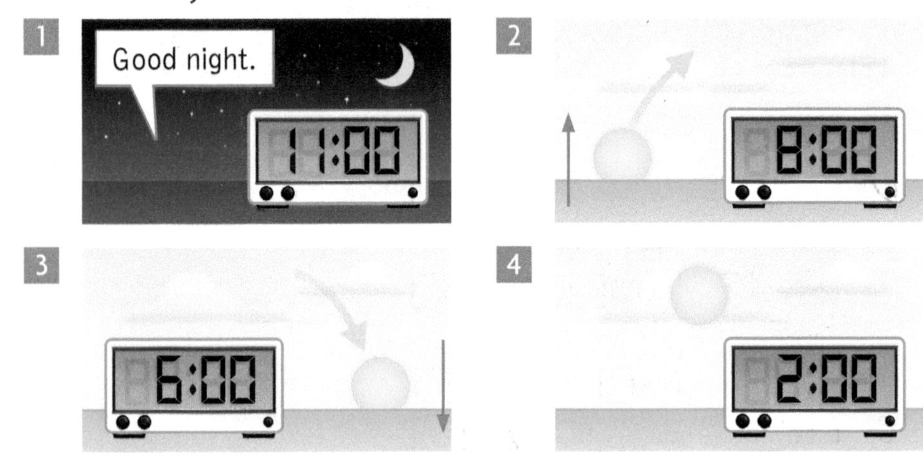

SOUND AND SPELLING: VOWEL SOUNDS

27 0.23 Look. Listen and say.

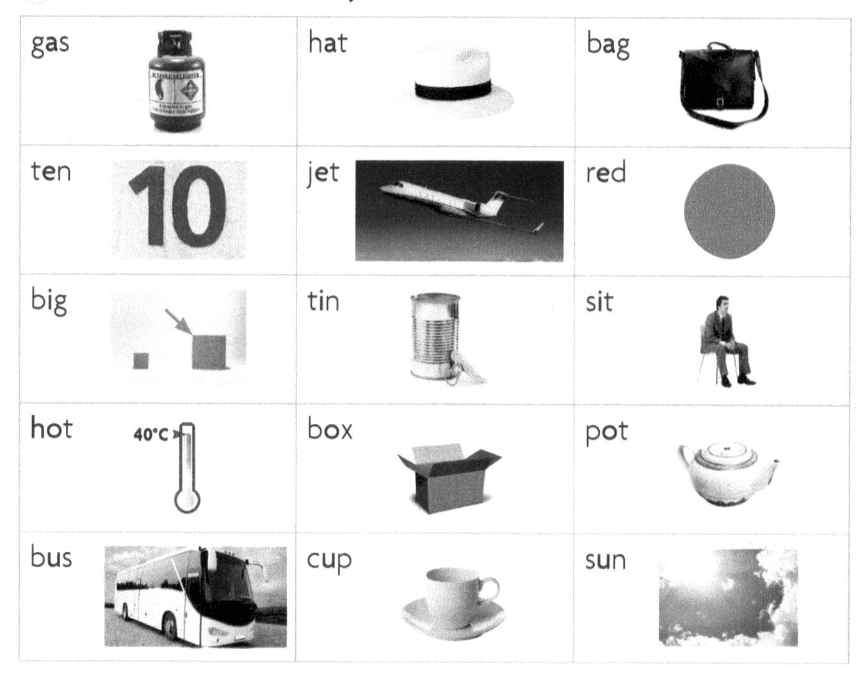

gas	hat	bag
ten	jet	red
big	tin	sit
hot	box	pot
bus	cup	sun

28 0.24 Listen and (circle).

1	hat	(hot)	hut	2	tan	ten	tin
3	big	bag	bug	4	cap	cop	cup
5	red	rid	rod	6	pet	pit	pot

29 Look, read and write. Say.

1 b _u_ s 2 t __ xi 3 d __ ctor 4 c __ ffee

5 s __ lad 6 l __ mon 7 v __ deo 8 m __ ssage

30 0.25 Listen and write ✔ or ✗. Then listen again and check.

1 hat ✔ taxi ✔ radio ✗
2 coffee ☐ hello ☐ doctor ☐
3 you ☐ bus ☐ sun ☐
4 seven ☐ ten ☐ evening ☐
5 nine ☐ video ☐ big ☐

LEARNING OBJECTIVES

Listening	Names, phone numbers and email addresses Spelling
Speaking	Ask for study objects you need Talk about names, phone numbers and email addresses
Reading	An email Names, phone numbers and email addresses
Writing	Write a list of study objects you need Write your name, phone number and email address
Watch and remember	A video about people and countries

MEETING PEOPLE UNIT 1

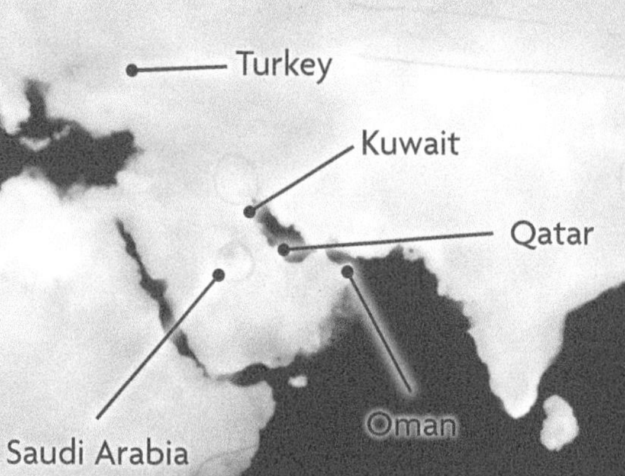

UNLOCK YOUR KNOWLEDGE

1 Look. Where is your country?

2 What's the name of your country in English?

LISTENING AND READING 1

PREPARING TO READ

1 Match. Then say.

N	u
T	t
U	y
Y	n

READING FOR GENERAL UNDERSTANDING

2 🔊 1.1 Read and listen. Then say.

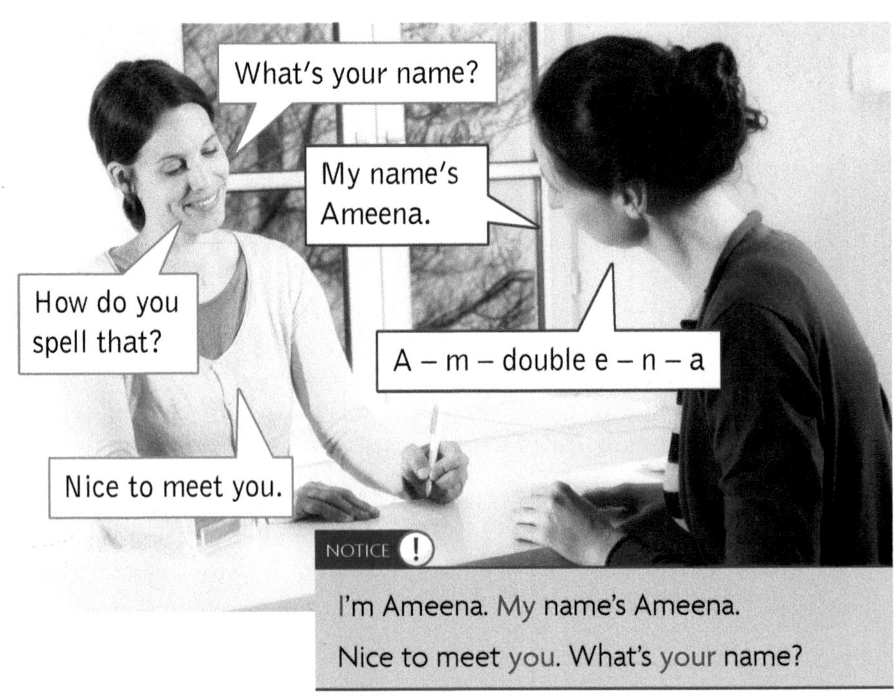

NOTICE !

I'm Ameena. My name's Ameena.

Nice to meet you. What's your name?

ACADEMIC WRITING SKILLS

3 Underline the CAPITAL letters.

NAME	NAME	NAME	NAME
Murat	Ameena	Sultan	Rosa
	Pedro	Karem	

LISTENING FOR KEY INFORMATION

4 1.2 Listen and write. Then say.

NAME

K h a l i f a

NAME

__ a __ i __ m

NAME

__ __ f a __ l

NAME

Y __ s e __ i __

NOTICE !

Ameena = A – m – double e – n – a

SOUND AND SPELLING: *e*

5 1.3 Listen and say.

hello spell meet English

SPEAKING AND WRITING

6 Ask and answer. Listen and write.

NAME	NAME	NAME
____________	____________	____________

REMEMBER !

Hi! / Hello!
What's your name?
My name's ... / I'm ...
How do you spell that?
Nice to meet you.

LISTENING AND READING 2

VOCABULARY: ID

1 1.4 Read and listen. Then match.

Me: **Leyla Atalay**
My email: **leyla97@mail.edu**
My phone number: **0774 566 212**

Jenny
online

Name: **Jenny Baker**
Email: **bakerjenny@mymail.co.uk**
Phone: **0774 902 154**

Sultan
online

Name: **Sultan Al Zayani**
Email: **s.zayani@mymail.com**
Phone: **0714 332 503**

	phone number	s.zayani@mymail.com
1 (name icon)	name	Jenny Baker
2 (email icon)	email address	0774 566 212
3 (phone icon)		

NOTICE !

0774 = double 7   0774 = oh, zero

LISTENING FOR DETAIL

2 1.5 Listen and underline. Then say.

What's your phone number?   My number is ...

1	Leyla	0774 566 212	0774 902 154
2	Jenny	0714 332 503	0774 902 154
3	Sultan	0774 566 212	0714 332 503

READING FOR DETAIL

3 Look at 1. Read. Then circle *Yes* or *No*.

1	My name is Leyla. My phone number is 0774 566 212.	Yes	No
2	Her name is Jenny Atalay.	Yes	No
3	His email address is zayani@mymail.com.	Yes	No
4	His phone number is 0714 332 503.		

GRAMMAR: POSSESSIVE ADJECTIVES

4 1.6 Listen and read. Then write.

His	name is	Sultan.
Her		Jenny.
My		________.

His name is Sultan.

Her name is Jenny.

5 1.7 Listen and circle. Then write.

1 His (His / Her) name is Utku.

2 ________ (His / Her) phone number is 0763 456 299.

3 ________ (His / Her) email address is u98@mymail.co.uk.

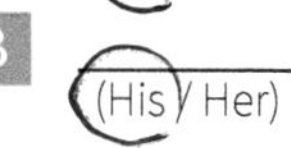

4 ________ (His / Her) name is Sakura.

5 ________ (His / Her) phone number is 0544 343 009.

6 ________ (His / Her) email address is sakura.k@mail.jp.

ACADEMIC WRITING SKILLS

6 Circle . and then underline the CAPITAL letters.

1 My name is Sara. My phone number is 0889 543 010.

2 His name is Mike. His phone number is 0782 822 513.

3 Her name is Aseel. Her email address is aseel.w@mymail.co.uk.

WRITING

7 Write. Read and check.

My name is Shirzad.
My phone number is 07787085711
My email address is shirzad@ali Mli.

SPEAKING AND WRITING

8 Ask and write. Then say.

Your partner:
His name is sarkat.
His phone number is 07712372231

Your partner:
Her name is AAAa.
Her phone number is 07977987198

REMEMBER !

What's your name?
What's your phone number?
His / Her name is ...
His / Her phone number is ...

LISTENING AND READING 3

VOCABULARY: COUNTRIES

1 1.8 Listen and point. Then say.

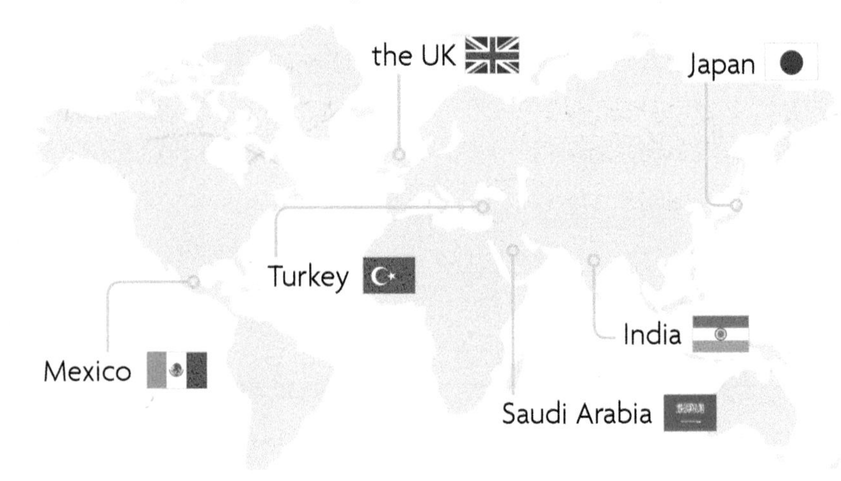

PRONUNCIATION FOR LISTENING

2 1.9 Listen and say.

Turkey Japan the UK Mexico India Saudi Arabia

ACADEMIC WRITING SKILLS

3 Write the CAPITAL letters.

I ndia S audi A rabia M exico
the U K J apan T urkey

NOTICE !

Mexico Japan Turkey

LISTENING FOR KEY INFORMATION

4 1.10 Listen. Circle the country.

Where are you from?

1

I'm from
Turkey / Mexico.

2

I'm from
Saudi Arabia / India.

3

I'm from
Mexico / Japan.

4

I'm from
Turkey / Saudi Arabia.

5

I'm from
the UK / Japan.

6

I'm from
Saudi Arabia / Turkey.

SPEAKING

5 Ask and answer.

Where are you from?

I'm from ...

6 1.11 Read and listen. Then say.

He is a **student.**

She is a **teacher.**

7 1.12 Read and circle. Then listen and check.

UNIVERSITY OF CAMBRIDGE

STUDENT ID CARD

First name: **Saeed**
Family name: **Al Shahrani**
Country: **Saudi Arabia**

UNIVERSITY OF CAMBRIDGE

TEACHER ID CARD

First name: **Emma**
Family name: **Jackson**
Country: **UK**

1 Saeed is a *teacher / student*.

2 His first name is *Saeed / Al Shahrani*.

3 He is from *the UK / Saudi Arabia*.

4 Emma is a *teacher / student*.

5 Her family name is *Jackson / Emma*.

6 She is from *the UK / Saudi Arabia*.

8 1.13 Listen and read.

	be	
I	**am**	a student.
He She	**is**	from Japan. a teacher.

NOTICE !

I'm a student.	=	I am a student.
She's a teacher.	=	She is a teacher.
He's from Japan.	=	He is from Japan.

9 1.14 Listen and circle. Then write.

1 I ________ a student. (am / is)

2 She ________ from Turkey. (am / is)

3 He ________ a teacher. (am / is)

4 I ________ from India. (am / is)

10 Write.

You

I ________ a ________.
I ________ from ________

11 Look at **10** and say. Then listen and write.

Your partner

________ ________ a ________________.
________ ________ from ________________.

WATCH AND REMEMBER

PART 1

BEFORE YOU WATCH

1 Look and match.

a ____________

b ____________

c ____________

1 the UK — a
2 Mexico — b
3 Saudi Arabia — c

2 1.15 Look at 1. Listen and check. Then write the country.

WATCH

3 Watch part 1 and circle.

1 Saif is *a teacher* / *a student*.
2 Carlos is *a teacher* / *a student*.
3 Elaine is *a teacher* / *a student*.

4 Match.

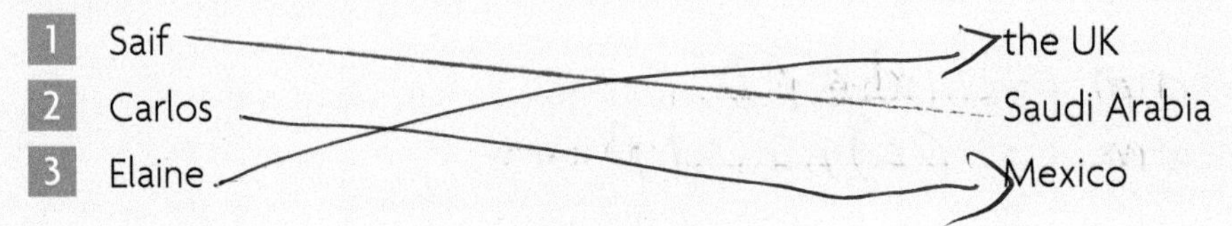

1 Saif — the UK
2 Carlos — Saudi Arabia
3 Elaine — Mexico

AFTER YOU WATCH

5 Read and write.

meet name's from

Saif: My ____________ Saif.
Carlos: I'm ____________ Mexico City.
Elaine: Nice to ____________ you.

PART 2

6 1.16 Look. Write. Then listen and check.

UNIVERSITY LIBRARY
STUDENT LIBRARY CARD

First ______ :
______ **name:**
Phone ______ :
Email address:

7 Watch part 2. Read and circle.

1 Demir is his *first name / family name*.
2 Topuz is his *first name / family name*.

8 1.17 Read and circle. Listen and check. Then write.

1 *He's / His* ______ Demir.
2 *He's / His* ______ family name is Topuz.
3 *He's / His* ______ from Ankara.
4 *He's / His* ______ email address is dtopuz@universitymail.edu.tr.

PART 3

9 Watch part 3. Say. Then write.

1 Saif is from ______ .
2 Carlos is from ______ .
3 Elaine is a ______ .

10 Write. Then watch parts 1–3 and check.

London Mexico City Ankara ~~Riyadh~~

1 He's from ______ , in Saudi Arabia.
2 He's from ______ , in Mexico.
3 She's from ______ , in the UK.
4 He's from ______ , in Turkey.

11 Ask and answer. Then write.

Where are you from?

I'm from … , in … .

BEFORE YOU WATCH

WATCH

AFTER YOU WATCH

REMEMBER

MORE VOCABULARY: CITY NAMES

ASK AND ANSWER

LANGUAGE FOCUS

VOCABULARY: STUDY OBJECTS

1 1.18 Listen and point. Then say.

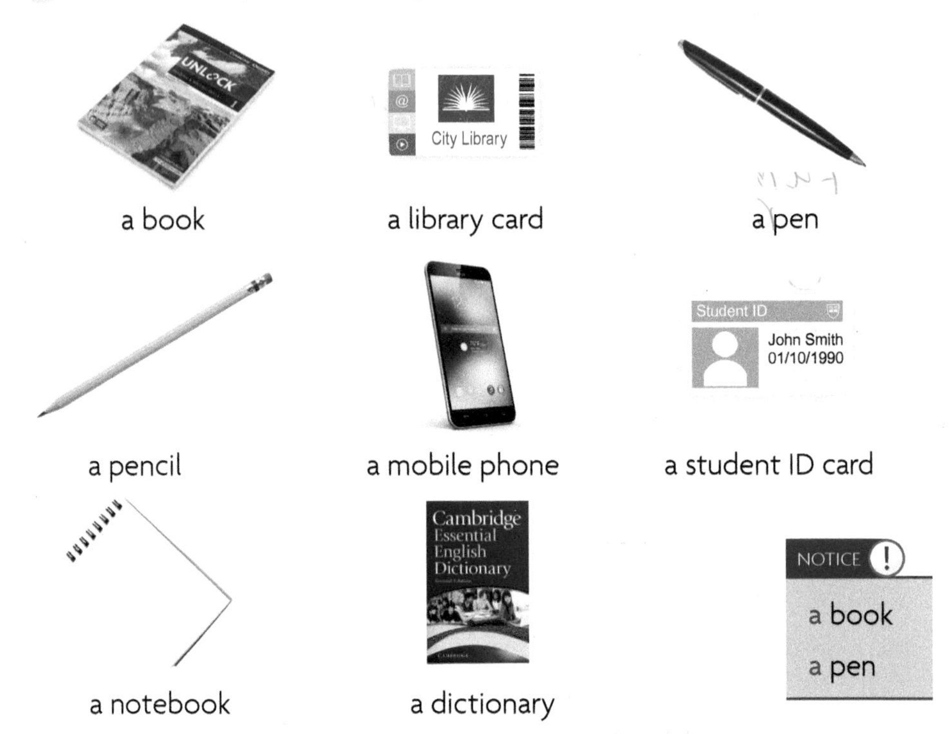
UNLOCK
City Library
Student ID
John Smith
01/10/1990
Cambridge
Essential
English
Dictionary

a book
a library card
a pen
a pencil
a mobile phone
a student ID card
a notebook
a dictionary

NOTICE !

a book
a pen

SPEAKING

2 1.19 Listen and read. Then say.

Excuse me.
Can I have a pen, please?
Here you are.
Thank you.
No. I'm sorry.
Excuse me.
Can I have your library card, please?

NOTICE !

Can I have a pen, please?
Can I have your library card, please?

LISTENING AND WRITING

3 1.20 Write. Then listen and check.

1 Can I have your ______, please?

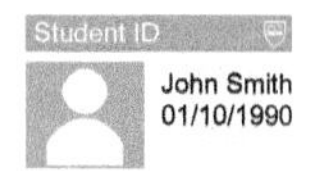

2 Can I have your student ______, please?

3 Can I have a ______, please?

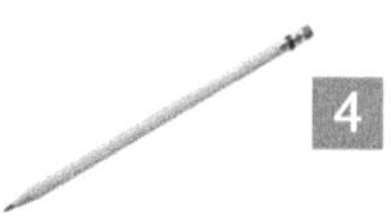

4 Can I have a ______, please?

5 Can I have your ______, please?

SPEAKING

4 Ask and answer.

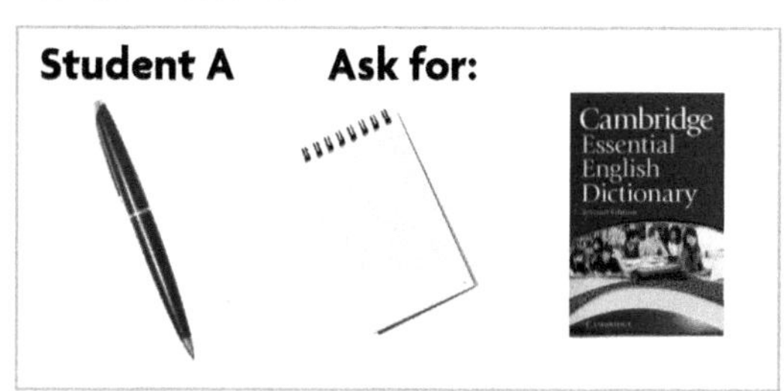

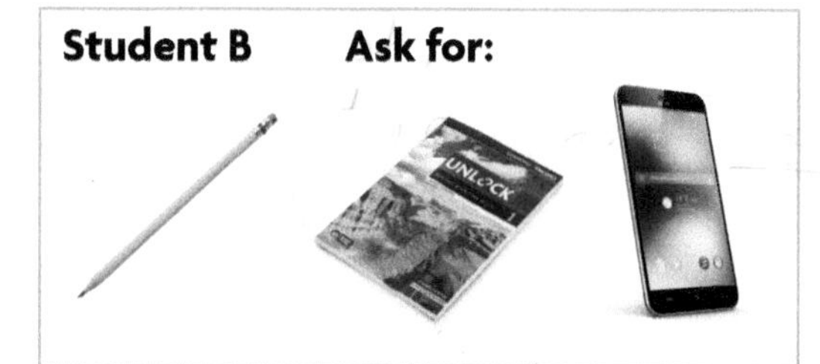

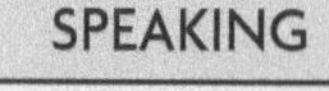

Excuse me. Can I have your ..., please?
Here you are. ✔
No. I'm sorry. ✗
Thank you.

WRITING

5 Look at **1** and write. Then check.

For my English class, I need

- a dictionary
- ______
- ______
- ______
- ______
- ______

ACADEMIC LISTENING AND SPEAKING

PREPARING TO LISTEN

1 Read and match.

1 first name — Bozer
2 family name — 0799 011 345
3 country — Burak
4 phone number — b.bozer@myemail.com
5 email address — Turkey

what is yor first name
what is yor first name
what

USING VISUALS TO PREDICT CONTENT

2 Look. Then read and circle.

Gabriela is *a student* / *a teacher*.
She needs *a pen* / *a student ID card* / *a mobile phone*.

NOTICE !

alopez@myemail.com — at
alopez@myemail.com — dot

LISTENING FOR MAIN IDEAS

3 1.21 Look at 2. Listen and check.

LISTENING FOR DETAIL

4 1.21 Listen again. Circle *Yes* or *No*.

1	Her first name is Gabriela.	Yes	No
2	Her family name is Lorenz.	Yes	No
3	She is from the UK.	Yes	No
4	Her phone number is 0832 556 436.	Yes	No
5	Her email address is alopez@mail.co.uk.	Yes	No

LISTENING FOR KEY INFORMATION

5 1.21 Listen again and write.

STUDENT ID CARD APPLICATION FORM

First name: Gabriela
Family name: ____________
Country: ____________
Phone number: ____________
Email address: alopez@____________

PRONUNCIATION FOR SPEAKING

6 1.22 Listen and say.

1 What's your first name?
2 What's your family name?
3 How do you spell that?
4 Where are you from?
5 What's your phone number?
6 What's your email address?

NOTICE !

What's your first name? My first name is Angela.
What's your phone number? My phone number is 01229 679 318.

SPEAKING TASK

7 Ask and answer. Write. Then swap.
Student A: You need a student ID card. Answer questions.
Student B: Ask questions. Write.

REMEMBER !

What's your ... ?
My ... is ...
Where are you from?
I'm from ...

STUDENT ID CARD APPLICATION FORM

First name: ____________
Family name: ____________
Country: ____________
Phone number: ____________
Email address: ____________

Hello.

Hi. I need a student ID card.

Yes, of course. What's ...?

ACADEMIC READING AND WRITING

USING VISUALS TO PREDICT CONTENT

1 Look and circle.

He is *a student / a teacher.*

He needs a *pencil / library card.*

READING FOR MAIN IDEAS

2 1.23 Read and listen. Look at 1 and check.

To: University Library
From: h.murase@uni.co.jp
Subject: library card

Reply Forward

Hi,

I'm a new student. I need a library card.

My first name is Haruto. My family name is Murase.
I'm from Japan. My phone number is 0443 020 894.
My email address is h.murase@uni.co.jp.

I can come to the library on Monday.

Thank you.

Haruto

READING FOR DETAIL

3 Look at 2. Read again and circle *Yes* or *No*.

1	His first name is Haruto.	(Yes)	No
2	He needs an ID card.	Yes	No
3	His family name is Murase.	Yes	No
4	His phone number is 0443 200 894.	Yes	No
5	His email address is h.musare@uni.co.jp.	Yes	No

4 1.24 Write. Then listen and check.

1	n _a_ m _e_	2	c __ __ ntry
3	ph __ n __	4	__ m __ __ l
5	b __ __ k	6	p __ nc __ l
7	p __ n	8	d __ ct __ __ n __ ry

5 Read and write.

STUDENT LIBRARY CARD APPLICATION FORM

First name: Salim
Family name: Al Hazmi
Country: Saudi Arabia
Phone number: 0678 0998 152
Email address: s.hazmi@myemail.com

My first name is Salim ______________ .

My family name is ______________ .

I am from ______________ .

My phone number is ______________ .

My email address is ______________ @ ______________ .

6 Check the CAPITAL letters.

1. ~~i~~ I am a student.
2. i am from mexico.
3. my family name is sanchez.
4. my email address is r.sanchez@myemail.com.

CRITICAL THINKING: APPLY

7 Write about you.

LIBRARY CARD APPLICATION FORM

First name: ____________________

Family name: ____________________

Country: ____________________

Phone number: ____________________

Email address: __________ @ __________

WRITING TASK

8 Look at 7. Write about you.

My first name is ____________________.

My family ________ is ____________________.

________ am from ____________________.

________ am a ____________________.

My ________ number is ____________________.

________ email address is __________ @ __________.

REMEMBER !

First names: **Abdullah**, **Burak**, **Gabriela**
Family names: **Al Hazmi**, **Bozer**, **Lopez**
Countries: **Saudi Arabia**, **Turkey**, **Mexico**

9 Swap and check.

OBJECTIVES REVIEW

I can ...

understand names, phone numbers and email addresses.	☐
understand spelling.	☐
ask for study objects I need.	☐
talk about names, phone numbers and email addresses.	☐
read an email.	☐
read names, phone numbers and email addresses.	☐
write my name, phone number and email address.	☐
write a list of study objects I need.	☐

WORDLIST

book	notebook
country	pen
dictionary	pencil
email address	phone number
family name	Saudi Arabia
first name	spell
India	student
Japan	student ID card
library card	teacher
Mexico	the United Kingdom (the UK)
mobile phone	Turkey
name	

LEARNING OBJECTIVES

Listening	People and things Families
Speaking	Say numbers 1–100 Ask and answer questions about people and things
Reading	Profile Text with photos
Writing	Write numbers 1–100 Write about your family
Watch and remember	A video about families and things

PEOPLE AND THINGS UNIT 2

UNLOCK YOUR KNOWLEDGE

1 Look. Count the people (1, 2, 3 ...).

2 Count the people in your family.

LISTENING AND READING 1

VOCABULARY: FAMILY

1 2.1 Listen and point. Then say.

grandmother

grandfather

grandmother

grandfather

father

mother

brother

sister

brother

2 2.2 Read and listen. Then look at **1** and write ✔ or ✗.

1 I'm Ahmed.

2 This is my mother.

3 This is my father.

4 This is my grandfather.

5 This is my grandmother.

6 This is my sister.

7 This is my brother.

Who's this?

LISTENING FOR DETAIL

3 2.3 Listen and match.

1 mother	Yusuf
2 father	Sara
3 grandfather	Sena
4 grandmother	Rana
5 sister	Tariq
6 brother	Hasan

NOTICE !

Who's this? = Who is this?

SOUND AND SPELLING: *th*

4 2.4 Underline *th*. Then listen and say.

1 mother
2 father
3 brother
4 grandmother
5 grandfather
6 this

5 Look at 1. Ask and answer.

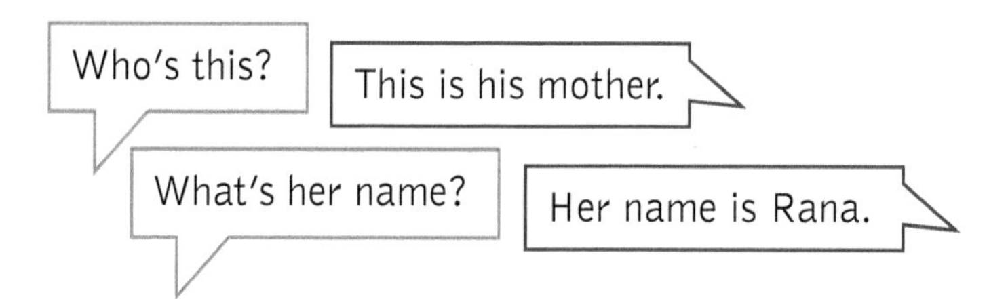

Who's this?
This is his mother.
What's her name?
Her name is Rana.

6 2.5 Listen and match. Then circle the CAPITAL letters.

2 Dr Farrel

3 Mr Erkol

7 2.6 Read and circle. Listen and check. Then write.

1 This is my teacher, ______ (Mr / Mrs) Lewis.

2 This is my teacher, ______ (Mr / Mrs) Johnson.

3 This is my teacher, ______ (Mr / Mrs) Young.

4 This is my doctor, ______ (Dr / Mrs) Richardson.

8 2.6 Look at 7. Listen and say.

9 Look at page 206.

NOTICE !

This is Mia Young / Mrs Young / ~~Mrs Mia~~.

SPEAKING

LISTENING FOR KEY INFORMATION

READING FOR KEY INFORMATION

WRITING AND SPEAKING

LISTENING AND READING 2

USING VISUALS TO PREDICT CONTENT

1 2.7 Look and (circle) *Yes* or *No*. Listen and check.

Hamad and Nasser

Mr Cole

Mrs Nolan

1 Hamad and Nasser are brothers. (Yes) No

2 Mr Cole and Mrs Nolan are students. Yes (No)

NOTICE !

I'm from /
She's from
Saudi Arabia.

We're from /
They're from
Saudi Arabia.

READING FOR KEY INFORMATION

2 2.7 Read and listen. Then write ✓ or ✗.

I'm Hamad and this is Nasser. We're brothers. We're students from Saudi Arabia.

This is Mr Cole and this is Mrs Nolan. They're teachers. They're from the UK.

1 Hamad and Nasser

[✗] teachers [✓] students [✓] from the UK

2 Mr Cole and Mrs Nolan

[ ] teachers [✓] brothers [✓] from Saudi Arabia

GRAMMAR: VERB *BE*: *WE* AND *THEY*

3 2.8 Listen and read. Then say.

We are students.

They are teachers.

We	are	students.
They		teachers.

NOTICE !

We're students. = We are students.

They're teachers. = They are teachers.

4 2.9 Read and circle. Listen and check. Then write.

1 We are students. (We / I)

2 ______ are from Japan. (I / We)

3 ______ are teachers. (She / They)

4 ______ are from Turkey. (They / I)

LISTENING FOR KEY INFORMATION

5 2.10 Listen, read and circle.

Our names are Silvia and Patricia. We are from Mexico. Our *mother / teacher* is Mrs Moreno. Our *university / family* is in Mexico.

Silvia and Patricia

They are *teachers / students*. Their names are Silvia and Patricia.

Mrs Moreno

GRAMMAR: *OUR* AND *THEIR*

6 2.11 Listen and read. Then say.

Our	names are Silvia and Patricia. teacher is Mrs Moreno.	Their	names are Silvia and Patricia. teacher is Mrs Moreno.

7 2.12 Read and circle. Listen and check. Then write.

1 They are students. Their (Our / Their) names are Silvia and Patricia. ______ (Our / Their) teacher is Mrs Moreno.

2 We are brothers. ______ (Our / Their) names are Hamad and Nasser. ______ (Our / Their) family is from Saudi Arabia.

WRITING AND SPEAKING

8 Write. Then say.

Our names are shirzad and skad. We are ______.

Our teacher is ______. ______ is from ______.

REMEMBER !

We are ... / Our names are ...
They are ... / Their names are ...
Mr / Mrs ...

LISTENING AND READING 3

VOCABULARY: MY THINGS

1 2.13 Listen and point. Then say.

car

television

computer

mobile phone

camera

bag

READING FOR NUMBERS

2 Look, read and circle.

How many ... do you have?

1 I have five cameras

camera / *cameras*.

2 I have eight ____________

bag / *bags*.

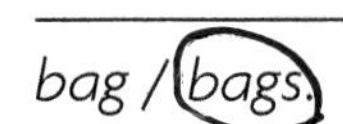

3 We have one ____________

car / *cars*.

4 We have six ____________

computer / *computers*.

3 2.14 Look at 2. Listen and check. Then write and say.

ACADEMIC WRITING SKILLS

4 2.15 Write. Then listen and check. Say.

1 one	2 two	3 three
4 four	5 five	6 six
7 seven	8 eight	9 nine
10 ten		

LISTENING FOR KEY INFORMATION

5 2.16 Listen and circle. Then write.

1 I have ___two___ cars. (two / three)

2 I have __________ computers. (six / ten)

3 I have __________ cameras. (three / four)

4 I have __________ bags. (five / six)

5 I have __________ televisions. (three / four)

PRONUNCIATION FOR SPEAKING

6 2.17 Listen and say. Ask and answer.

How many cars do you have?

I have two cars.

1 How many cars do you have? 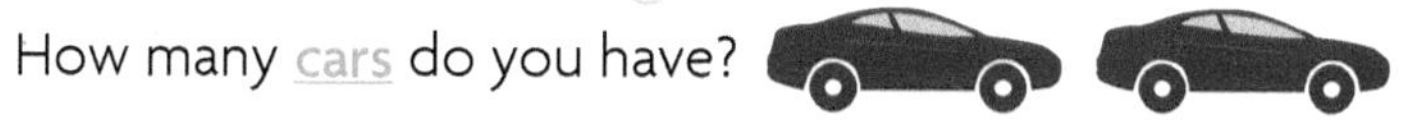

2 How many cameras do you have? 

3 How many televisions do you have? 

4 How many bags do you have? 

5 How many computers do you have? 

SPEAKING AND WRITING

7 Ask and answer. Write the numbers.

Student Survey: People and things
How many ... do you have?

a __________

a __________

a __________

a __________

a __________

REMEMBER !

How many ... do you have?
I have ...
We have ...

WATCH AND REMEMBER

PART 1

BEFORE YOU WATCH

1 Look. Match.

a

b

c

1 mother — a
2 grandmother — b
3 brother — c

2 2.18 Look at 1. Listen and check. Then write.

WATCH

3 Watch part 1 and circle.

1 Hachiro has one *brother / sister*.
2 His *father / grandfather* is 71.
3 His *mother / grandmother* is 66.

AFTER YOU WATCH

4 Read and write.

is one ~~I'm~~ old My

I'm Hachiro. I have ________ brother.
________ brother ________ 6 years ________ .

PART 2

BEFORE YOU WATCH

5 Look. Match.

a

b

c

1 one computer — a
2 three televisions — b
3 two cars — c

6 2.19 Look at 5. Listen and check. Then write.

WATCH

7 Watch part 2 and circle.

1 Sheila is from *the UK / the USA*.
2 Anna is *a student / a teacher*.
3 Sheila has *one / two* bag.

AFTER YOU WATCH

8 Read and write.

computer camera mobile phone

Sheila: I have one ______.
David: I have one ______.
Anna: I have one ______.

PART 3

REMEMBER

9 Watch part 3. Say. Then write.

1 Hachiro has ______ brother.
2 The Smith family have ______ computers.
3 The Smith family have ______ televisions.

MORE VOCABULARY: FAMILY

10 Match.

1 Anna — father
2 David — daughter
3 James — mother
4 Sheila — son

NOTICE !

Sheila has one son.
His name is ...

And she has one daughter. Her name is ...

ASK AND ANSWER

11 Ask and answer.

How many ... do you have?

I have ...

LANGUAGE FOCUS

VOCABULARY: NUMBERS 11–100

1 2.20 Write. Then listen and check. Then say.

11	eleven	12	twelve	13	thirteen
14	fo _u_ rteen	15	fifteen	16	s ___ xteen
17	s ___ venteen	18	e ___ ghteen	19	nin ___ teen

NOTICE !

sixteen seventeen nineteen

2 2.21 Listen and point. Then say.

20	twenty	30	thirty	40	forty
50	fifty	60	sixty	70	seventy
80	eighty	90	ninety	100	one hundred
21	twenty-one	22	twenty-two	23	twenty-three
24	twenty-four	25	twenty-five	26	twenty-six
27	twenty-seven	28	twenty-eight	29	twenty-nine

NOTICE !

21 twenty-one 22 twenty-two

PRONUNCIATION FOR LISTENING

3 2.22 Listen and say.

● ⬤ thirteen	⬤ ● thirty	● ⬤ fourteen	⬤ ● forty
● ⬤ fifteen	⬤ ● fifty	● ⬤ sixteen	⬤ ● sixty
● ● ⬤ seventeen	⬤ ● ● seventy	● ⬤ eighteen	⬤ ● eighty
● ⬤ nineteen	⬤ ● ninety		

SPEAKING AND WRITING

4 Say. Then write.

31	thirty-one	32	______
43	______	54	______
65	______	76	______
87	______	98	______

LISTENING AND WRITING

5 2.23 Listen and circle. Then write.

You and your family

1 How old are you?
Eighteen years old.
(80 / 18)

2 How old is your mother?
_______ years old.
(48 / 84)

3 How old is your father?
_______ years old.
(51 / 57)

4 How old is your grandfather?
_______ years old.
(91 / 61)

5 How old is your brother?
_______ years old.
(13 / 30)

READING FOR KEY INFORMATION

6 2.24 Read and circle. Then listen and check.

1 How old is your *mobile phone / father*? Two years old.
2 How old is your *computer / grandmother*? One hundred years old.
3 How old is your *car / grandfather*? Twenty-two years old.
4 How old is your *mother / bag*? Forty-seven years old.

SPEAKING AND WRITING

7 Ask and answer. Listen and write.

mother father sister brother
grandmother grandfather

You and your family

You? seventeen

Your _______ ? _______

Your _______ ? _______

Your _______ ? _______

Your _______ ? _______

REMEMBER !

How old are you?
How old is your ... ?
... years old.

ACADEMIC LISTENING AND SPEAKING

USING VISUALS TO PREDICT CONTENT

1 2.25 Look and circle. Then listen and check.

Ercan has *two / three* cars.

Mr Rosales is his *teacher / father*.

LISTENING FOR KEY INFORMATION

2 2.25 Listen again and circle.

1 Mr Rosales is from *Mexico / Turkey*.

2 He is *forty / thirty* years old.

3 The car is *eleven / twelve* years old.

4 The Nissan car is from *Japan / the UK*.

CRITICAL THINKING: UNDERSTAND

3 2.25 Listen again and write.

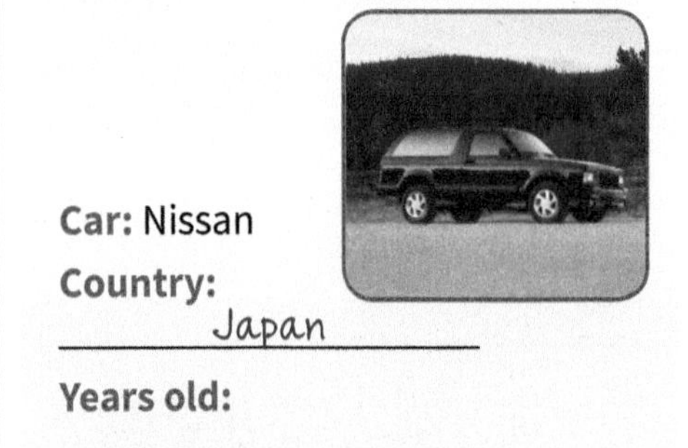

Car: Nissan

Country: Japan

Years old: ____________

Car: Jaguar

Country: ____________

Years old: ____________

CRITICAL THINKING: REMEMBER

4 Read and write about your things.

Mobile phone: ____________________

Country: ____________________

Years old: ____________________

Computer: ____________________

Country: ____________________

Years old: ____________________

Car: ____________________

Country: ____________________

Years old: ____________________

____

____

____

PRONUNCIATION FOR SPEAKING

5 2.26 Listen and say.

1 This is my car.
2 My car is twelve years old.
3 How many cars do you have?
4 How old is your car?
5 How many computers do you have?

REMEMBER !

This is my ...
My car is a Nissan.
My ... is from Japan.
My ... is ... years old.
I have ...

SPEAKING TASK

6 Look at 4. Listen, ask and write. Answer.

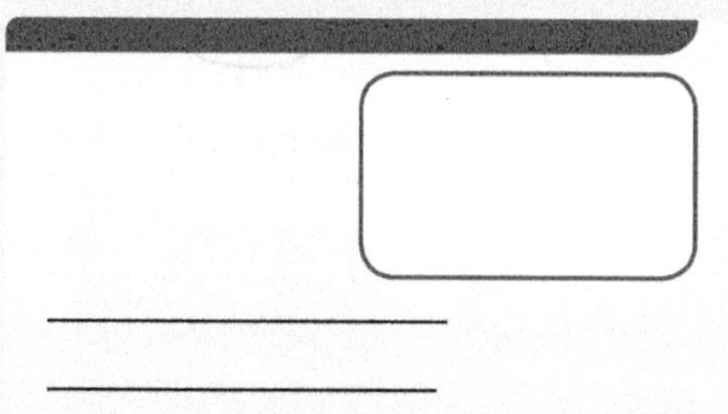

____

____

____

____

____

____

ACADEMIC READING AND WRITING

PREPARING TO READ

1 Read and write.

friends brother

We are ______________ and sister.

We are ______________ .

USING VISUALS TO PREDICT CONTENT

2 Look at 3 and circle. Then read and check.

1 Maria and Yolanda are *sisters* / *brothers*.
2 Asma and Khadijah are *sisters* / *friends*.
3 Sou and Minato are from *Japan* / *Turkey*.

READING FOR KEY INFORMATION

3 2.27 Read and listen. Circle.

www.cambridgeuniversity.uk/ourstudents

Home | Our Class | Our Teachers | Our Students

MARIA

YOLANDA

ASMA

KHADIJAH

MELIS

SOU

MINATO

Welcome to English 001!

This is our class. Maria and Yolanda are sisters. Maria is seventeen years old and Yolanda is eighteen. Asma is twenty-five years old. Khadijah is her sister. Sou and Minato are friends from Japan.

Our teacher is Mrs Smith. She is from the UK. Our university is eighty years old. We have five computers and one hundred books.

1 Maria is *17* / *18* years old.
2 Yolanda is *17* / *18* years old.
3 Asma is *25* / *35* years old.
4 They have *5* / *6* computers.
5 They have *80* / *100* books.

ACADEMIC WRITING SKILLS

4 2.28 Write. Then listen and check.

1 s _i_ st _e_ r
2 fr ___ ___ nd
3 br ___ th ___ r
4 m ___ th ___ r
5 f ___ th ___ r
6 e ___ ghte ___ n
7 th ___ rt ___ -s ___ v ___ n
8 f ___ ft ___ -f ___ v ___

CRITICAL THINKING: UNDERSTAND

5 Read and write.

This is my family.
This is my mother, Lucia. She is 45 years old.
This is my father, Jim. He is 50 years old.
I have two sisters and one brother.
Mia and Tanya are my sisters. Mia is 12 years old.
Tanya is 15 years old.
This is my brother, Ben. He is 18 years old.
My name is Chris and I am 23 years old.
We are from the UK.

mother

Name: ___________

Years old: ___________

father

Name: ___________

Years old: ___________

sister

Name: ___________

Years old: ___________

sister

Name: ___________

Years old: ___________

brother

Name: ___________

Years old: ___________

me

Name: ___________

Years old: ___________

ACADEMIC WRITING SKILLS

6 Read and circle *and*.

1 Mia (and) Tanya are my sisters.
2 I have two sisters and one brother.
3 Maria and Yolanda are from Mexico.
4 My name is Chris and I am twenty-three years old.

7 2.29 Write. Then listen and check.

1 Lisa _and Amy are_ my sisters. (are / Amy / and)

2 Noora ____________ students. (and / Fatima / are)

3 Chris ____________ my brother and sister. (Lee / and / are)

4 Erin ____________ my brothers. (are / Rin / and)

CRITICAL THINKING: CREATE

8 Write.

mother
Name: ____________
Years old: ____________

father
Name: ____________
Years old: ____________

____
Name: ____________
Years old: ____________

____
Name: ____________
Years old: ____________

____
Name: ____________
Years old: ____________

WRITING TASK

REMEMBER !

Mia and Tanya are my sisters.
I have two sisters and one brother.

9 Look at 8. Write about your family.

My name is ____________ .
This is my family.
This is my ____________ , ____________ .
She is ____________ years old.
This is my ____________ , ____________ .
He is ____________ years old.
I have ________ ________ and ________ ________ .
My ____________ is ____________ years old.
________ ________ is ________ ________ old.
We are from ____________ .

10 Swap and check.

OBJECTIVES REVIEW

I can ...

listen for information about people and things.	☐
listen about a family.	☐
say numbers 1–100.	☐
ask and answer questions about people and things (*How old ... It's ... She's from ...*).	☐
read a profile.	☐
read with photos.	☐
write numbers 1–100.	☐
write about my family.	☐

WORDLIST

bag	grandfather
brother	grandmother
camera	mobile phone
car	mother
computer	Mr
Dr	Mrs
family	sister
father	television

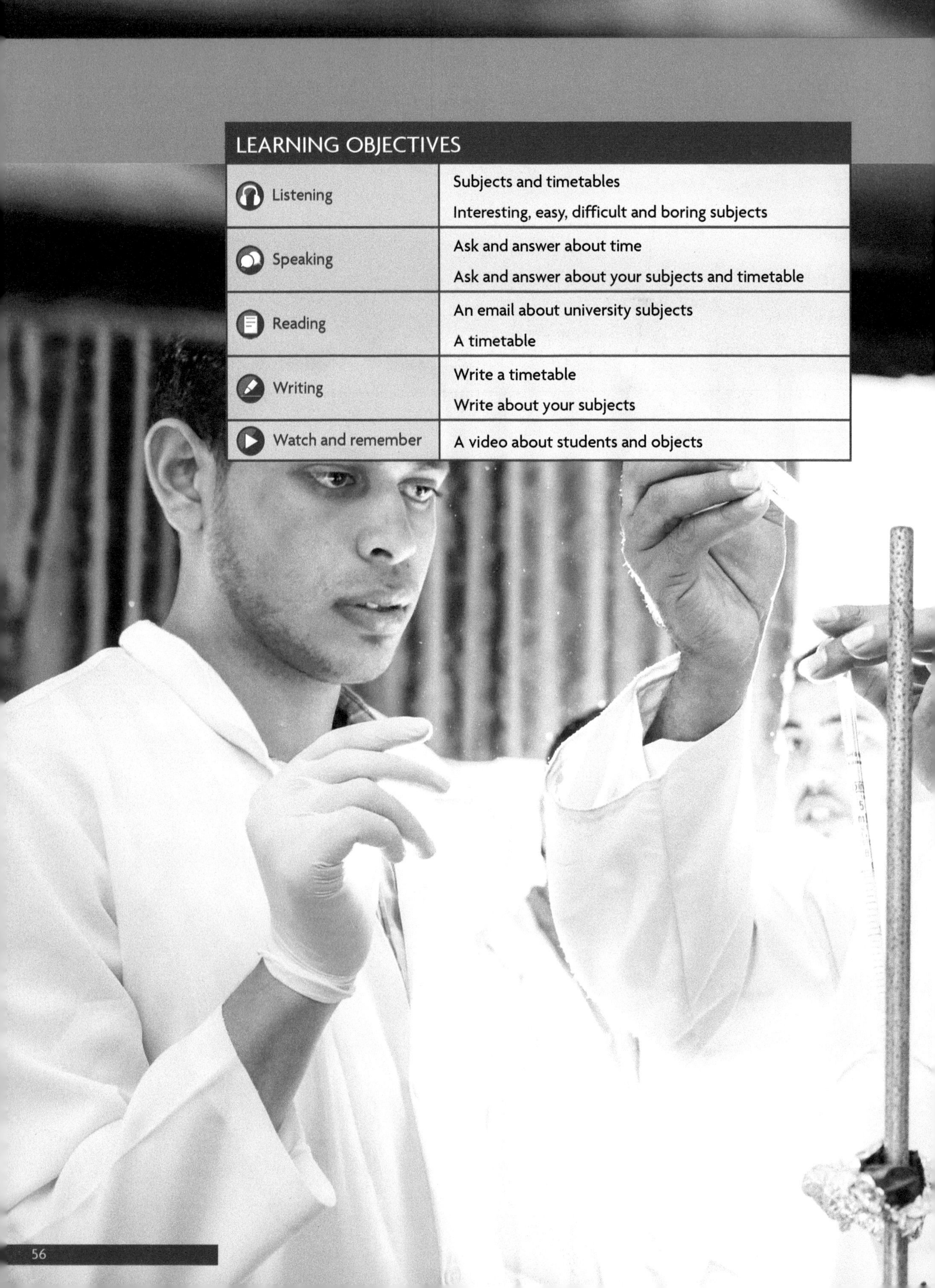

LEARNING OBJECTIVES

Listening	Subjects and timetables Interesting, easy, difficult and boring subjects
Speaking	Ask and answer about time Ask and answer about your subjects and timetable
Reading	An email about university subjects A timetable
Writing	Write a timetable Write about your subjects
Watch and remember	A video about students and objects

UNIVERSITY LIFE UNIT 3

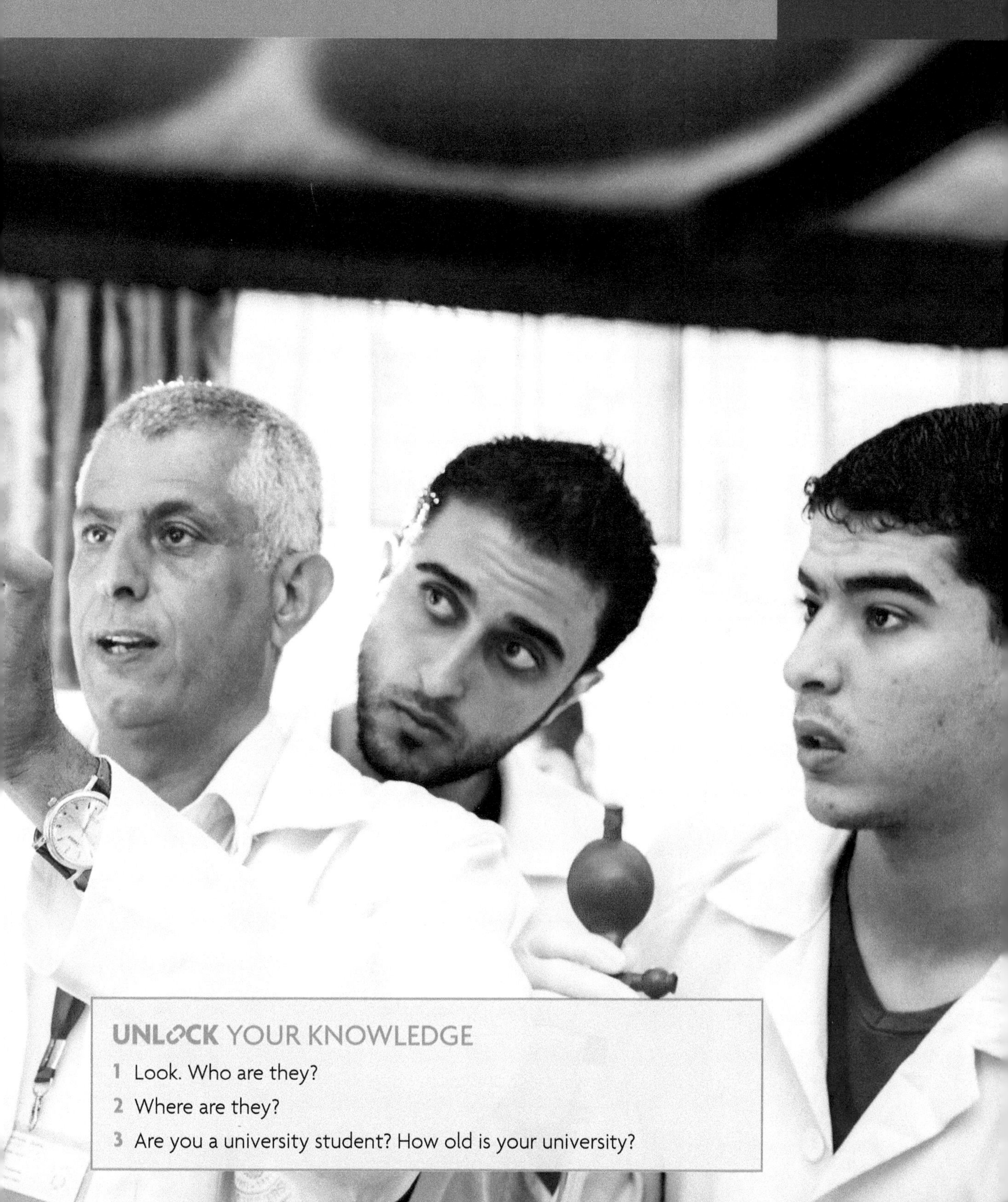

UNLOCK YOUR KNOWLEDGE

1 Look. Who are they?
2 Where are they?
3 Are you a university student? How old is your university?

LISTENING AND READING 1

VOCABULARY: SUBJECTS

1 3.1 Listen and point. Then say.

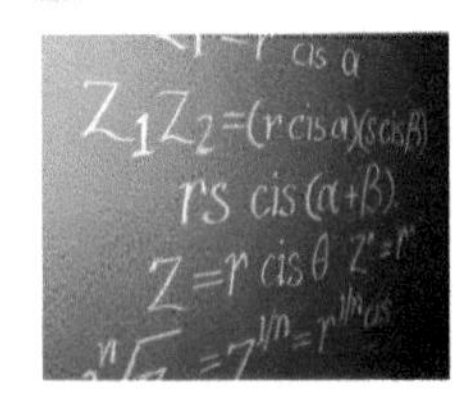

Maths

Chemistry

English

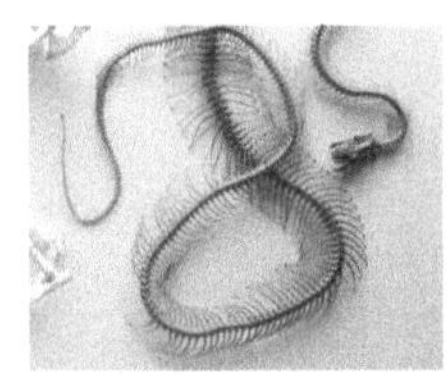

Biology

History

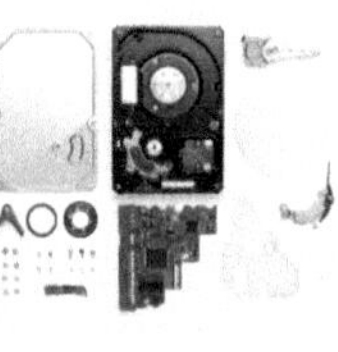

IT

Business

Japanese

ACADEMIC WRITING SKILLS

2 Write the CAPITAL letters.

1 M aths 2 ___ hemistry 3 ___ nglish 4 ___ iology
5 ___ istory 6 ___ usiness 7 ___ T 8 ___ apanese

SOUND AND SPELLING: *sh*, *ch*

3 3.2 Write the letter. Listen and say.

1 Englis ___ 2 teac ___ er 3 C ___ emistry

LISTENING FOR KEY INFORMATION

4 3.3 Listen and circle.

What subjects do you study?

Maths Biology Business IT

History Business English Japanese

English Chemistry Maths IT

History Biology Chemistry English

5 3.4 Listen and read. Circle *Yes* or *No*.

1	I study Maths, English and Business.	Yes	(No)
2	I study Biology, English and Japanese.	Yes	No
3	I study English, History and IT.	Yes	No
4	I study Biology, Chemistry and English.	Yes	No

6 Circle **,** and and.

1 I study Biology, English (and) Japanese.

2 I study English, History and IT.

3 I study Maths, English and IT.

7 3.5 Read and write. Then listen and check. Say.

1 I study English, __________ and __________.

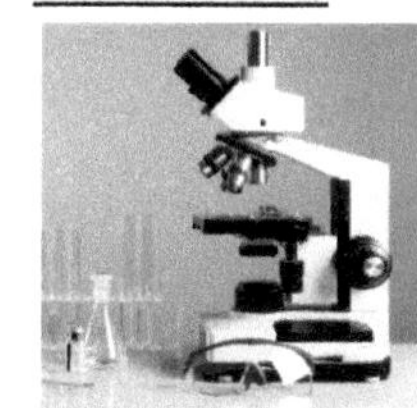
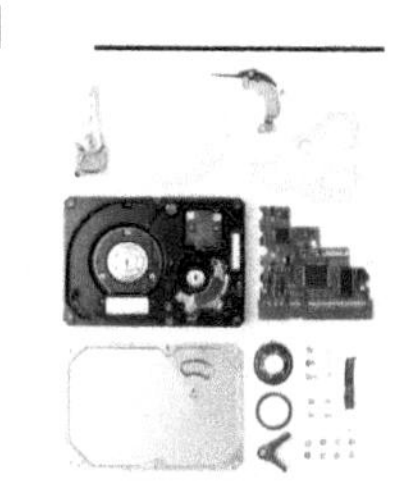

2 I study Japanese, __________ and __________.

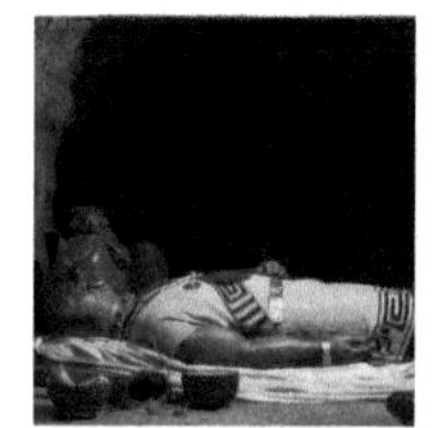
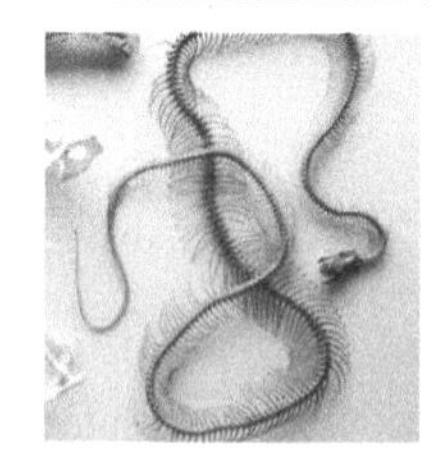

3 I study English, __________ and __________.

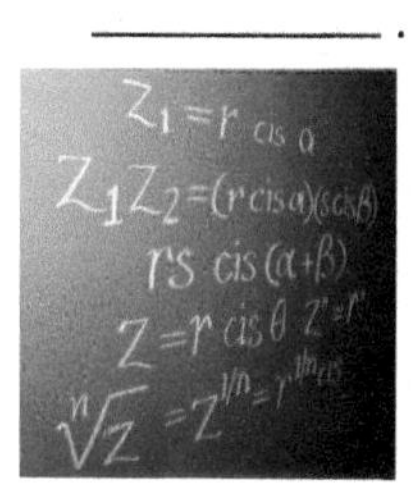

8 Student A: Look at page 200.

Student B: Look at page 203.

LISTENING AND READING 2

VOCABULARY: DAYS OF THE WEEK

1 3.6 Listen and point. Then say.

Sunday	Monday	Tuesday	Wednesday	Thursday	Friday	Saturday
1	2	3	4	5	6	7

ACADEMIC WRITING SKILLS

2 Write the CAPITAL letters.

1 S unday 2 __ onday 3 __ uesday 4 __ ednesday
5 __ hursday 6 __ riday 7 __ aturday

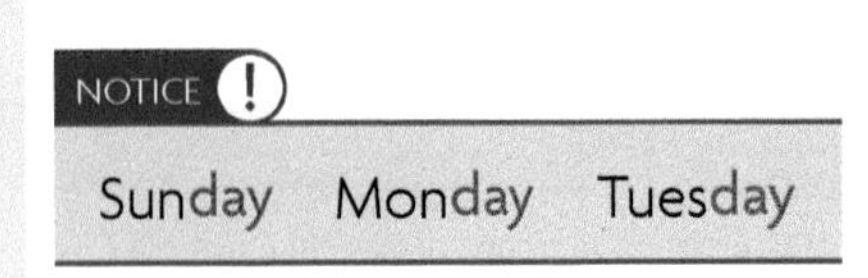

3 Write the days.

CLASS: QA631
TIMETABLE: Science Foundation Programme

	Sunday	______	Tuesday	Wednesday	______
MORNING	English Room ______	History Room 11	IT Room 24	Chemistry Room 21	Biology Room ______
12:00–1:00					
AFTERNOON	History Room 13	Chemistry Room 21	Maths Room ______	English Room 11	Business Room 18

READING FOR KEY INFORMATION

4 3.7 Look at 3. Read and match. Then listen and check.

1 Business class — Wednesday morning
2 Chemistry class — Thursday afternoon
3 IT class — Room 24

LISTENING FOR DETAIL

5 3.8 Look at 3. Listen and write.

GRAMMAR: *WHEN / WHERE* AND *IN / ON*

6 3.9 Listen and read.

When is our English class?	**On** Sunday morning.
Where is our English class?	**In** room 11.

7 3.10 Read and circle. Then listen and check. Write.

1 **A:** Where is our IT class?
(When / Where)

B: In room 11.

2 **A:** When is your History class?

B: ________ Tuesday morning.
(In / On)

3 **A:** Where is our Chemistry class?

B: ________ room 18.
(In / On)

4 **A:** ________ is your Business class?
(When / Where)

B: On Monday afternoon.

WRITING AND SPEAKING

8 Write. Ask and answer.

SUBJECTS	DAY	MORNING	AFTERNOON	ROOM
ENGLISH				
BUSINESS				
CHEMISTRY				

REMEMBER !

When is your ... class?
Where is your ... class?
On ... morning / afternoon.
In room ...

LISTENING AND READING 3

VOCABULARY: ADJECTIVES

1 3.11 Listen and point. Then say.

boring

interesting

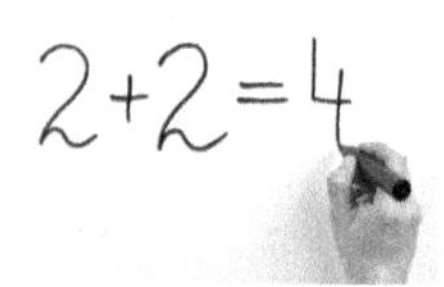

easy

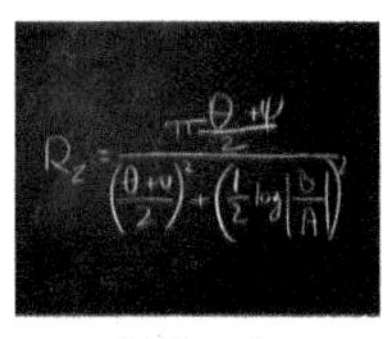

difficult

LISTENING FOR KEY INFORMATION

2 3.12 Listen and write *1*, *2* or *3*.

☐

Toki
I study Business and IT.

☐

☐

Tahir
Rashid
I study Maths, English and Chemistry.

LISTENING FOR DETAIL

3 3.12 Listen again and circle.

1 **Maths** (easy) / difficult

2 **IT** boring / interesting

3 **English** easy / difficult

GRAMMAR: VERB *BE*: *IT*

4 3.13 Listen and read.

It	is	interesting. difficult.

It	is	not	boring. easy.

5 3.14 Read and circle. Listen and check. Then write.

1 Chemistry is not difficult. It ___is___ easy. (is / is not)

2 Biology is not boring. It __________ interesting. (is / is not)

3 History is interesting. It __________ boring. (is / is not)

4 Business is easy. It __________ difficult. (is / is not)

NOTICE !

It's interesting. =
It is interesting.

It isn't boring. =
It is not boring.

SOUND AND SPELLING: *s*

6 3.15 Listen and say.

It's ... isn't ...

It's boring. It's difficult. It isn't boring. It isn't difficult.

7 3.16 Listen and circle. Then say.

1 *It's / isn't* interesting.

2 *It 's / isn't* easy.

3 *It 's / isn't* boring.

4 *It 's / isn't* difficult.

SPEAKING

8 Ask and circle.

What's ... like?	It's ...	It isn't ...
English	easy / difficult	boring / interesting
Maths	easy / difficult	boring / interesting
__________	easy / difficult	boring / interesting

REMEMBER !

What's ... like?
It's easy.
It isn't easy.

READING AND WRITING

9 Look at 8. Then read and write.

English

It __________ easy.

It __________ difficult.

__________ boring.

__________ interesting.

Maths

It __________ easy.

It __________ difficult.

__________ boring.

__________ interesting.

WATCH AND REMEMBER

PART 1

BEFORE YOU WATCH

1 Look. Match.

a

b

c

_______________ _______________ _______________

1	Japanese	a
2	Business	b
3	IT	c

2 3.17 Look at 1. Listen and check. Then write.

WATCH

3 Watch part 1 and circle.

1 Mira studies *Business* / *Maths* / *History*.
2 Faisal studies *Biology* / *Chemistry* / *IT*.
3 Fathima studies *Business* / *IT* / *Japanese*.
4 Emma studies *Biology* / *Chemistry* / *Maths*.

AFTER YOU WATCH

4 Read and write.

study interesting ~~name~~ student

Hello, my ___name___ is Faisal. I'm a _______________ in Jeddah, in Saudi Arabia. I _______________ IT. It's very _______________!

PART 2

5 Look. Then write.

1

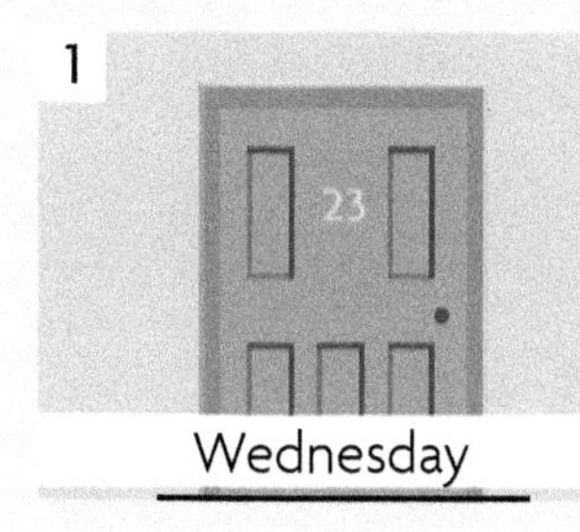

Wednesday

2

56

Tuesday

3

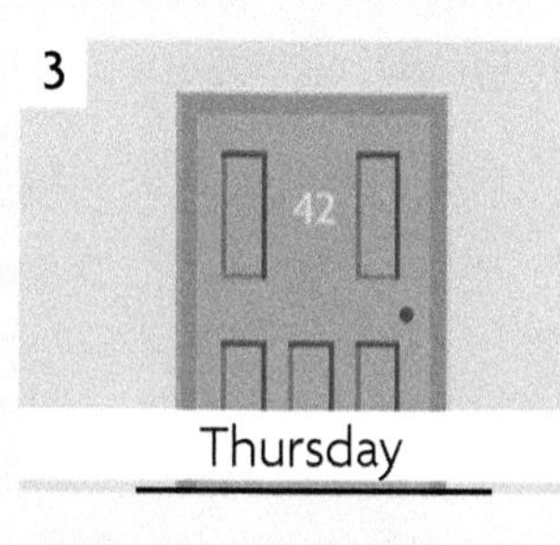

Thursday

1. My class is on Wednesday in room 23.
2. My class is on ____________ in ____________ ________ .
3. My class is on ____________ in room ________ .

6 Watch part 2. Read and circle.

1. **Mira:** My class is in room *4* / *24* / *(42)*.
2. **Faisal:** My class is on *Monday* / *Tuesday* / *Wednesday*.
3. **Fathima:** My class is on *Sunday* / *Monday* / *Tuesday*.
4. **Emma:** My class is on *Friday* / *Wednesday* / *Thursday*.

7 Read and correct the Chemistry timetable.

Sunday	Monday	Tuesday	Wednesday	Thursday
No class	Chemistry Room ~~8~~ 1	Chemistry Room 12	Chemistry Room 23	Chemistry Room 5

PART 3

8 Watch part 3. Say. Then write.

1. Mira studies ____________ .
2. Faisal studies ____________ .
3. Fathima studies ____________ .
4. Emma studies ____________ .

9 Look. Then write.

first second third ~~fourth~~

④ fourth floor
③ ____________ floor

② ____________ floor
① ____________ floor

10 Ask and answer.

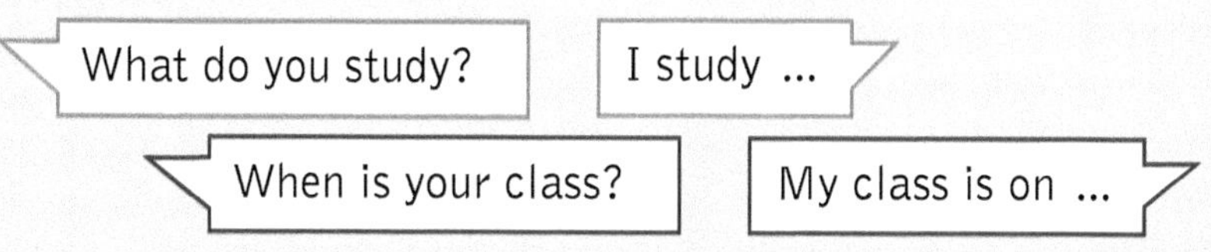

What do you study?
I study ...
When is your class?
My class is on ...

BEFORE YOU WATCH

WATCH

AFTER YOU WATCH

REMEMBER

MORE VOCABULARY: *What floor is it on?*

ASK AND ANSWER

LANGUAGE FOCUS

VOCABULARY: TIME

1 3.18 Listen and point. Then say.

nine o'clock

five o'clock

seven-thirty

ten-thirty

2 3.19 Read and match. Listen.

What time is it?

6:00	9:30	8:00	4:30
A	B	C	D

1 It's six o'clock. A

2 It's four-thirty. ☐

3 It's eight o'clock. ☐

4 It's nine-thirty. ☐

SPEAKING

3 Say.

What time is it?

8:00 11:00 2:30 12:30

LISTENING AND WRITING

4 3.20 Listen and read. Write the times.

10:30
What time is our IT class?
It's at ____ :00.
What time is it?
It's 10: ____ .
Oh, no. We're late!

NOTICE !

What time is it? It's ... o'clock.

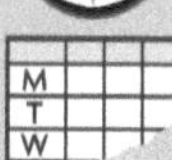

What time is our IT class? It's at ten o'clock.

PRONUNCIATION FOR SPEAKING

5 3.21 Listen and say.

It's at six o'clock.

It's at twelve o'clock.

It's at three-thirty.

It's at six-thirty.

LISTENING FOR DETAIL

6 3.22 Listen and circle *Yes* or *No*.

1	What time is it? It's 7:30.	Yes	(No)
2	What time is our Maths class? It's at 3:00.	Yes	No
3	What time is our Chemistry class? It's at 9:30.	Yes	No

SPEAKING

7 Student A: Look at page 200.

Student B: Look at page 203.

ACADEMIC LISTENING AND SPEAKING

PREPARING TO LISTEN

1 Match. Then say.

1	What subjects do you study?	It's on Wednesday at 3 o'clock.
2	When is your History class?	I study English, Maths and IT.
3	Where is your IT class?	It isn't easy.
4	What's Biology like?	It's in room 16.

NOTICE !

It's on Wednesday at 3 o'clock.

2 3.23 Read and write. Then listen and check. on at

1 It's _on_ Monday ______ 9:30.
2 It's ______ 10:00 ______ Tuesday.
3 It's ______ Friday ______ 1:30.
4 It's ______ 3:00 ______ Thursday.

LISTENING FOR MAIN IDEAS

3 3.24 Listen and circle.

1 Amal and Sarah are *sisters / teachers / students.*
2 They study *English / Business / Biology.*

LISTENING FOR KEY INFORMATION

4 3.24 Listen again and circle.

Amal is a student.
Her Business class is on *Tuesday / Thursday* afternoon at *2:30 / 1:30*. It's in room *33 / 43*.
Her Business class is not *difficult / easy*.

CRITICAL THINKING: UNDERSTAND

5 Look at 4. Write.

STUDENT NAME: Amal Sabry
CLASS: GH642
DAY: Tuesday

TIME	SUBJECT	ROOM
9:00–10:30	Maths	35
11:00–12:00	IT	24
______ –3:00	______	______

PRONUNCIATION FOR SPEAKING

6 3.25 Listen and say.

When is your English class?
What time is your Maths class?
Where is your IT class?
What's your Chemistry class like?

CRITICAL THINKING: EVALUATE

7 Write. Swap and check.

STUDENT NAME: ______
CLASS: GH642
DAY: ______

TIME	SUBJECT	ROOM
______	English	______
______	Biology	______
______	Chemistry	______

SPEAKING TASK

8 Look at 7. Ask and answer.

REMEMBER !

When is your ... class?
Where is your ... class?
What time is your ... class?

ACADEMIC READING AND WRITING

PREPARING TO READ

1 3.26 Listen and point. Then say.

email

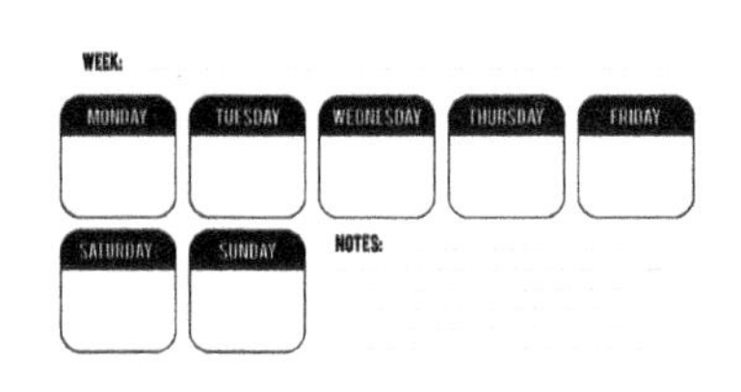

timetable

question

READING FOR MAIN IDEAS

2 3.27 Read and listen. Then circle.

1 The email is **from** *a student / a teacher.*

2 The email is **about** *a class / a timetable.*

From: dr.mohamed.khan@uni.ac.ae Reply Forward
Subject: your timetable

Dear students,

Please look at your new timetable.

Maths is on Sunday and Tuesday at 11 o'clock.

The English class on Tuesday is not in room 12. It is in room 22.

The Chemistry class is in room 14. It is not in room 8.

The IT class on Thursday is not in room 23. It is in room 13.

Please email me with any questions.

Regards,

Dr Mohamed Khan

SCANNING FOR KEY INFORMATION

3 Look at **2**. Read and correct the timetable.

TIME	Sunday	Monday	Tuesday	Wednesday	Thursday
9:00–10:30	English Room 12	English Room 12	English Room 12	English Room 12	English Room 12
11:00–12:30	~~Business~~ Maths Room 4	Chemistry Room 8	History Room 11	Chemistry Room 8	English Room 12
1:30–3:00	IT Room 23	Biology Room 8	History Room 12	Biology Room 8	IT Room 23

CRITICAL THINKING: ANALYZE

4 3.28 Listen and read. Then write.

I study English, Maths and Chemistry.
My English class is on Monday and Tuesday at 9 o'clock in room 16.
My Maths class is on Sunday and Wednesday at 1 o'clock in room 21.
My Chemistry class is on Thursday at 10:30 in room 9.

NAME: Noshin Mirza
CLASS: F0B21
Student timetable

SUBJECT	______	Maths	Chemistry
WHEN	Monday ______ 9:00 – 11:00	Sunday ______ 1:00 – 3:00	______ ______ – 12:30
WHERE	Room 16	Room ______	Room ______

ACADEMIC WRITING SKILLS

5 Read and circle. Then write.

1 English is __on__ Monday. (in / **on** / at)

2 IT is ______ room 23. (in / on / at)

3 Chemistry is ______ 11 o'clock. (in / on / at)

4 Maths is ______ Tuesday. (in / on / at)

5 Japanese is ______ room 12. (in / on / at)

6 Biology is ______ 1:30. (in / on / at)

English is on Monday and Tuesday at 9 o'clock in room 16.

when?

what time?

where?

CRITICAL THINKING: CREATE

6 Write your English timetable for three classes.

NAME: __________

CLASS: F0B21

English timetable

WRITING TASK

7 Look at 6. Write about you.

This ____________________ my English timetable.
My English class is on ____________________ at
____________________ in room ____________________ .
My ____________________ ____________________ is on
____________________ at ____________________ in room
____________________ .
____________________ ____________________
____________________ is ____________________
____________________ at ____________________
____________________ room ____________________ .

8 Swap and check.

OBJECTIVES REVIEW

I can ...

- listen about subjects and timetables. ☐
- listen about interesting, easy, difficult and boring subjects. ☐
- ask and answer about time. ☐
- ask and answer about my subjects and timetable. ☐
- read an email about university subjects. ☐
- read a timetable. ☐
- write a timetable. ☐
- write about my subjects. ☐

WORDLIST

Biology	Japanese
boring	Maths
Business	Monday
Chemistry	o'clock
day	room
difficult	Saturday
easy	subject
English	Sunday
Friday	Thursday
History	time
interesting	Tuesday
IT	Wednesday

LEARNING OBJECTIVES

Listening	Questions with *what*, *where* and *who* A country or a city
Speaking	Answer questions with *what*, *where* and *who* Ask and answer questions about your country and city
Reading	A country or a city Sentences with *and*
Writing	Write sentences with *and* Write about your country or a city
Watch and remember	A video about old and new places

DIFFERENT COUNTRIES UNIT 4

UNLOCK YOUR KNOWLEDGE

Look and circle.

1 This is in *Mexico / Japan / Oman*.
2 Is this place *boring / interesting*?
3 Say three countries in English.

LISTENING AND READING 1

VOCABULARY: DESCRIBING COUNTRIES

1 4.1 Listen and point. Then say.

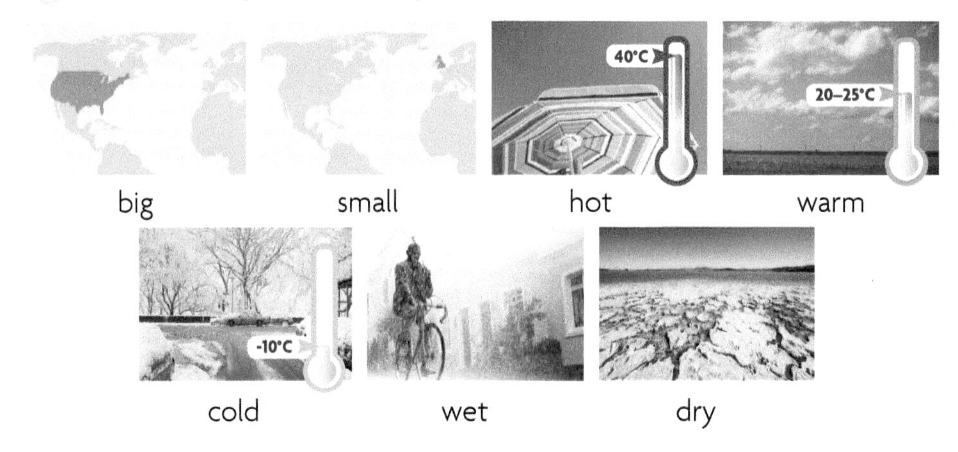

SOUND AND SPELLING: *w*, *v*

2 4.2 Write ***w*** or ***v***. Then listen and say.

1 _w_ et
2 ___ here
3 tele ___ ision
4 ___ hat
5 ___ ideo
6 ___ i-Fi
7 e ___ ening
8 ___ arm

READING FOR KEY INFORMATION

3 4.3 Look, read and circle. Then listen and check.

1 Canada is (*big*) / *small*.
2 It's *hot* / *cold* and *wet* / *dry*.

3 Singapore is *big* / *small*.
4 It's *hot* / *cold* and *wet* / *dry*.

PRONUNCIATION FOR LISTENING

LISTENING FOR KEY INFORMATION

WRITING AND SPEAKING

4 4.4 Listen and say.

It's hot and dry. 

It's cold and wet. 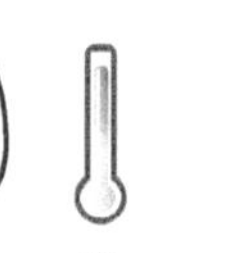

It's warm and dry. 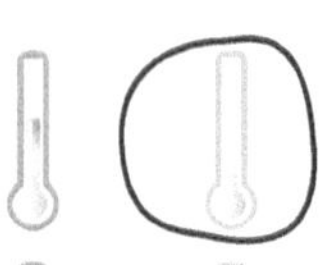 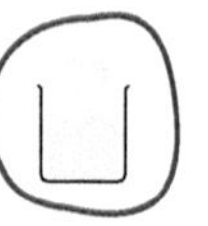 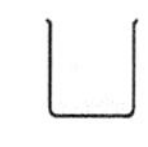

5 4.5 Listen and circle. Then say.

What's the UK like?

The UK is small. It's cold and wet.

1 the UK    

2 Turkey   

3 Japan

4 India

6 Look. Write. Then say.

BRAZIL

Country: Brazil

SAUDI ARABIA

Country: Saudi Arabia

1 Brazil is big. It is ______ and ______.

2 Saudi Arabia is ______. It is ______ and ______.

7 Write. Then say.

My country is ______. It is ______ and ______.

LISTENING AND READING 2

PREPARING TO LISTEN

1 4.6 Look and match. Then listen and say.

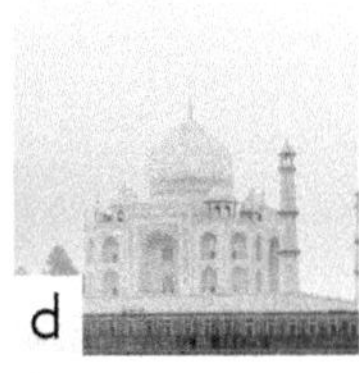

1 It's in India. d

2 They're in Egypt. ☐

3 It's in the USA. ☐

4 They're from Canada. ☐

5 It's from Japan. ☐

READING FOR DETAIL

2 4.7 Read and circle. Then listen and check.

1 It isn't in Saudi Arabia. It's in *Turkey / Mexico*.

2 It isn't in the USA. It's in *Egypt / Sudan*.

3 They aren't from Brazil. They're from *Mexico / Japan*.

4 It isn't from Canada. It's from *Egypt / India*.

NOTICE !

It's in Japan.

It's from Japan.

PRONUNCIATION FOR SPEAKING

3 4.8 Listen and say. Then look at 2 and say.

It isn't in the UK. It's in France.

He isn't from Mexico. He's from Canada.

They aren't in Saudi Arabia. They're in Turkey.

GRAMMAR: VERB *BE* NEGATIVE

4 4.9 Listen and read. Then say.

I	am not	in from	Canada. Saudi Arabia. Mexico. Egypt. the USA. Japan. the UK.
It She He	is not		
We You They	are not		

5 4.10 Read and circle. Listen and check. Then write.

NOTICE !

It isn't in Saudi Arabia. = It is not in Saudi Arabia.

They aren't from India. = They are not from India.

1 It is not in Canada. (is not / are not)

It ________ in the UK. (is / are)

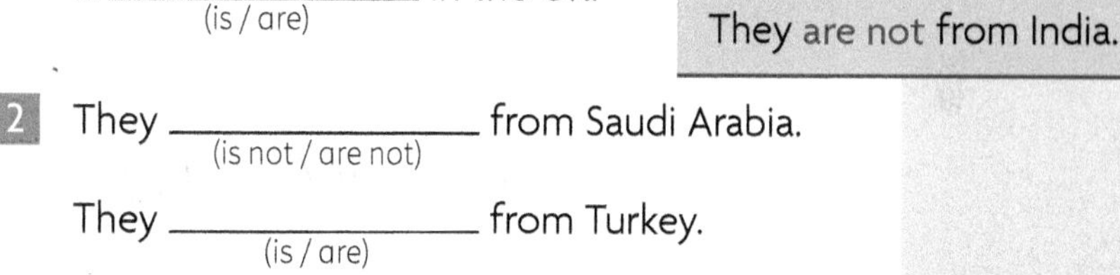

2 They ________ from Saudi Arabia. (is not / are not)

They ________ from Turkey. (is / are)

3 He is't from Mexico. (is not / are not)

He's ________ from Brazil. (is / are)

ACADEMIC WRITING SKILLS

6 Write the CAPITAL letters and **.**.

1 it is not in Canada. it is in Turkey

2 it is not in the USA it is in Japan

SPEAKING

7 Look and say.

It isn't from Singapore. It's from India.

1 Singapore ✗ India ✓

2 the UK ✗ the USA ✓

3 Oman ✗ Malaysia ✓

4 Canada ✗ the UK ✓

LISTENING AND READING 3

VOCABULARY: DESCRIBING CITIES

1 4.11 Listen and point. Then say.

new

old

expensive

cheap

beautiful

clean

LISTENING FOR KEY INFORMATION

2 4.12 Look at the photographs. Listen and write *1*, *2* or *3*.

READING FOR DETAIL

3 4.12 Read and circle. Listen and check. Then write.

1 This is Seoul, in South Korea. It is old (new / old) and beautiful. It isn't cheap.

2 This is London, in the UK. It is cheap (cheap / expensive). It isn't clean (clean / beautiful).

3 This is Doha, in Qatar. It is new (old / new) and beautiful. It isn't cheap (cheap / expensive).

4 4.13 Look at 3. Read again and circle. Then listen and check.

1 Is Seoul old? Yes, it is. No, it isn't.
Is it cheap? Yes, it is. No, it isn't.

2 Is London expensive? Yes, it is. No, it isn't.
Is it clean? Yes, it is. No, it isn't.

3 Are Doha and Seoul beautiful? Yes, they are. No, they aren't.
Are they cheap? Yes, they are. No, they aren't.

SPEAKING

5 Look at 2. Point and say.

London is old and expensive.

Doha isn't old.

GRAMMAR: VERB *BE* QUESTIONS

6 4.14 Listen and read. Say.

Is	London	old?	Yes, it is.	No, it isn't.
	it	expensive?		
	he	from the UK?	Yes, he is.	No, he isn't.
	she	in Canada?	Yes, she is.	No, she isn't.
Are	Seoul and Doha	cheap?	Yes, they are.	No, they aren't.
	they	beautiful?		

7 4.15 Read and circle. Listen and check. Then write.

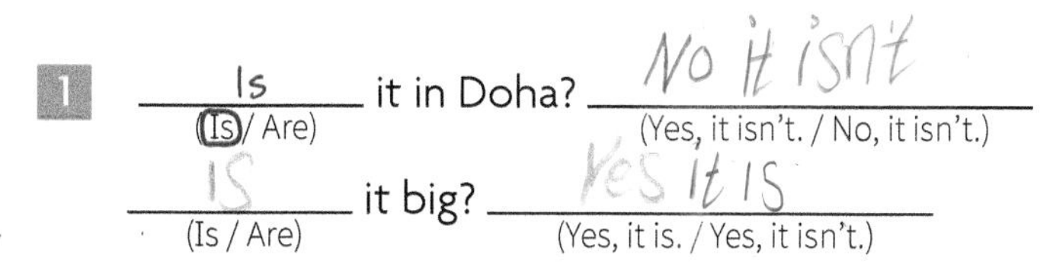

1 ___Is___ it in Doha? ___No it isnt___
(Is / Are) (Yes, it isn't. / No, it isn't.)

___IS___ it big? ___Yes it IS___
(Is / Are) (Yes, it is. / Yes, it isn't.)

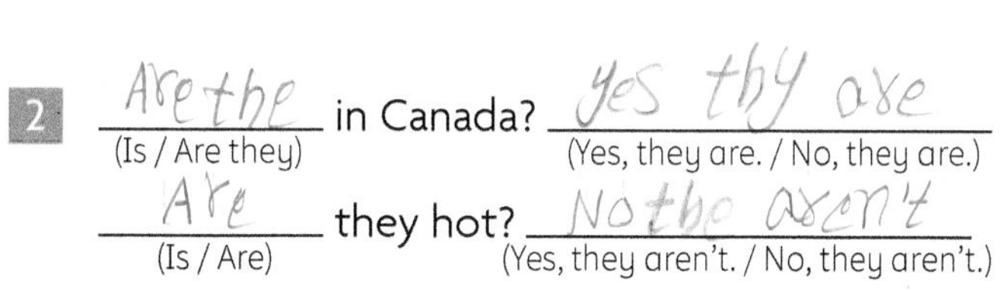

2 ___Are the___ in Canada? ___yes thy are___
(Is / Are they) (Yes, they are. / No, they are.)

___Are___ they hot? ___No the arent___
(Is / Are) (Yes, they aren't. / No, they aren't.)

NOTICE !

No, it isn't.
= No, it is not.

No, they aren't.
= No, they are not.

8 4.16 Listen and write the CAPITAL letters.

1 _D_ ubai 2 ___ ondon 3 ___ oha
4 ___ exico City 5 ___ stanbul 6 ___ okyo

ACADEMIC WRITING SKILLS

9 Look and write. Then ask and answer.

Dubai in the United Arab Emirates

___Is it___ old?
_______________ cheap?
_______________ beautiful?
_______________ big?

WRITING AND SPEAKING

10 Student A: Look at page 200.
Student B: Look at page 203.
Student C: Look at page 206.

SPEAKING

WATCH AND REMEMBER

PART 1

BEFORE YOU WATCH

1 Look. Match.

a

a old Town

b

a new city

c

a big Town

d

a small Town

1	big	a
2	new	b
3	small	c
4	old	d

2 4.17 Look at 1. Listen and check. Then write.

WATCH

3 Watch Part 1 and circle.

1 The 'Pearl' is a *new / old* city.

2 Mexico City is *big / small*.

3 The palace is *new / old*.

AFTER YOU WATCH

4 Read and write.

warm ~~Where's~~ Who's new Where's

A: Where's this?

B: This is Doha, in Qatar. It's warm and dry in Doha.

A: Who's this?

B: This is my brother.

A: Where's this?

B: It's in Doha. It's the 'Pearl'.

A: Is it new ?

B: Yes, it is.

PART 2

5 Look. Match. Then write.

a

b

c

d

________ ________ ________ ________

1 cold	a
2 wet	b
3 hot	c
4 dry	d

6 Watch part 2. Match.

1 Muscat, in Oman	wet and cold
2 London, in the UK	very cold
3 Seoul, in South Korea	hot and dry

7 Write.

My city is __________ and __________ .

PART 3

8 Watch part 3. Say. Then write.

city Doha London Seoul

1 The 'Pearl' is a new city.
2 It's hot and dry in Doha.
3 It's wet and cold in London.
4 It's very cold in Seoul.

9 Read and circle.

1 My city has a fort. Yes / No
2 My city has a palace. Yes / No

NOTICE !

interesting **place** in my city

beautiful **palace** for kings and queens

10 Ask and answer.

I'm from ... , in ...

What's it like?

It's ...

BEFORE YOU WATCH
WATCH
AFTER YOU WATCH
REMEMBER
MORE VOCABULARY: PLACES
ASK AND ANSWER

LANGUAGE FOCUS

VOCABULARY: *WH-* QUESTIONS

1 4.18 Match. Listen and say.

1 Where? ☐ 2 What? ☐ 3 Who? ☐

a

b

c

SPEAKING

2 4.19 Listen and match. Then say.

1 What's this?	It's in Kenya.
2 Where's this?	This is our driver.
3 Who's this?	It's an elephant.

4 What's this?	His name's Abdullah.
5 Where's this?	It's in Muscat.
6 Who's this?	This is oud from Oman.

NOTICE !

What's = What is

Where's = Where is

Who's = Who is

3 4.20 Listen and say.

What's this? Where's this? Who's this?

4 4.21 Look and write. Listen and check.

Where's this?

what is this?

who's this?

5 4.22 Look and write. Listen and check.

It is New Delhi, in India.

This is dal.

His name is Sashem.

it is Kerala, in India.

it is a sari.

her name is Srabanti.

6 Look at 4. Ask and answer.

This is ...

His name's ...

Where's this? What's this? Who's this?

It's in ...

ACADEMIC LISTENING AND SPEAKING

PREPARING TO LISTEN

1 4.23 Read and circle. Listen and check.

La Boca in Buenos Aires

1. Argentina is *big* / *small*.
2. Buenos Aires is a *country* / *city*.
3. La Boca is *interesting* / *boring*.

LISTENING FOR KEY INFORMATION

2 4.24 Listen and circle.

1. Natalia is from *Argentina* / *Mexico*.
2. Argentina is *hot and dry* / *wet*.
3. Buenos Aires is old and *expensive* / *beautiful*.
4. La Boca isn't *old* / *new*.
5. Buenos Aires isn't *warm* / *cold*.
6. Buenos Aires is *interesting* / *clean*.

CRITICAL THINKING: UNDERSTAND

3 4.24 Write. Listen again and check.

dry old city beautiful expensive ~~big~~

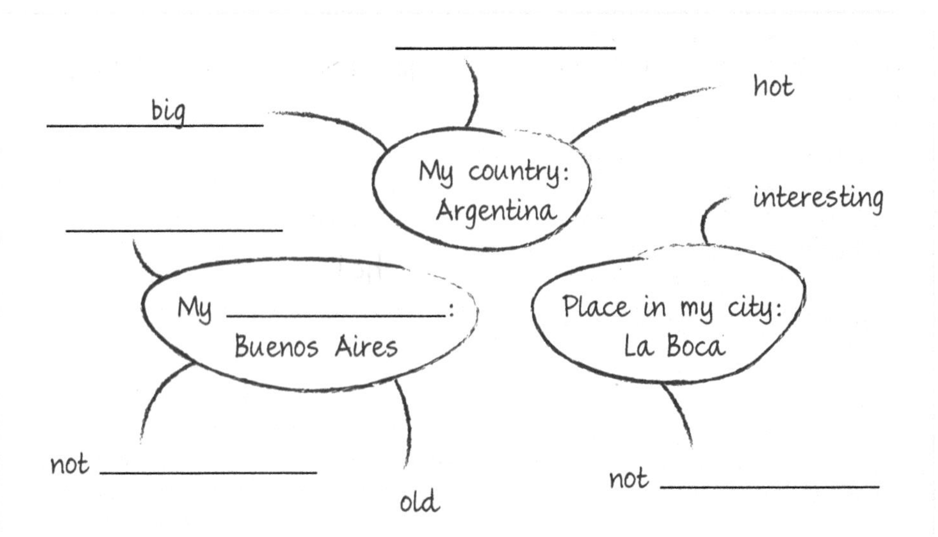

CRITICAL THINKING: CREATE

4 Write about your country. Swap and talk.

PRONUNCIATION FOR SPEAKING

5 4.25 Listen and say.

1	hot	Is it hot?	2	beautiful	Is it beautiful?
3	expensive	Is it expensive?	4	cold	Is it cold?
5	big	Is it big?			

SPEAKING TASK

6 Look at 4. Say. Ask and answer.

REMEMBER !

My country is ... / My city is ...
Is it hot in ... ? Is it expensive?
Yes, it is. / No, it isn't.

ACADEMIC READING AND WRITING

SCANNING FOR KEY INFORMATION

1 Look and circle. Read and check.

This is the Eiffel Tower. It is *big / small*.

This is the Louvre. It is *old / new*. It is in *London / Paris*.

FRANCE

the area:
643,801 km²

population:
66,660,000 people

This is France. France is a country in Europe.

Paris is a city in France. It is big. Paris is beautiful. It is expensive. The Eiffel Tower and the Louvre are in Paris. They are interesting. The Eiffel Tower is big. It is not new. The Louvre is old and beautiful. It is not boring.

Paris-Sorbonne University is in Paris. It is big and old. Students at the Sorbonne study Chemistry, Business and IT.

READING FOR DETAIL

2 4.26 Read 1 and listen. Circle *Yes* or *No*.

1	Paris is a country in France.	Yes	(No)
2	Paris is beautiful.	Yes	No
3	The Eiffel Tower and the Louvre are interesting.	Yes	No
4	Students at Paris-Sorbonne University study English, Business and IT.	Yes	No

3 4.27 Write. Then listen and check.

1 c _o_ _u_ ntry 2 c __ ty 3 b __ __ __ t __ f __ l
4 w __ rm 5 __ nt __ r __ st __ ng 6 sm __ ll
7 ch __ __ p 8 __ xp __ ns __ v __

4 Read and write.

place ~~country~~ city

_____country_____ : France – warm, not cold
_______________ : Paris – beautiful, clean, not cheap
_______________ : Eiffel Tower – big, interesting, not new

5 4.28 Look. Then write. Listen and check.

France is a country in Europe. **It** is warm. **It** is not cold.
Paris is a city in France. **It** is beautiful and clean. **It** is not cheap.
The Eiffel Tower is in Paris. **It** is big and interesting. **It** is not new.

Dubai is a city. __It__ is hot and dry.
______ is big and new. ______ is not cheap.
The Burj Khalifa is in Dubai. ______ is big.
______ is beautiful and new.

CRITICAL THINKING: CREATE

6 Write about a country.

Country: ______________ –
______________ , not ______________
City: ______________ –
______________ , ______________ , not ______________
Place: ______________ –
______________ , ______________ , not ______________

WRITING TASK

7 Look at 6. Write.

______________ is a country. It is ______________ . It is not ______________ .

______________ is a city in ______________ . It ______________ ______________ and ______________ . It ______________ not ______________ .

______________ is in ______________ . ______________ ______________ ______________ and ______________ . ______________ ______________ not ______________ .

8 Swap and check.

OBJECTIVES REVIEW

I can ...

- understand questions with *what*, *where* and *who*. ☐
- listen about a country and city. ☐
- answer questions with *what*, *where* and *who*. ☐
- ask and answer questions about my country and city. ☐
- read about a country and city. ☐
- read sentences with *and*. ☐
- write sentences with *and*. ☐
- write about my country and city. ☐

WORDLIST

beautiful	expensive
big	hot
cheap	new
city	old
clean	place
cold	small
country	warm
dry	wet

LEARNING OBJECTIVES

Listening	*Yes / No* questions Job
Speaking	Talk about your day Talk about jobs
Reading	Months in a calendar A flyer for a course
Writing	Write the names of the months Write about your studies
Watch and remember	A video about jobs and holidays

WORK UNIT 5

UNLOCK YOUR KNOWLEDGE

Look and circle.

1 They are *doctors / teachers.*

2 What's it like? *interesting / boring / easy / difficult*

3 Are you a student? What subjects do you study? What's it like?

LISTENING AND READING 1

VOCABULARY: JOBS

1 5.1 Listen and point. Then say.

a police officer

a pilot

a photographer

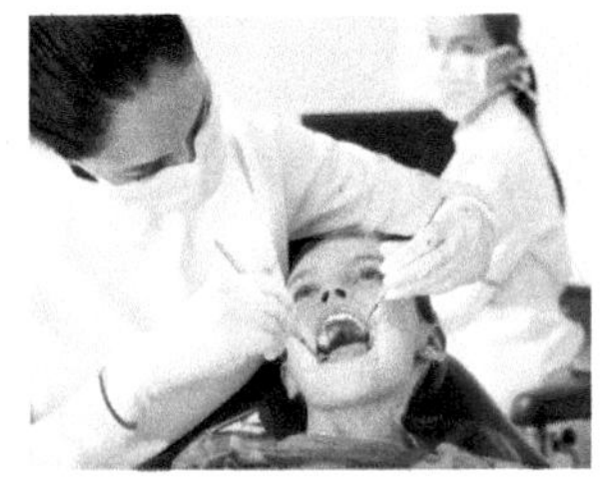
a dentist

a bank manager

a nurse

PRONUNCIATION FOR SPEAKING

2 5.2 Look and listen. Then say.

●	●•	● •	● • •	• ● • •	• ● ● • •
nurse	pilot	dentist	manager	photographer	police officer

READING FOR KEY INFORMATION

3 5.3 Read and circle. Listen and check.

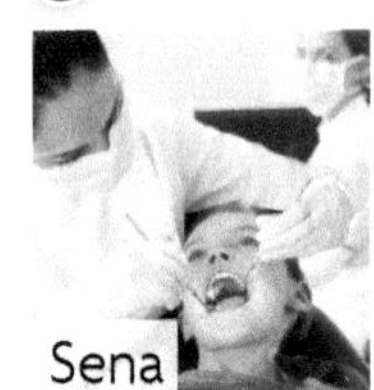
Sena

1 Is she a nurse? Yes, she is. No, she isn't.

Atilla

2 Is he a police officer? Yes, he is. No, he isn't.

Joel

3 Is he a pilot? Yes, he is. No, he isn't.

Kate

4 Is she a bank manager? Yes, she is. No, she isn't.

LISTENING FOR DETAIL

4 5.3 Listen again and match.

1 Sena — bank manager
2 Atilla — police officer in Ankara
3 Joel — sister
4 Kate — friend from the USA

SPEAKING

5 Look at 1. Ask and answer.

Is she a dentist?
Yes, she is.

Is he a pilot?
No, he isn't. He's a photographer.

ACADEMIC WRITING SKILLS

6 Write ? or . .

1 Is she a nurse ?
2 Is he a dentist ___
3 Yes, he is ___
4 Yes, she is ___
5 Is he a pilot ___

SOUND AND SPELLING: *ph, f, ff*

7 5.4 Look. Then listen and write *ph*, *f* or *ff*.

1 father
2 phone
3 co ___ ___ ee
4 ___ ___ otogra ___ ___ er
5 ___ riend

WRITING

8 Write about two people.

Name: Abdullah H	Name: Shirzad
Job: He is my frend He is student	Job: He is my brother He is student in Cheshire college

SPEAKING

9 Look at 8. Say. Ask and answer.

REMEMBER !

This is my ...
Is he / she a ... ?
Yes, he / she is.
No, he / she isn't.
He's / She's a ...

LISTENING AND READING 2

VOCABULARY: MY DAY

1 5.5 Listen and point. Then say.

go to work

go to university

go to the library

go home

start work / classes

finish work / classes

meet friends

LISTENING FOR KEY INFORMATION

2 5.6 Listen and circle *Yes* or *No*.

1. Her name is Valeria. Yes No
2. She is from Mexico. Yes No
3. She is a teacher. Yes No

READING FOR KEY INFORMATION

3 5.6 Read and write. Then listen again and check.

~~university~~ friends the library classes

Tuesday		Wednesday	
7:30	go to university	8:30	start work
8:00	start classes	4:30	finish work
3:00	finish ________	5:00	go to ________
3:30	meet ________		

ACADEMIC WRITING SKILLS

4 Write the CAPITAL letters.

1 I i study maths at cambridge university.

2 i study business at riyadh university.

NOTICE !

I study at Cambridge University.

GRAMMAR: PRESENT SIMPLE AFFIRMATIVE

5 5.7 Listen and read. Then say.

I	study	Business.
You	start	work at 9 o'clock.
We	meet	friends.
You	go	home at 5:30.
They	finish	classes at 3 o'clock.

6 5.8 Write. Listen and check. Then say.

1 I start work at 7:00.
(work / I / start)

2 ______ at 3:30.
(I / work / finish)

3 ______ at 4:00.
(go / home / I)

4 ______ at 8:30.
(start / We / classes)

5 ______ at 3:30.
(finish / classes / We)

WRITING

7 Write.

~~go to university~~ go to the library finish classes go home meet friends start classes

DAY: ______ **DAY:** ______

Time		Time	
____	go to university	____	____
____	____	____	____
____	____	____	____

SOUND AND SPELLING: *o*

8 5.9 Listen and say.

coffee officer
go home
work word

SPEAKING AND WRITING

9 Look at page 206.

LISTENING AND READING 3

VOCABULARY: WORK

1 5.10 Listen and point. Then say.

take photographs

read emails

write emails

help people

meet people

travel to different countries

work in the city

SOUND AND SPELLING: VOWEL SOUNDS WITH TWO LETTERS

2 5.11 Write. Then listen and check. Say.

1 r ___ ___ d
2 em ___ ___ l
3 m ___ ___ t
4 p ___ ___ ple
5 countr ___ ___ s

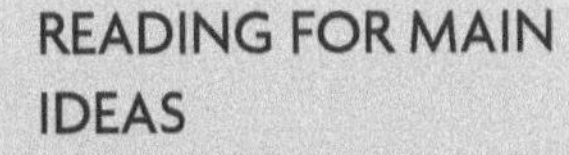

READING FOR MAIN IDEAS

3 5.12 Read and listen. Then match the photographs.

A a doctor

B a photographer

C a bank manager

1 Kate starts work at *8:00 / 9:00* in the evening. She works at night. She helps *students / people*.

2 Aki starts work at 9:00. He works *in the city / at university*. He reads and writes emails. He meets people. He finishes work at *5:00 / 5:30*.

3 Salim travels to different countries. He takes photographs. He works *at night / in the afternoon* and in the morning. His camera is big and *new / expensive*.

NOTICE !

in the city
the afternoon
the morning

at night
university

LISTENING FOR KEY INFORMATION

4 5.12 Look at 3. Listen again and circle.

5 5.13 Read and match. Then listen and say.

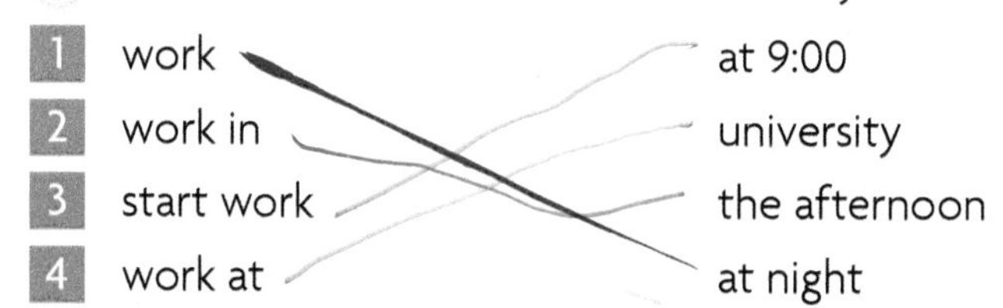

1 work — at 9:00
2 work in — university
3 start work — the afternoon
4 work at — at night

6 5.14 Listen and read. Then say.

He	works	in the city.
	reads	emails.
	travels	to different countries.
She	reads	books.
	helps	students.
	meets	people.

GRAMMAR: PRESENT SIMPLE AFFIRMATIVE *HE* AND *SHE*

7 5.15 Write. Then listen and check.

1 He starts (start) work at 7:00.
2 He reads (read) books.
3 He Write (write) emails.

4 She start (start) work at 6:30.
5 She help (help) people.
6 She Work (work) in the morning.

WRITING AND SPEAKING

8 Student A: Look at page 200.

Student B: Look at page 203.

WATCH AND REMEMBER

PART 1

BEFORE YOU WATCH

1 Look. Match.

a

b

c

d

1 a pilot — a
2 a nurse — b
3 a doctor — c
4 a photographer — d

2 5.16 Look at 1. Listen and check. Then write.

WATCH

3 Watch part 1 and circle.

1 Neil is a *bank manager* / *pilot*.
2 Aadab is a *doctor* / *nurse*.
3 The photographers have *a nice* / *an interesting* job.

AFTER YOU WATCH

4 5.17 Read and circle. Then listen and check.

A: Who are they? Are they *photographs* / *photographers*?

B: Yes, they are. They take *photographs* / *photographers* of *boring* / *interesting* people.

A: What's it like?

B: It's a *nice* / *new* job!

PART 2

5 5.18 Listen and point. Then say.

work

go on holiday

go to university

6 Watch part 2 and circle.

1. William goes on holiday *in the UK* / *Switzerland*.
2. Saad works in *Riyadh* / *Jeddah*.
3. Safiya goes to university in *Dammam* / *London*.

7 Write about you.

I'm a ______________ . I go on holiday in ______________ .

PART 3

8 Watch part 3. Say. Write.

June January a nurse a pilot

1. Neil is a pilot.
2. Aadab isn't a nurse.
3. William goes on holiday in January.
4. Saad goes on holiday in June.

9 Look. Match. Then write.

a

b

c

1. a waiter — c
2. an actor
3. a driver

a
b
c

10 Ask and answer.

Are you a waiter?

No, I'm not. I'm a ...

BEFORE YOU WATCH

WATCH

AFTER YOU WATCH

REMEMBER

MORE VOCABULARY: JOBS

ASK AND ANSWER

LANGUAGE FOCUS

VOCABULARY: MONTHS

1 5.19 Listen and point. Then say.

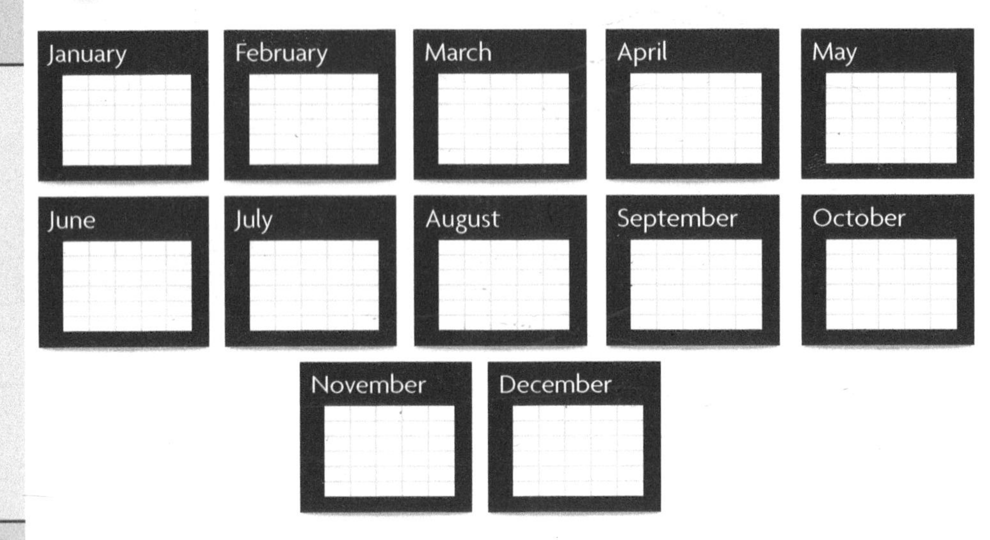

ACADEMIC WRITING SKILLS

2 Look at 1. Underline the CAPITAL letters.

PREPARING TO LISTEN

3 5.20 Look and match. Then listen.

a

b

December
classes finish
winter holiday starts
c

August
university starts
d

1 The **winter holiday** is in December. c

2 The **first day of** university is in August.

3 The English **exam** is in May.

4 The **summer holiday** starts in June.

4 5.21 Listen and circle. Then say.

1	When is the summer holiday?	In May.	In July.
2	When is the first day of university?	In September.	In October.
3	When is the Maths exam?	In November.	In February.
4	When is the English exam?	In March.	In December.
5	When is the winter holiday?	In April.	In January.

5 5.22 Listen and write. Then say.

1	A __ __ i __	2	Augu __ __
3	O __ __ ober	4	Fe __ __ uary
5	Se __ __ ember	6	Nove __ __ er

NOTICE !

in January.

in October.

6 Look at 4. Read and write.

September	first day of university
	English exam
	Maths exam
	winter holiday
	summer holiday

REMEMBER !

When is the ... ?

In February.

7 Student A: Look at page 201.

Student B: Look at page 204.

LISTENING FOR KEY INFORMATION

ACADEMIC WRITING SKILLS

READING AND WRITING

SPEAKING

ACADEMIC LISTENING AND SPEAKING

USING VISUALS TO PREDICT CONTENT

1 5.23 Look and match. Then listen and check.

Maitha is a **manager**.

1 She is
2 She works in
3 She reads and writes

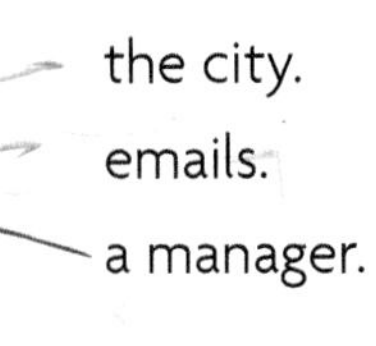

the city.
emails.
a manager.

John is a **pilot**.

4 He is
5 He travels to
6 He works

interesting places.
a pilot.
at night.

LISTENING FOR DETAIL

2 5.23 Listen again and circle *Yes* or *No*.

1	Maitha is from Turkey.	Yes	No
2	She starts work at 10 o'clock.	Yes	No
3	She meets university managers.	Yes	No
4	She finishes work at 7:30.	Yes	No
5	John is from the USA.	Yes	No
6	He starts work at different times.	Yes	No

CRITICAL THINKING: REMEMBER

3 5.23 Write. Then listen again and check.

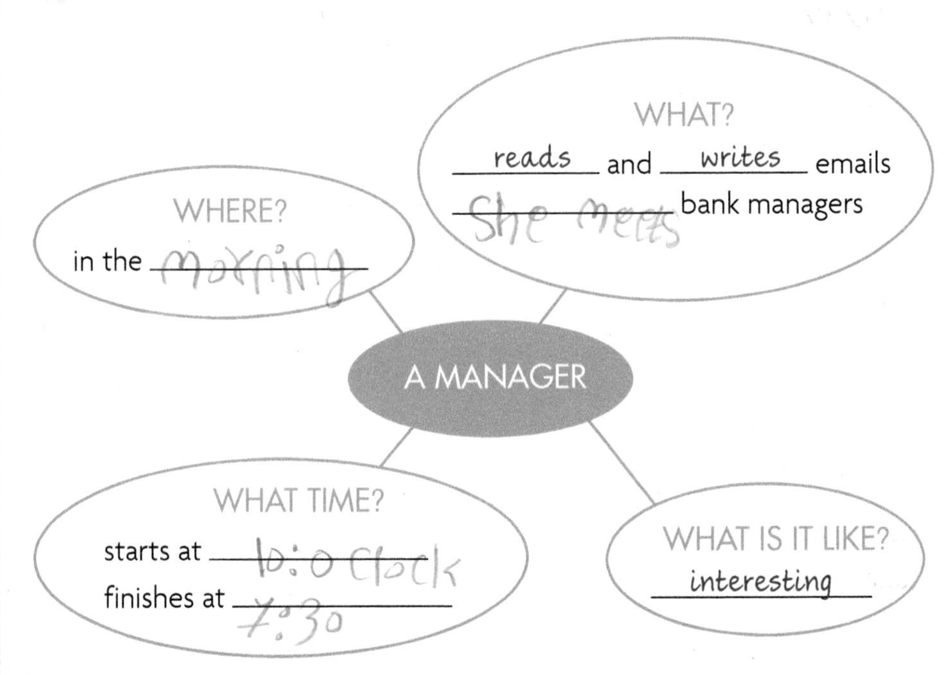

CRITICAL THINKING: ANALYZE

4 Circle one job. Then circle *where*, *what* and *what is it like*.

teacher

bank manager

photographer

pilot

Where?

in the city / at a bank / at university / in different countries

What?

travels to different countries / helps people / meets interesting people / helps students / reads and writes emails

What is it like?

interesting / boring / easy / difficult

NOTICE !

at university

at a bank

PREPARING TO SPEAK

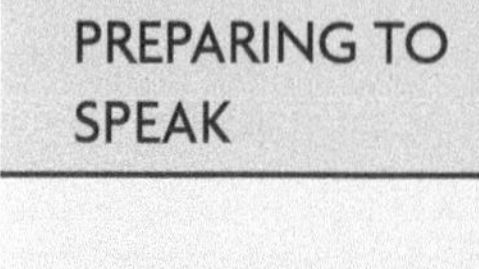

5 Write about a job from 4. Swap. Then ask and answer.

Where? at university

What? helps students

a teacher

What time?
starts at 9:15
finishes at 3:00

What is it like? boring

PRONUNCIATION FOR SPEAKING

6 5.24 Listen and say.

Is it interesting? Is it easy? Is it difficult? Is it boring?

SPEAKING TASK

7 Look at 5 and talk.

A teacher works at university. She helps ...

Is it interesting? Is it easy?

ACADEMIC READING AND WRITING

PREPARING TO READ

1 Look and match.

1 Wi-Fi ☐
2 Word® ☐
3 PowerPoint® ☐
4 video ☐

a 
b 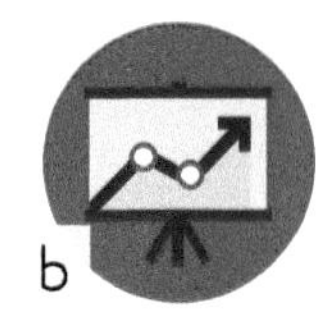
c
d 

READING FOR MAIN IDEAS

2 Read and circle.

It's about computer *jobs / classes*.

COMPUTER CLASSES!!!

When? Tuesdays, Thursdays

What time? 4:30 – 6:30

Where? Room 23

In this class, we study:

- emails
- Microsoft Word® and
- PowerPoint®

The classes are with Mr Bahlia and Mr Patel. We start in October. The classes finish in December. The exam is in January.

Sign up soon!

READING FOR DETAIL

3 5.25 Look at 2. Read and listen. Then circle *Yes* or *No*.

1 The classes are on Wednesdays. Yes No

2 They start at 4:30. Yes No

3 They finish at 5:30. Yes No

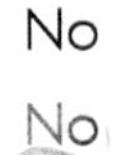

4 They are in room 28. Yes No

5 The classes start in October. Yes No

6 The exam is in December. Yes No

4 Look at **2**. Read and tick ✔.

In this class, they study:

mobile phones	☐	photographs	☐	emails	☐
computers	☐	Wi-Fi	☐	videos	☐
Microsoft Word®	☑	PowerPoint®	☐		

5 5.26 Write. Then listen and say.

1 f _ n _ sh   2 st _ rt   3 st _ dy
4 w _ rk   5 st _ d _ nt

6 Look and read. Write.

Ganesh

2017	IT student
2021	IT teacher

You

__________ __________
__________ __________

Ganesh

7 Read and write.

I am an IT student.
I study at Tesla University in Mumbai.
I study IT, Maths and English.
My classes start in September and finish in June.
In the afternoon, I go to the library and meet friends.
In the evening, I go home and read books.

study at Tesla University
in __________
study IT __________,
__________ and
____

classes start in
____
classes finish in
____

IT student

in the afternoon
go to __________
meet __________

in the evening
go __________
read __________

CRITICAL THINKING: CREATE

8 Write about your studies.

study at ______________________
in ______________________
study ______________________

classes start in
____
classes finish in
____

student

in the afternoon
____
____

in the evening
____
____

ACADEMIC WRITING SKILLS

9 Look. Then write.

I go to the library. **I meet** friends.
I go to the library **and meet** friends.

I go home. I read books.
I ______________ and read ______________ .
My classes start in September.
My classes finish in June.
My classes start ______________ and ______________ .

NOTICE !
I go to the library and meet friends.

WRITING TASK

10 Look at 8. Write about your studies.

I am a student.
I study at ______________ in ______________ .
I study ______________ and ______________ .
My classes start ______________ and ______________ .
In the afternoon, I go ______________ and ______________ .
In the evening, I ______________ and ______________ .

11 Swap and check.

OBJECTIVES REVIEW

I can ...

- understand *Yes* / *No* questions. ☐
- listen about a job. ☐
- talk about my day. ☐
- talk about jobs. ☐
- read months in a calendar. ☐
- read a flyer for a course. ☐
- write the names of the months. ☐
- write about my studies. ☐

WORDLIST

April	May
August	meet friends
bank manager	meet people
December	November
dentist	nurse
exam	October
February	photographer
finish work / classes	pilot
first day of university	police officer
go home	read emails
go to university	September
go to the library	start work / classes
go to work	summer holiday
help people	take photographs
January	travel to different countries
July	winter holiday
June	work in the city
March	write emails

LEARNING OBJECTIVES

Listening	A survey report about food What people do in a day
Speaking	Ask and answer *How are you?* Talk about food and drinks
Reading	Food and health in different countries What people do in a day
Writing	Complete a survey about your food Write about what you eat
Watch and remember	A video about food and drink

FOOD AND HEALTH UNIT 6

UNLOCK YOUR KNOWLEDGE

1 Look. Where is it?
2 Is food in this photograph cheap or expensive?
3 Is food cheap or expensive in your country?

LISTENING AND READING 1

VOCABULARY: FOOD

1 6.1 Listen and point. Then say.

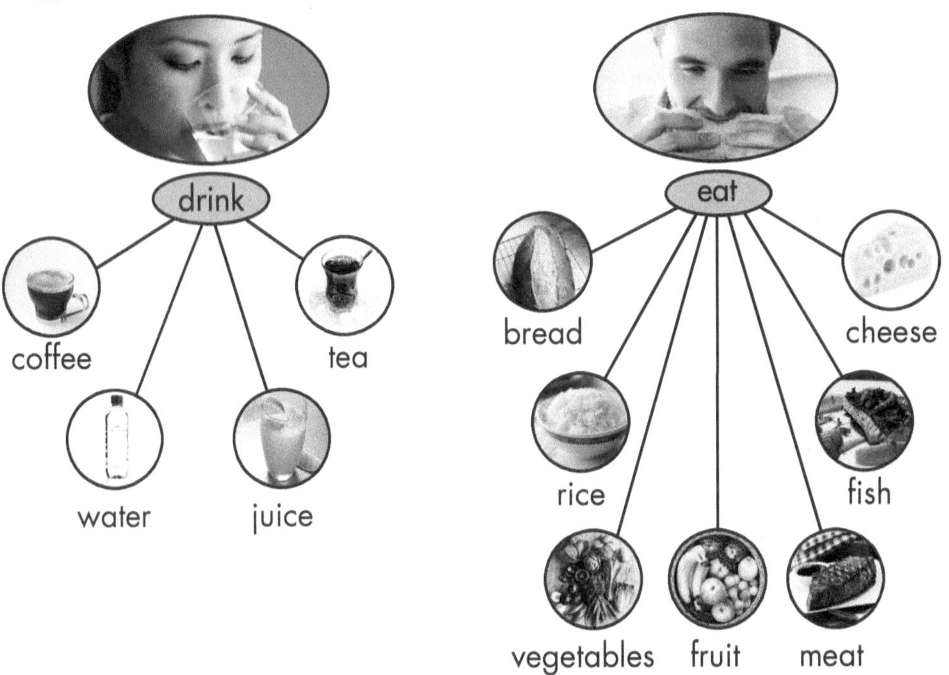

LISTENING FOR DETAIL

2 6.2 Listen and match.

Naomi from France

A

Vinood from India

B

3 6.2 Read and circle. Then listen again and check.

Naomi:

I eat **bread** / *fruit* and cheese.
I eat potatoes and *fish* / **meat.**
I don't eat **rice** / *potatoes.*
I drink **coffee** / *tea* and water.
I don't drink **juice** / *coffee.*

Vinood:

I eat **rice** and **fish** / *meat.* I eat
bread and vegetables / *cheese.*
I don't eat *rice* / **meat.**
I drink *coffee* / **tea and water.**
I don't drink juice / *water.*

NOTICE !

I don't eat rice. = I do not eat rice.

4 Look at 1. Say.

I eat rice. I don't eat fish.

I drink coffee. I don't drink tea.

5 6.3 Write. Then listen and check.

1 d r ink
2 f r uit

3 b r ead

6 Look at 1 and write. Then check.

I eat meat and rice.
I do not eat bread.
I drink water and juice.
I do not drink tea.

7 Look at page 207.

LISTENING AND READING 2

VOCABULARY: DAILY ROUTINE

1 6.4 Listen and point. Then say.

get up

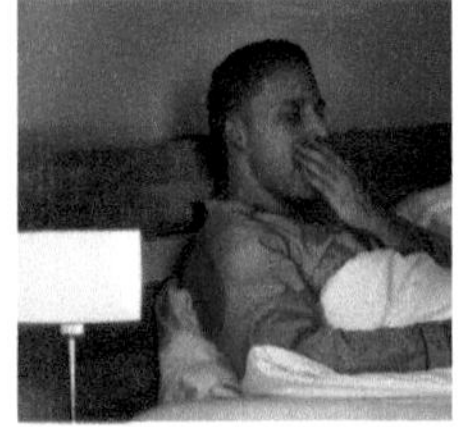

go to bed

have breakfast

have lunch

have dinner

drive to work

walk to university

SOUND AND SPELLING: *ea*

2 6.5 Say and match. Then listen and check.

1	tea	meat
2	tea	eat
3	bread	breakfast

LISTENING FOR DETAIL

3 6.6 Listen and circle.

Mia and Lena have
breakfast / lunch / dinner
with their friends.

READING FOR DETAIL

4 6.6 Read and listen again. Then match.

I'm Mia and this is my sister Lena. We go to university in New York. We get up at 6:30 and have breakfast at 7:00. I drink coffee. Lena doesn't drink coffee. She drinks tea.

We walk to university. We don't drive. I have lunch with my friends at 12:30. Lena has lunch with her friends. We finish classes at 4:00 and go home.

We have dinner at 7:30. Lena goes to bed at 10:00. I go to bed at 11:00.

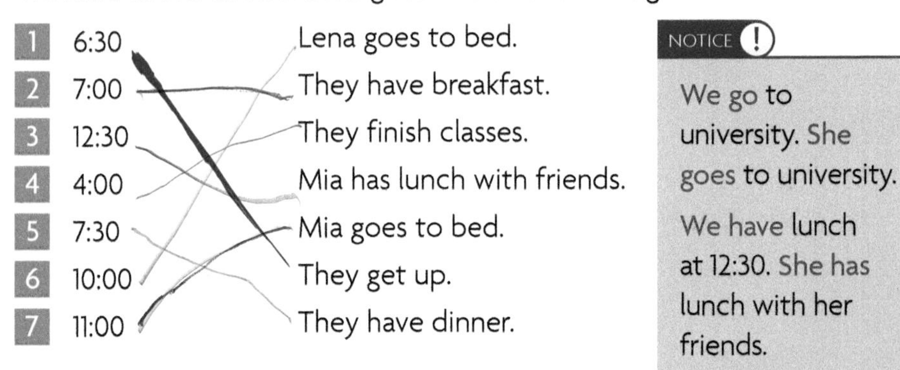

1	6:30	Lena goes to bed.
2	7:00	They have breakfast.
3	12:30	They finish classes.
4	4:00	Mia has lunch with friends.
5	7:30	Mia goes to bed.
6	10:00	They get up.
7	11:00	They have dinner.

NOTICE !

We go to university. She goes to university.

We have lunch at 12:30. She has lunch with her friends.

GRAMMAR: *DON'T* AND *DOESN'T*

5 6.7 Listen and read. Then say.

I We You They	do not	drink coffee. walk to university. get up at 7:00. study.
He She	does not	drive to work. eat bread.

6 6.8 Read and circle. Listen and check. Then write.

1 They ______________ get up at 9:30.
(does not / do not)

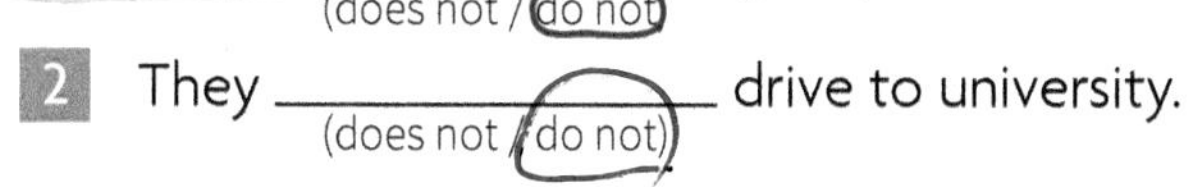

2 They ______________ drive to university.
(does not / do not)

3 He ______________ walk to work.
(does not / do not)

4 He ______________ have lunch at home.
(does not / do not)

WRITING AND SPEAKING

7 Look at 1 and say. Then listen and write.

I get up at 8:00. I don't have breakfast.

Name: Mia
gets up at 6:30
has breakfast at 7:00
goes to university at ______________
has lunch at 11:30
finishes university at 4:00
has dinner at 7:30
goes to bed at 11:00

SPEAKING

8 Look at 7 and say.

REMEMBER !

He / She gets up at 8:00.
He / She doesn't have breakfast.

LISTENING AND READING 3

VOCABULARY: HEALTH

1 6.9 Listen and point. Then say.

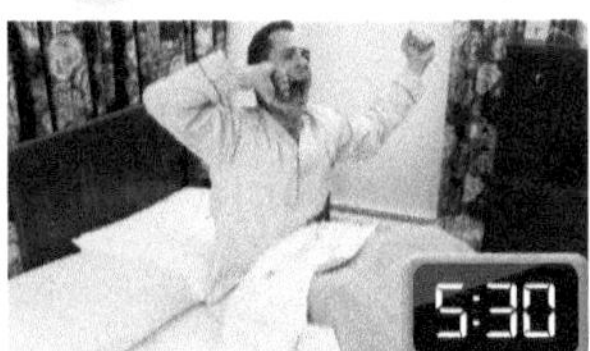

get up early

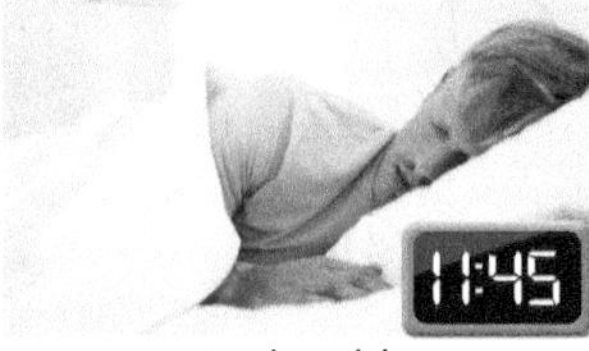

go to bed late

drink green tea

eat fruit and vegetables

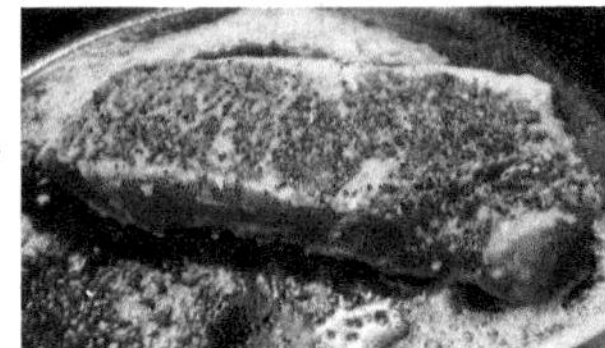
eat red meat

drink coffee with milk and sugar

SPEAKING

2 Look at 1. Say.

I eat fruit and vegetables. I get up early.

I don't eat fruit and vegetables. I don't get up early.

SCANNING FOR KEY INFORMATION

3 Read and circle.

1 People in *Canada / Japan* go to bed at 12:49 and get up at 6:30.

2 People in *Canada / Japan* go to bed at 11:30 and get up at 7:33.

Food and Health: Japan and Canada

	go to bed	get up
people in Japan	12:49	6:30
people in Canada	11:30	7:33

A lot of people in Japan go to bed late and get up early. They eat a lot of *fish / meat*. Some people eat red meat. They eat a lot of fruit and vegetables. Not a lot of people drink *tea / coffee* with milk and sugar.

People in Canada go to bed early and get up early. A lot of people eat red meat and *rice / potatoes*. They eat a lot of bread. Not a lot of people eat rice. Some people drink *green tea / juice*.

Food from Japan

Food from Canada

LISTENING FOR KEY INFORMATION

4 6.10 Look at 3. Listen, read and circle.

GRAMMAR: *A LOT OF, SOME, NOT A LOT OF*

5 6.11 Listen and read. Then say.

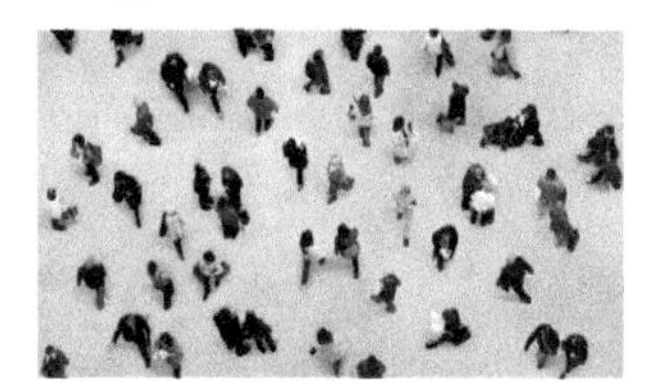

A lot of people

Some people

Not a lot of people

A lot of Some Not a lot of	people	eat	fish. red meat. rice.

NOTICE !

A lot of people go to bed late.

They eat a lot of fruit and vegetables.

READING FOR DETAIL

6 Look at 3. Read again and circle. Then write.

Japan

People eat ___a lot of___ fish. (a lot of / some)

______ people eat red meat. (Some / A lot of)

___Not a lot of___ people drink coffee with milk and sugar. (A lot of / Not a lot of)

Canada

___A lot of___ people eat red meat and potatoes. (A lot of / Not a lot of)

People eat ___a lot of___ bread. (some / a lot of)

___Some___ people drink green tea. (Not a lot of / Some)

WRITING

7 Write about people in your country. Swap and check.

	a lot of people	**some people**	**not a lot of people**
eat	rice, meat.	Vegetables	
drink	tea	Milk	Win

SPEAKING

8 Look at 7. Say.

A lot of people in Turkey drink tea with sugar.

Not a lot of people drink green tea.

REMEMBER !

A lot of people eat / drink ...
Some people eat / drink ...
Not a lot of people eat / drink ...

WATCH AND REMEMBER

PART 1

BEFORE YOU WATCH

1 Look. Then write.

lunch breakfast dinner

a

for ____________

b

for ____________

c

for ____________

2 6.12 Look at **1**. Listen and check.

WATCH

3 Watch part 1 and circle.

1 Gamze gets up *early* / *late*.
2 She drinks *tea* / *coffee* for breakfast.
3 She has a *cheap* / *expensive* lunch.
4 Gamze and Oya have *rice* / *noodles* for dinner.
5 Kashif gets up *early* / *late*.
6 Dubai has a lot of *libraries* / *markets*.
7 Kashif eats *fish* / *meat* and *vegetables* for lunch.

AFTER YOU WATCH

4 Read and write.

eat cheap Some expensive dinner ~~lot~~

1 A ____lot____ of people in Turkey eat meat for lunch or ____dinner____.
2 ____Some____ people in Istanbul have a big and ____expensive____ dinner. They eat meat for dinner too.
3 I have dinner with Oya. For dinner we ____eat____ noodles. We are students and noodles are ____cheap____!

PART 2

5 Look. Match.

a

b

c

1 coffee — a
2 green tea — b
3 a lot of coffee — c

6 6.13 Look at 5. Listen and check. Then write.

7 Watch part 2 and write **A** (Amy) or **G** (grandfather).

a lot of coffee	G	cheese	G	green tea	A
bread	G	fruit	A	sugar	G

PART 3

8 Watch part 3. Say. Write.

vegetables ~~salad~~ market cheese fruit

1 Gamze eats salad with cheese and olives for breakfast.
2 Kashif eats a lot of fruit and vegetables.
3 The grandfather goes to the market.

9 Look. Match. Then write.

a

b

c

1 dates — a
2 olives — b
3 noodles — c

10 Ask and answer.

What do you have for *breakfast / lunch / dinner?*

I *eat / drink* ... for *breakfast / lunch / dinner.*

LANGUAGE FOCUS

VOCABULARY: FEELINGS

1 6.14 Listen and point. Then say.

fine

not bad

not well

hungry

great

busy

tired

2 6.15 Look and circle. Listen and check. Then write.

1 I'm not well .
(fine / not well)

2 I'm __________ .
(fine / great)

3 I'm __________ .
(not bad / tired)

4 I'm __________ .
(busy / fine)

5 I'm __________ .
(not well / hungry)

6 I'm __________ .
(tired / great)

USING VISUALS TO PREDICT CONTENT

3 Look. Then read and circle.

1 B: I'm *fine* / *tired*. And you?
A: I'm *not bad* / *great*. Thank you.

2 B: I'm *fine* / *not well*.
A: *Thank you.* / *I'm sorry.*

3 B: I'm *great* / *hungry*.
A: *Me too.* / *And you?* Let's have lunch.

4 B: I'm *busy* / *not well*. I have a lot of classes.
A: *Me too.* I have a lot of work. I'm *tired* / *fine*.

LISTENING FOR KEY INFORMATION

4 6.16 Look at 3. Listen and check.

PRONUNCIATION FOR SPEAKING

5 6.17 Listen and say.

I'm great. I'm not bad. I'm not well.
I'm fine. I'm tired. I'm busy.

SPEAKING

6 Say.

REMEMBER !

How are you?
I'm ...
I'm fine. Thank you.
And you?
I'm sorry.
Me too!
Let's have lunch.

ACADEMIC LISTENING AND SPEAKING

PREPARING TO LISTEN

1 Look and match.

a 

b 

c

1 He eats some fruit and vegetables. ___
2 He doesn't eat a lot of fruit and vegetables. ___
3 He eats a lot of fruit and vegetables. ___

CRITICAL THINKING: UNDERSTAND

2 6.18 Look and circle. Then listen and check.

FOOD SURVEY

Please answer about what you eat and drink.

Name: Mark Jones

	a lot of	some	not a lot of
coffee	✔		
water			
tea		✔	
juice			
sugar	✔		
fruit and vegetables			
fish			✔
red meat			

1 Mark drinks a lot of *juice / coffee.*
2 He drinks some *water / tea.*
3 He doesn't eat a lot of *fish / red meat.*

CRITICAL THINKING: APPLY

3 Read. Look at 2 and tick ✔ the survey.

I don't drink a lot of water.

I don't drink a lot of juice.

I eat some fruit and vegetables.

I eat a lot of red meat.

LISTENING FOR DETAIL

4 6.18 Listen again and circle *Yes* or *No*.

1 Mark drinks coffee at night. Yes No
2 He drinks tea in the evenings. Yes No
3 He drinks coffee and tea with sugar. Yes No
4 He eats a lot of fruit and vegetables. Yes No
5 He eats some red meat. Yes No

CRITICAL THINKING: APPLY

5 Answer about you. Write and tick ✓.

FOOD SURVEY

I eat and drink ...

Name: Helal

	a lot of	some	not a lot of
coffee			✓
water	✓		
tea		✓	
juice	✓		
sugar			✓
fruit and vegetables		✓	
fish		✓	
red meat	✓		+

PRONUNCIATION FOR SPEAKING

6 6.19 Read and listen. Then say.

I drink a lot of coffee.
I don't drink a lot of water.
I eat a lot of sugar.
I eat some fish.

SPEAKING TASK

7 Look at 5 and say.

REMEMBER !

I drink a lot of ...
I eat some ...
I don't eat a lot of ...

ACADEMIC READING AND WRITING

PREPARING TO READ

1 6.20 Read and match. Then listen and say.

A 

B 

1 This is healthy.

2 This is not healthy.

NOTICE !

People eat fish for breakfast / lunch / dinner.

Fish is good for you.

USING VISUALS TO PREDICT CONTENT

2 Look. Then read and circle.

1 *A lot of / Some / Not a lot of* people in South Korea are healthy.

2 *A lot of / Some / Not a lot of* people in the USA are not healthy.

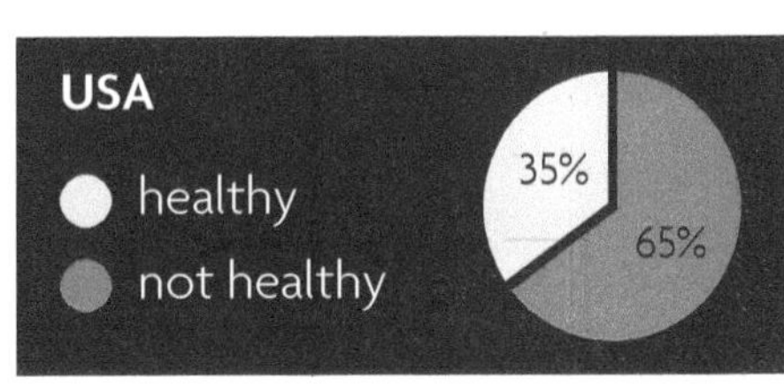

READING FOR DETAIL

3 6.21 Read and listen. Then circle *Yes* or *No*.

Food and Health: South Korea and the USA

A lot of people in South Korea are healthy. They do not eat a lot of sugar. For breakfast, they eat a lot of fruit and vegetables. They eat fish for lunch and dinner. Fish is good for you.

A lot of people in South Korea are tired. They go to bed late at night and get up early.

Some people in the USA are not healthy. For breakfast, they eat a lot of sugar and bread. They eat red meat for lunch and dinner. It is not good for you.

A lot of people are busy, but they are not tired. They go to bed early and they get up late.

1	People in South Korea eat a lot of sugar.	Yes	No
2	In South Korea, people eat fish for breakfast.	Yes	No
3	People in South Korea get up early.	Yes	No
4	Some people in the USA eat sugar for breakfast.	Yes	No
5	A lot of people have fish for lunch in the USA.	Yes	No
6	People in the USA go to bed early.	Yes	No

4 6.22 Look at 3. Read and write. Then listen and check.

red meat fish late bread early ~~fruit~~

South Korea

For breakfast, they eat ___fruit___ and vegetables.

For lunch and dinner, they eat ___Fish___ .

They get up ___early___ .

the USA

For breakfast, they eat sugar and ___bread___ .

For lunch and dinner, they eat ___red meat___ .

They get up ___late___ .

ACADEMIC WRITING SKILLS

5 6.23 Write the letters. Listen and check.

1 ch_e_ _e_se 2 fr__ __t 3 v__g__t__bl__s

4 m__ __t 5 f__sh 6 s__g__r

7 br__ __d 8 r__c__

CRITICAL THINKING: APPLY

6 Look and read. Write.

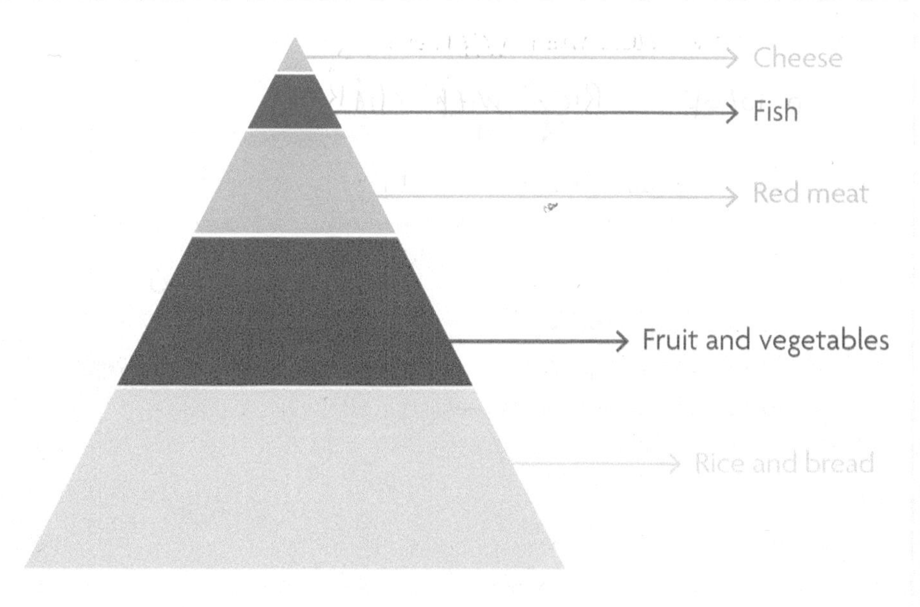

I eat a lot of rice and ___bread___ .

I eat a lot of fruit and ___Vegetables___ .

I eat some ___Red___ ___meat___ .

I do not eat a lot of ___fish___ .

I do not eat a lot of ___Cheese___ .

CRITICAL THINKING: CREATE

7 Write about your food. Swap and talk.

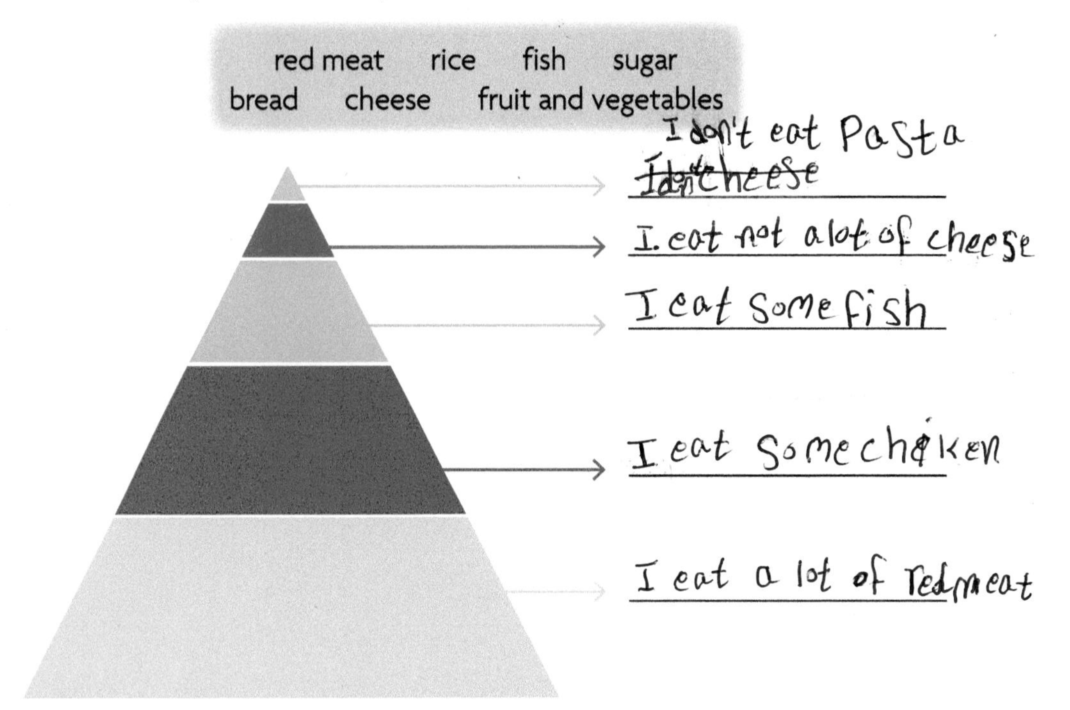

red meat rice fish sugar
bread cheese fruit and vegetables
I don't eat Pasta
~~Idon cheese~~
I eat not a lot of cheese
I eat Some fish
I eat Some chiken
I eat a lot of Redmeat

WRITING TASK

8 Look at **7**. Write.

I eat a lot of read meat with rice.

I eat a lot of Rice with chiken.

I eat some ________________.

I do not eat a lot of ________________.

I ________________ ________________ eat a lot of ________________.

9 Swap and check.

OBJECTIVES REVIEW

I can ...

listen to a survey report about food.	☐
listen about what people do in a day.	☐
ask and answer *How are you?*.	☐
talk about food and drinks.	☐
read about food and health in different countries.	☐
read about what people do in a day.	☐
complete a survey about my food.	☐
write about what I eat.	☐

WORDLIST

bread	green tea
busy	have breakfast
cheese	have dinner
coffee	have lunch
coffee with milk and sugar	healthy
drink	hungry
drive to work	juice
eat	meat
fine	not bad
fish	not well
fruit	red meat
fruit and vegetables	rice
get up	tea
get up early	tired
go to bed	vegetables
go to bed late	walk to university
great	water

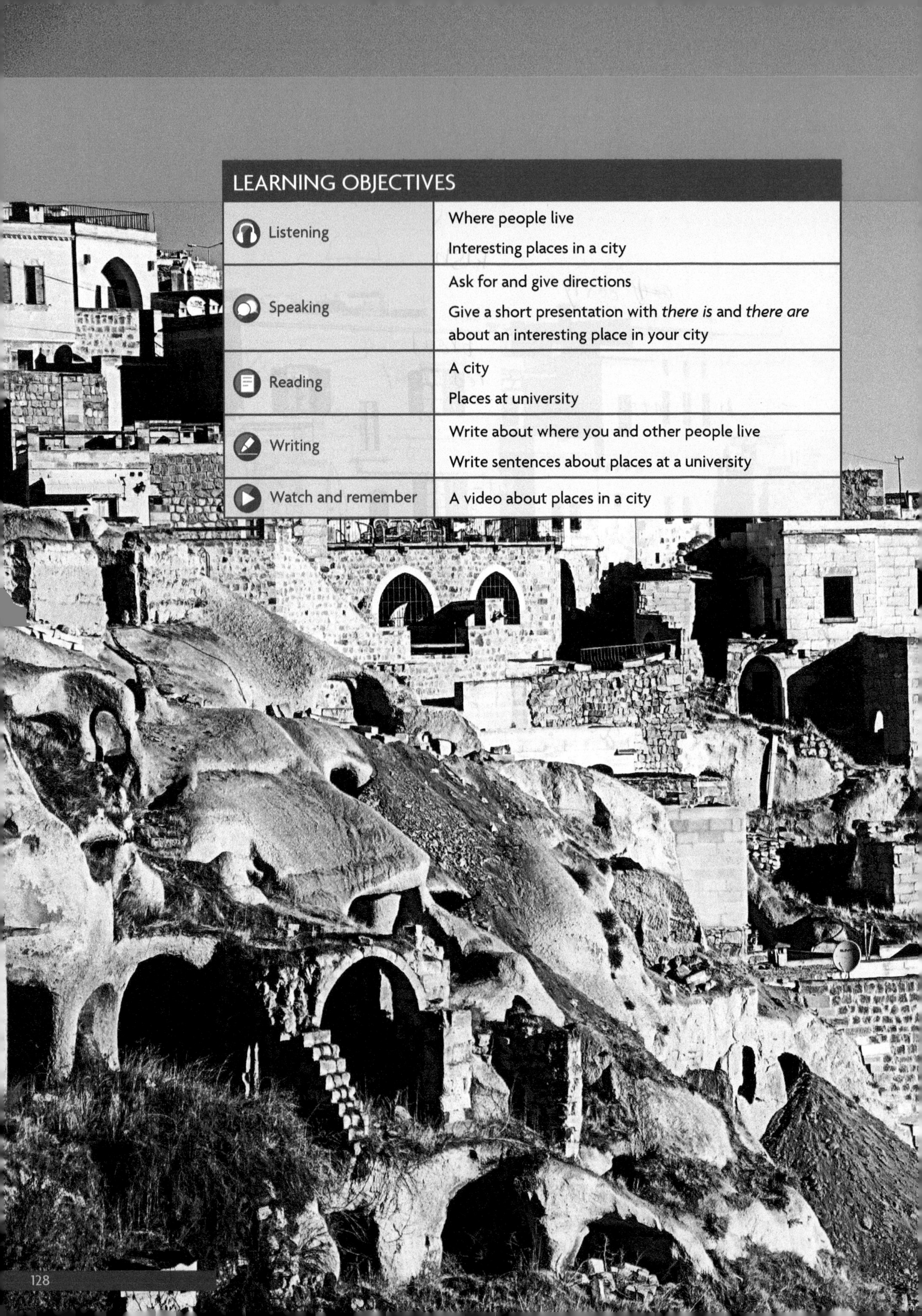

LEARNING OBJECTIVES

Listening	Where people live Interesting places in a city
Speaking	Ask for and give directions Give a short presentation with *there is* and *there are* about an interesting place in your city
Reading	A city Places at university
Writing	Write about where you and other people live Write sentences about places at a university
Watch and remember	A video about places in a city

PLACES UNIT 7

UNLOCK YOUR KNOWLEDGE

Look and circle. Then talk.

1 This place is

a beautiful b interesting c cold d warm

e old f new g clean

2 It is in *Argentina / Turkey / Canada.*

LISTENING AND READING 1

VOCABULARY: PLACES IN A CITY 1

1 7.1 Listen and point. Then say.

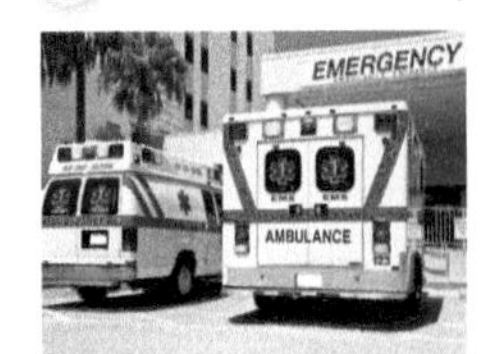

a hospital

a beach

a train station

a shopping centre

a park

an airport

an office building

SOUND AND SPELLING: *r*

2 7.2 Listen and say.

train room three centre park airport

LISTENING FOR KEY INFORMATION

3 7.3 Listen and write *1*, *2* or *3*.

a Tokyo

b Jeddah

c New York

4 7.3 Listen again and circle.

Asma

I live in Jeddah. I live near a beach and *a shopping centre* / *a hospital*. I don't live near a train station.

Taito

I live in Tokyo. I live near a train station and *an office building* / *a shopping centre*. I don't live near a park.

Steve

I live in New York. I live near an airport and *an office building* / *a hospital*. I don't live near a beach.

NOTICE !

I live near a train station.

I live near an office building.

I live near an airport.

SPEAKING

5 Look and say.

1

I live near a train station.

I **don't** live near an airport.

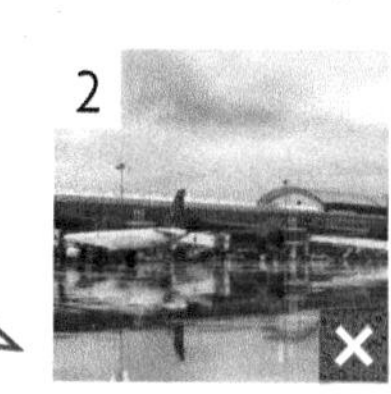
2

3

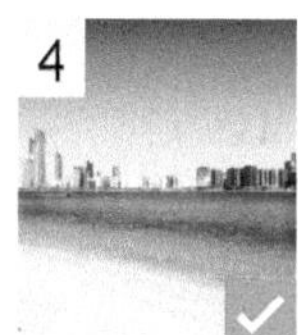
4

5

6

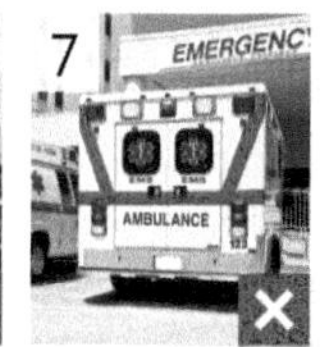
7

8

READING FOR DETAIL

6 Look and read. Then (circle) *Yes* or *No*.

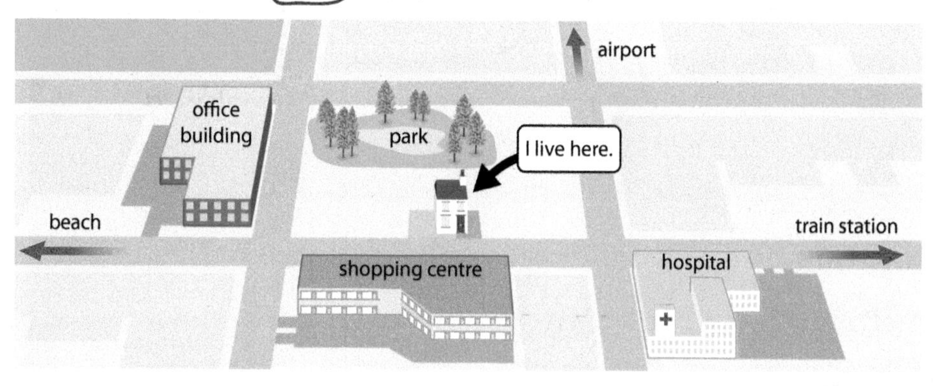

1	I live near a park.	(Yes)	No
2	I live near a shopping centre.	(Yes)	No
3	I do not live near an airport.	(Yes)	No
4	I live near a beach.	Yes	(No)
5	I do not live near an office building.	Yes	(No)
6	I live near a hospital.	(Yes)	No
7	I live near a train station.	Yes	(No)

WRITING

7 Look and write. Swap and check.

1

2

3

1 I live near a hospital **and** an airport.

2 I live near a Park and office building

3 I don't live near a Shoping on a trinstation

REMEMBER !

I live near ... and ...

SPEAKING AND WRITING

8 Student A: Look at page 201.

Student B: Look at page 204.

LISTENING AND READING 2

VOCABULARY: PLACES IN A CITY 2

1 7.4 Listen and point. Then say.

a restaurant

a factory

a hotel

a shop

a house

USING VISUALS TO PREDICT CONTENT

2 Look at the photographs in 3 and (circle).

This is Brighton. Brighton is *a hotel / a city*. It's really beautiful.

LISTENING FOR KEY INFORMATION

3 7.5 Listen, read and (circle).

ABOUT THE CITY | HOTELS | RESTAURANTS | AIRPORT

This is Brighton.

Brighton is a city in *India / the UK*. A lot of people travel to Brighton in *the summer / winter*. There are some beaches and parks. There are a lot of restaurants and hotels near the beaches. There is a train station and a *big / new* shopping centre.

Students from different countries study in Brighton. There are *two / three* universities. Students live in houses near the universities. There are a lot of shops and restaurants for the students.

There are some factories near Brighton. And there is an airport.

Brighton is really beautiful.

Brighton Wheel

Brighton Racecourse

READING FOR DETAIL

4 Look at 3. Read and (circle).

1 Brighton has some *beaches / banks*.

2 It has a lot of *restaurants / universities*.

3 It has *two airports / an airport*.

4 Brighton is a *new / beautiful* city.

NOTICE !

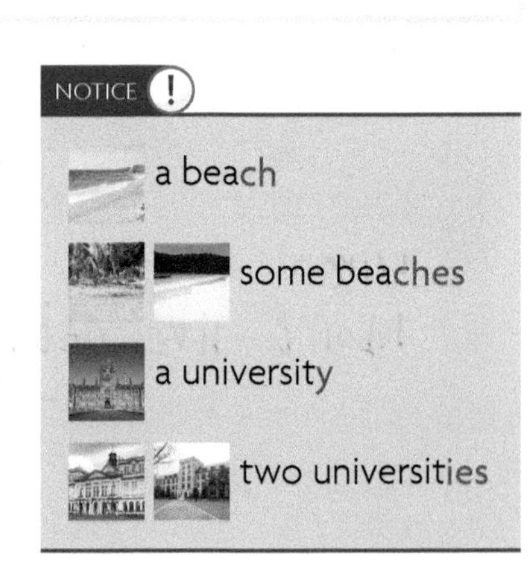

GRAMMAR: *THERE IS / THERE ARE*

5 7.6 Listen and read. Then say.

There	is	a train station.
		an airport.
	are	some hotels.
		five shops.
		a lot of restaurants.

6 Read and circle. Then look at 3 and check.

1 There *is* / *are* some beaches.
2 There *is* / *are* a lot of restaurants.
3 There *is* / *are* a train station.
4 There *is* / *are* a shopping centre.
5 There *is* / *are* two universities.
6 There *is* / *are* an airport.

7 7.7 Read and circle. Listen and check. Then write.

1 There is a factory in my city. (a factory / some factories)
2 There are ______ . (a library / two libraries)
3 There are ______ in my city. (a beach / some beaches)
4 There is ______ . (a university / some universities)
5 There are ______ in my city. (a hotel / a lot of hotels)

WRITING

8 Write about your city. Swap and check.

This is ~~city~~ cable .
There is ~~are some~~ mountains in my city.
There are some ______ .
~~There aresome~~ a lot of Building in my city.
And sea are Parks .

SPEAKING

9 Look at 8. Talk about your city.

REMEMBER !

There is a / an ... There are some / a lot of ...

LISTENING AND READING 3

VOCABULARY: FAMOUS PLACES

1 7.8 Listen and point. Then say.

an old street

an interesting market

a busy square

a famous stadium

tall buildings

LISTENING FOR KEY INFORMATION

2 7.9 Listen and match.

1 Ali is from *Rabat / Marrakesh*.

2 Carmen is from *Rio de Janeiro / Salvador*.

READING FOR DETAIL

3 7.9 Read and listen again. Then write.

Ali

I'm Ali. I live in Marrakesh. It's a beautiful city. There are a lot of old streets and buildings. I live near a busy square – the Jemaa el-Fnaa square. It's a famous place. There is an interesting market.

a market in Marrakesh

b Jemaa el-Fnaa square

c streets in Marrakesh

d beaches in Rio

e buildings in Rio de Janeiro

f Maracanã Stadium in Rio

My name's Carmen and I live in Rio de Janeiro. It's a big city. There are some beautiful beaches. There are a lot of tall buildings and new houses. I live near a famous stadium – the Maracanã Stadium.

Carmen

tall   old   ~~beautiful~~   famous   interesting   big

1 Marrakesh is a beautiful city.

2 A lot of streets in Marrakesh are old.

3 Ali lives near an interesting market.

4 Rio de Janeiro is a big city.

5 A lot of buildings in Rio are tall.

6 Carmen lives near a famous stadium.

GRAMMAR: ADJECTIVES

4 7.10 Listen and read. Then say.

			ADJECTIVE	PLACE
It	is	a an	beautiful old	city. street.
There	is	a an	busy interesting	square. market.
There	are	some a lot of	tall new	buildings. houses.

5 7.11 Write. Then listen and check.

the city of Rome

1 Rome is an old city.
(old / city. / an)

2 There are a lot of interesting buildings
(a lot of / buildings. / interesting)

3 There are ______
(streets. / beautiful / some)

4 The Colosseum is some beautiful street
(place. / famous / a)

5 There is a busy
(busy / a / square.)

SPEAKING

6 Match and say.

Oxford Street in London

1 It is — some — great — shops.
2 There is — a — old — street.
3 There is — a lot of — busy — shopping centre.
4 There are — a — famous — restaurant.
5 There are — a — expensive — buildings.

WRITING

7 Look at 6 and write.

1 It is a busy street.
2 ~~There is alotof shopping centre~~
3 ~~There are~~
4 ______
5 ______

WATCH AND REMEMBER

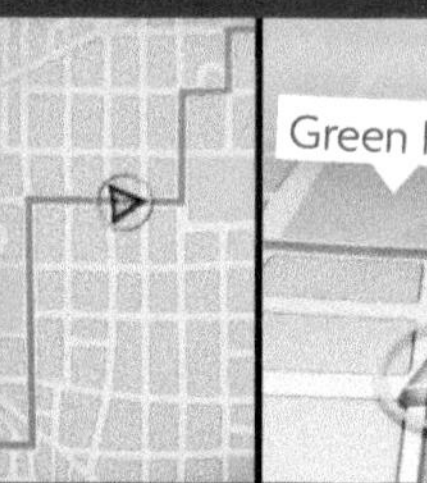

PART 1

BEFORE YOU WATCH

1 Look. Then write.

a hotel   an office building   a car factory   a shopping centre

a

b

c

d

2 7.12 Look at 1. Listen and check.

NOTICE !

~~The fishes are …~~

The fish are …

WATCH

3 Watch part 1 and circle.

1 Rashid lives in the *UAE* / *USA*.
2 There is a famous *factory* / *tall building* in Dubai.
3 There are a lot of *fish* / *vegetables* in the hotel.
4 Rashid says the hospitals are *good* / *busy*.
5 In Incheon there are a lot of *small* / *tall* buildings.
6 Ji-woo *drives* / *walks* to work.
7 There are beautiful *beaches* / *stadiums*.

AFTER YOU WATCH

4 Read and write.

expensive   big   interesting   tall   beautiful

In the UAE there are beaches, parks and tall buildings. There are a lot of shops and a big shopping centre. There are a lot of beautiful fish in the shopping centre! There are ______, ______ hotels. There are a lot of fish in the hotel too!

BEFORE YOU WATCH

WATCH

AFTER YOU WATCH

REMEMBER

MORE VOCABULARY: PLACES

ASK AND ANSWER

PART 2

5 7.13 Listen and point. Then say.

turn right

turn left

go straight on

6 Watch part 2 and choose map *a* or *b*.

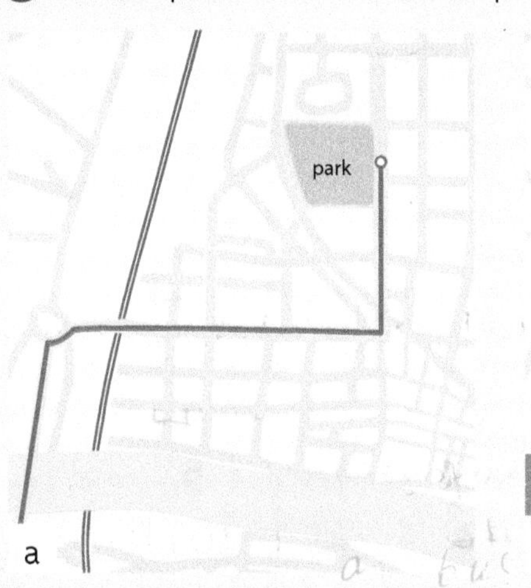

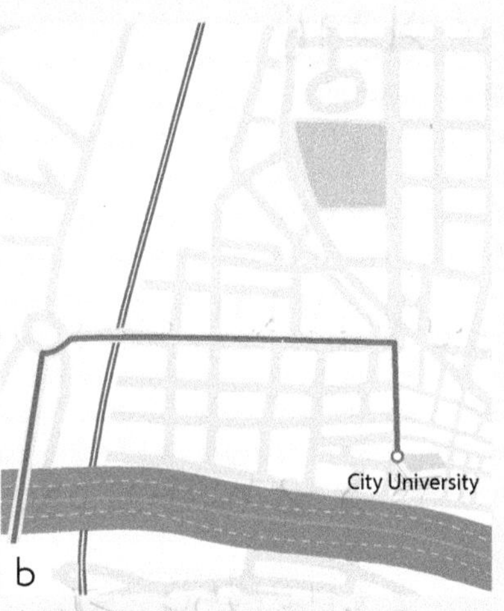

7 Watch part 2 again. Then write the numbers.

1 There is __one__ bridge.

2 There are ________ parks.

PART 3

8 Watch part 3. Say. Write.

1 In Dubai there is a famous tall ________________ .

2 The fish are in ________________ and ________________ .

3 There are ________________ in the factory.

4 Green Park is beautiful and ________________ .

9 Look. Then write.

bridge boats station

a

b

c

________________ metro ________________ ________________

10 Ask and answer. Then write.

Excuse me, where is ... Park?

Turn / go ...

LANGUAGE FOCUS

VOCABULARY: LOCATION

1 7.14 Listen and point. Then say.

on Green Street

on the right

on the left

next to the restaurant

between the hospital and the shop

near the park

2 Look at your location on the map. Read and circle *Yes* or *No*.

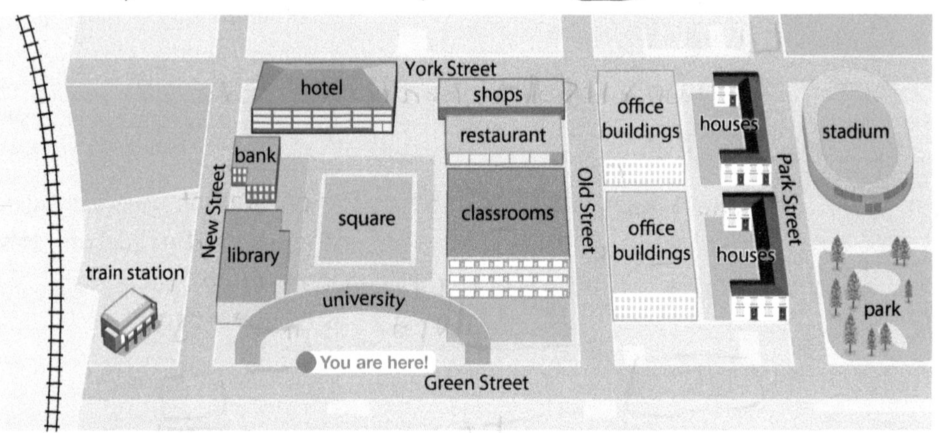

1	The office buildings are on the right.	(Yes)	No
2	The houses are on Park Street.	Yes	No
3	The bank is on the right.	Yes	No
4	The park is next to the library.	Yes	No
5	The restaurant is between the classrooms and the shops.	Yes	No
6	The train station is near the library.	Yes	No

READING AND WRITING

3 7.15 Read and circle. Listen and check. Then write.

1 The office buildings are ____on____ Old Street. ((on) / between)

2 The shops are ________ the restaurant. (next to / between)

3 The library is ________ the train station. (on the left / near)

4 The stadium is ________ . (next to / on the right)

5 The bank is ________ the library and the hotel. (between / on the right)

LISTENING FOR KEY INFORMATION

4 7.16 Listen and circle. Then say.

Excuse me. Where's the library?
It's *on New Street* / *on Park Street.*
I'm sorry. I don't understand. Where's that?
New Street is on the *right* / *left.* The library is next to the train station.
Thank you.
You're welcome.

NOTICE !

It's on New Street.

New Street is on the left.

Excuse me. / *Thank you.* Where's the bank?
It's on Market Street, near *the square* / *the stadium.* It's *between* / *on* two restaurants.
I'm sorry. Could you say that again please?
Yes. It's on Market Street between two restaurants.
29
Italia

PRONUNCIATION FOR LISTENING

5 7.17 Listen and say.

Where's the bank?

Where's the library?

It's near the square.

Could you say that again please?

SPEAKING

6 Student A: Look at page 201.

Student B: Look at page 204.

ACADEMIC LISTENING AND SPEAKING

USING VISUALS TO PREDICT THE CONTENT

1 Look and circle.

Advik from India

Chandni Chowk market

Chandni Chowk is a market in India. Chandni Chowk is *busy / new / old / small / expensive / cheap / tall.*

Rachel from Singapore

Orchard Road

Orchard Road is a street in Singapore. It is *old / new / clean / big / small / busy / interesting.*

LISTENING FOR DETAIL

2 7.18 Look at 1. Listen and check your answers.

3 7.18 Listen again and circle *Yes* or *No*.

1	Advik lives near Chandni Chowk.	Yes	No
2	There are a lot of big shops.	Yes	No
3	There are a lot of cheap restaurants.	Yes	No
4	Orchard Road is old.	Yes	No
5	There is a shopping centre.	Yes	No
6	It's an interesting place.	Yes	No

CRITICAL THINKING: REMEMBER

4 7.19 Look at Rachel's notes. Write. Then listen and check.

buildings new ~~street~~ shopping centre

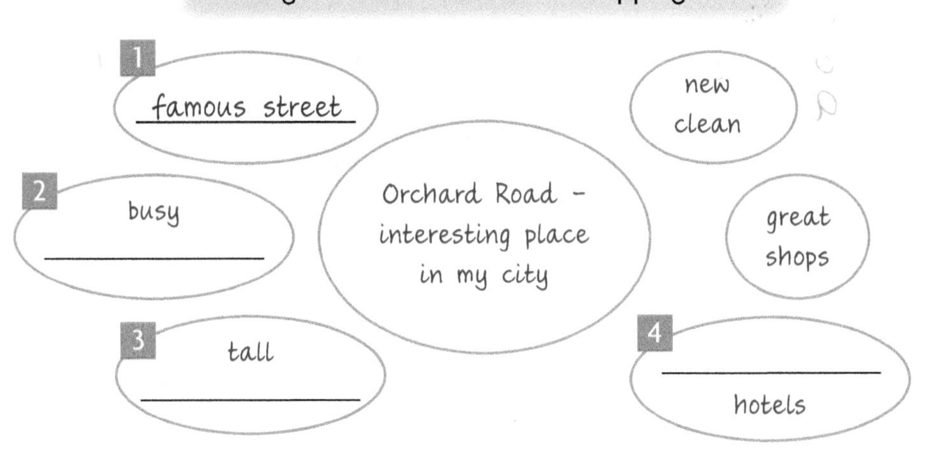

CRITICAL THINKING: APPLY

5 Write about an interesting place in your city.

cheap	expensive	small
big	tall	beautiful
famous	clean	busy

shops	restaurant	hotels
houses	beach	market
square	stadium	buildings

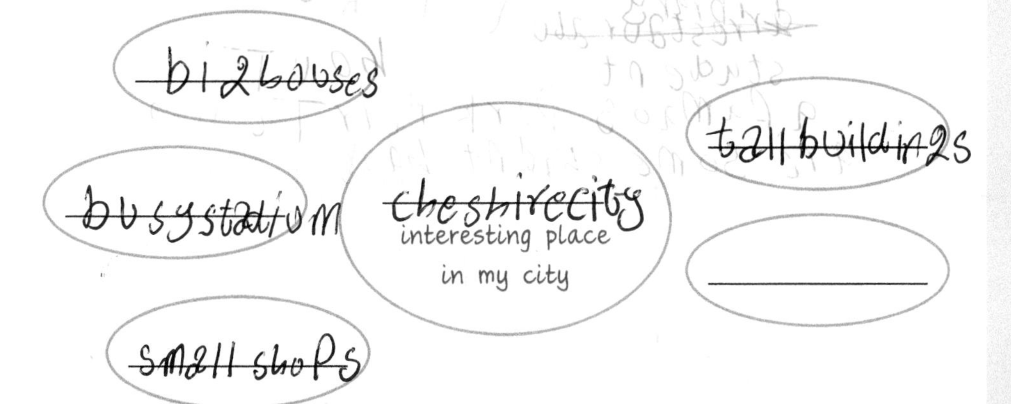

PRONUNCIATION FOR SPEAKING

6 7.20 Listen and say.

There's ... busy stadium
There's an interesting shop.
There's a tall building.

There are ... small shops
There are some great restaurants.
There are a lot of new houses.

SPEAKING TASK

7 Look at 5. Talk about an interesting place in your city.

REMEMBER !

I live near ... ... is an interesting place in my city.
There is ... There are ...

ACADEMIC READING AND WRITING

PREPARING TO READ

1 Look at the photographs and (circle).

The university has

a library / a beach / classrooms / student houses / a factory / office buildings.

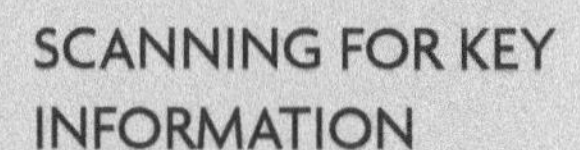

SCANNING FOR KEY INFORMATION

2 Read and underline *the city, student houses* and *library*.

Home | Our Students | Our Teachers

Welcome to Al Jazari University!

Our university is near the city centre on Volkan Street. There is a train station near the university, and it's next to the famous Al Jazari Park.

There are 2,000 students. They study Maths, Chemistry and Business. Some students live in student houses. There is a restaurant for the students with food from different countries. It is near their houses and it is really good. It is not expensive. There are also some shops.

Our library is next to the office buildings. It is 100 years old! There are a lot of interesting books. A lot of students study in the library in the evenings.

student houses

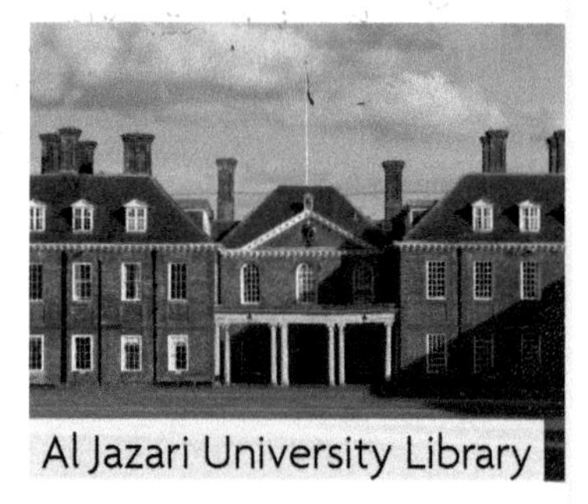

Al Jazari University Library

3 Look at 2 again. Then (circle) *Yes* or *No*.

1. Al Jazari University is in the city. (Yes) No
2. Al Jazari University does not have student houses. Yes (No)
3. There is an old library at the university. (Yes) No

4 7.21 Read 2 again and listen. Then write.

1. The university is near the city ___centre___.
2. The university is on Volkan ___street___.
3. ___2000___ students study Maths, Chemistry and Business.
4. The restaurant for the students is not ___expensive___.
5. A lot of students are in the ___library___ in the evenings.

READING FOR DETAIL

5 Look at **2**. Read again. Write on the map.

restaurant train station office buildings

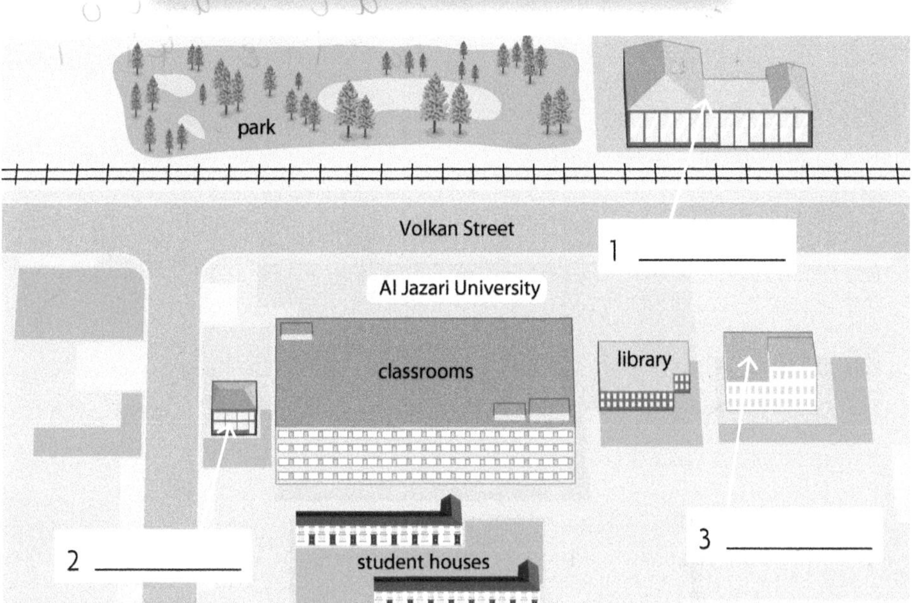

CRITICAL THINKING: ANALYZE

6 Read and underline the places. Read, look and tick ✔ the map.

1 The university is near a beautiful beach.
2 There is a famous park near the beach.
3 There is an old library next to the classrooms.
4 There are some student houses between the train station and the restaurant.
5 There is a good restaurant next to the student houses.

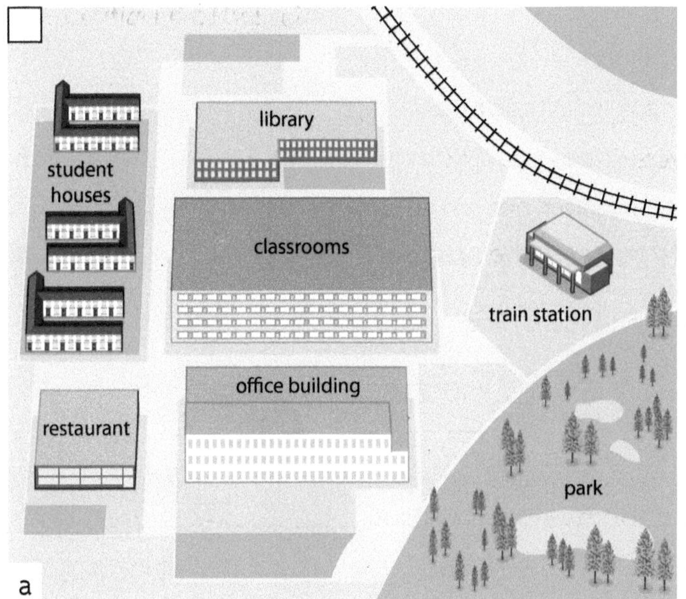

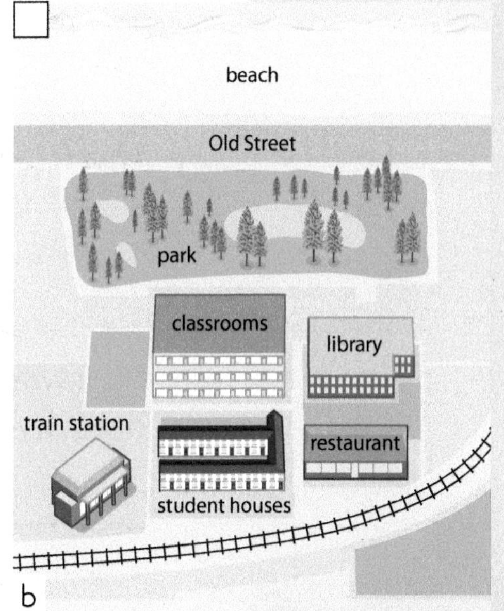

ACADEMIC WRITING SKILLS

7 7.22 Write the letters. Listen and check.

1 r _ st _ _ r _ nt
2 cl _ ssr _ _ ms
3 l _ br _ ry
4 tr _ _ n st _ t _ _ n
5 h _ _ s _
6 _ ff _ c _ b _ _ ld _ ng
7 p _ rk

CRITICAL THINKING: EVALUATE

8 Look at map *a* in 6. Then match.

1 train station	new
2 restaurant	beautiful
3 library	busy
4 office building	good
5 park	old

WRITING TASK

9 Look at map *a* in 6 and the words in 8. Write about a university.

The university is near the train ______________.
There is ______________ next to ______________.
There are ______________ near ______________.
There is ______________.
There ______________.

10 Swap and check.

OBJECTIVES REVIEW

I can ...

- understand where people live. ☐
- listen about interesting places in a city. ☐
- ask for and give directions. ☐
- give a short presentation with *there is* and *there are* about an interesting place in my city. ☐
- read about a city. ☐
- read about places at university. ☐
- write about where you and other people live. ☐
- write sentences about places at a university. ☐

WORDLIST

airport	office building
beach	old street
beautiful beaches	on the left
between	on the right
busy square	park
factory	restaurant
famous stadium	shop
hospital	shopping centre
hotel	tall buildings
house	train station
interesting market	You're welcome.
near	
next to	

LEARNING OBJECTIVES

Listening	Big numbers and currencies What people have and buy
Speaking	Ask and answer questions about shopping Talk about things you have and buy
Reading	How people spend money What people have
Writing	Write about how often you do things Write about how you spend your money
Watch and remember	A video about money and things people buy

SPENDING UNIT 8

UNLOCK YOUR KNOWLEDGE

Look and circle. Then talk.

1 Where is this shop?
   a Mexico   b Turkey   c Japan

2 What is in this shop?
   a bags   b food   c mobile phones

3 What famous shops do you know?

LISTENING AND READING 1

VOCABULARY: THINGS WE BUY

1 8.1 Listen and point. Then say.

a smartphone | a video game | a newspaper | a bank card

a laptop | a watch | a T-shirt | a tablet

SOUND AND SPELLING: *a*

2 8.2 Listen and say.

car → card
take → game
what → watch
bad → bag

3 8.3 Say and match. Then listen and check.

1	laptop	smartphone	watch
2	card	newspaper	market
3	game	wasp	name
4	what	bank	camera

LISTENING FOR GENERAL UNDERSTANDING

4 8.4 Listen and circle.

Tao and Jun talk about …

a watches and T-shirts.
b video games and tablets.
c newspapers and bank cards.

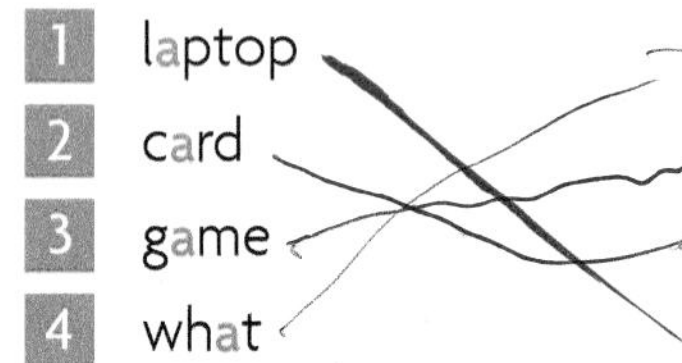

5 8.4 Read and circle. Then listen again and check.

Tao: It's a beautiful watch. Is it new?

Jun: Yes, it is.

Tao: How many *video games* / *watches* do you have?

Jun: I have three watches.

Tao: Oh, I don't have a watch. I look at the time on my smartphones and my *laptop* / *newspaper*.

Jun: How many *tablets* / *smartphones* do you have?

Tao: I have two smartphones. And is this a new T-shirt?

Jun: No, it isn't. It's *new* / *old*. I have a lot of *T-shirts* / *watches*.

6 8.5 Listen and read. Then say.

I have	a	great	camera.
	a	new	bag.
	an	old	car.

7 8.6 Write. Then listen and check.

1 I have a beautiful watch.
(a / watch. / beautiful)

2 I have ______
(smartphone. / expensive / an)

3 I have an old shirt
(old / T-shirt / an)

4 I have an ______
(interesting / an / newspaper.)

8 Ask, answer and write. Then say.

How many smartphones do you have?

I have two smartphones.

He doesn't have a smartphone.

Your partner

	How many ... ?		How many ... ?
smartphones laptops watches bank cards	2	T-shirts tablets video games cameras	

READING FOR GENERAL UNDERSTANDING

ACADEMIC WRITING SKILLS

SPEAKING AND WRITING

LISTENING AND READING 2

VOCABULARY: CALENDAR TIME

1 8.7 Listen and point. Then say.

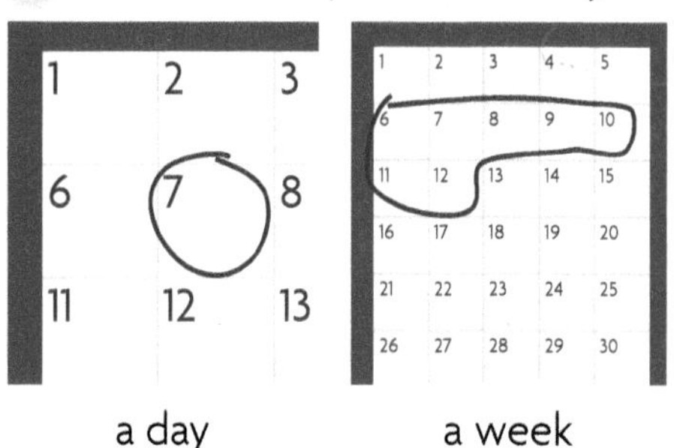

a day | a week | a month | a year

USING BACKGROUND KNOWLEDGE TO PREDICT CONTENT

2 8.8 Look at the photographs and circle. Then listen and check.

Enrique – a bank manager

Namareq – an English student

1 The bank manager buys …

coffee | dictionaries
a smartphone | a laptop

2 The student buys …

English books | tablets
cars | video games

READING FOR DETAIL

3 8.8 Read and listen. Then read again and match.

A: How often do you buy coffee?

Enrique – a bank manager: I buy coffee once a day. I buy a newspaper once a week. I buy a new smartphone twice a year and a new laptop once a year.

Namareq – an English student: I have a lot of English books and video games on my tablet. I buy a new book once a week. I buy a new game twice a month. I buy a new tablet once a year.

1 Enrique buys coffee | twice a year.
He buys a newspaper | once a week.
He buys a new smartphone | once a day.

2 Namareq buys a new book | twice a month.
She buys a new game | once a week.
She buys a new tablet | once a year.

GRAMMAR: FREQUENCY EXPRESSIONS 2

4 8.9 Listen and read. Then say.

I buy a book		day.
She buys bread	once a	week.
We walk to university	twice a	month.
They travel to different countries		year.

WRITING

5 8.10 Write. Then listen and check.

1 We buy T-shirts twice a year.
(buy T-shirts / twice a year. / We)

2 She buys smart Phone
(buys a smartphone / once a year. / She)

3 He buys coffee
(twice a day. / buys coffee / He)

4 They buy video games
(They / once a month. / buy video games)

5 ______________________
(once a week. / I / buy a newspaper)

SPEAKING

6 Look and say.

once a week twice a day once a day
twice a week once a month once a year

How often do you buy a newspaper?

I buy a newspaper twice a week.

LISTENING AND READING 3

VOCABULARY: SHOPPING

1 8.11 Listen and point. Then say.

go shopping

buy clothes

buy shoes

buy things on the internet

spend money

pay by cash

pay by card

READING FOR DETAIL

2 8.12 Look at 3. Read, listen and circle **two** places.

Rob buys things ...

a in the shopping centre.

b at the market.

c on the internet.

Rob Salim

LISTENING FOR KEY INFORMATION

3 8.12 Listen again and circle. Then say.

Salim: How often do you buy new clothes?

Rob: I buy new clothes *twice a year / once a month.*

Salim: Where do you buy your clothes?

Rob: I buy jeans and T-shirts *at the market / on the internet.*

Salim: Do you buy shoes on the internet?

Rob: *Yes, I do. / No, I don't.*

Salim: How often do you go shopping?

Rob: *Once a week. / Twice a week.* I spend a lot of money in this shopping centre.

Salim: Do you pay by bank card or by cash?

Rob: I pay *by card / by cash.* It's easy.

NOTICE !

buy clothes

pay by card

spend a lot on clothes

WRITING

4 Write about you. Swap and check.

~~go shopping~~ buy new clothes
buy new shoes buy things on the internet

once/twice a day
week month year

1 I go shopping every week.
2 ~~I go shopping in by evnig~~ once ~~ever~~ a week
3 ~~I buy new clothes year week~~ once a month
4

GRAMMAR: PRESENT SIMPLE QUESTIONS

5 8.13 Listen and read. Then say.

Question					Answer
How often	do	you	go	shopping?	Once a week.
			buy	new clothes?	Twice a year.
Where	do	you	buy	your clothes?	At the market.
			have	lunch?	At the restaurant.
	Do	you	pay	by cash?	Yes, I do.
			buy	things on the internet?	No, I don't.

6 8.14 Write. Then listen and check.

1 How often ___do you pay___ (pay) by card?
2 How often ______ (go) shopping?
3 Where ______ (buy) your shoes?
4 Where ______ (go) shopping?
5 ______ (spend) a lot of money on computers?
6 ______ (buy) a lot of clothes?

NOTICE !
spend on computers

SOUND AND SPELLING: *th, w, o*

7 8.15 Listen and say.

things month three
watch where
once twice

SPEAKING

8 Look at page 207.

WATCH AND REMEMBER

PART 1

BEFORE YOU WATCH

1 8.16 Listen and point. Then say.

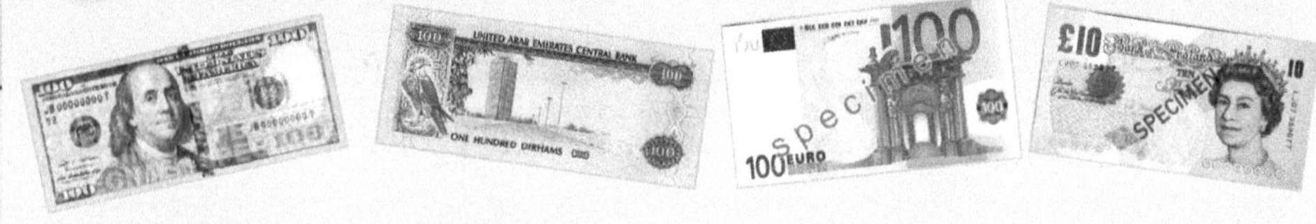

dollar dirham euro pound

WATCH

2 Watch part 1 and (circle).

1 Tom buys bread *once* / (*twice*) a week.
2 Tom pays one *pound* / *dollar* for bananas.
3 Luca buys fruit twice a *day* / *week*.
4 Luca pays *three* / *thirteen* euros for apples.
5 Eric buys fruit *once* / *twice* a week.
6 Eric pays six *dollars* / *euros* for apples.

AFTER YOU WATCH

3 Read and write.

pay ~~buy~~ cash pound

Tom: I ___buy___ five bananas. It's one pound. I buy a newspaper once a day.
Narrator: How much is a newspaper?
Tom: It's one ________ .
Narrator: Do you ________ for the bananas and newspaper by ________ ?
Tom: Yes, I do.

BEFORE YOU WATCH

PART 2

4 Look. Then write.

bank card laptop tablet video game

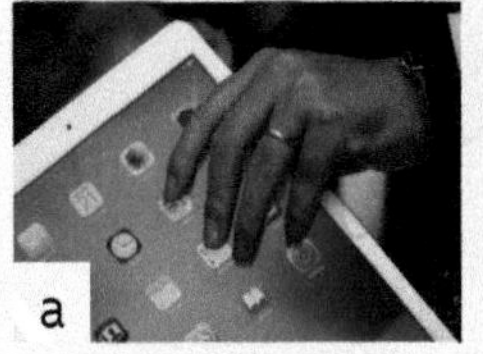
a

b

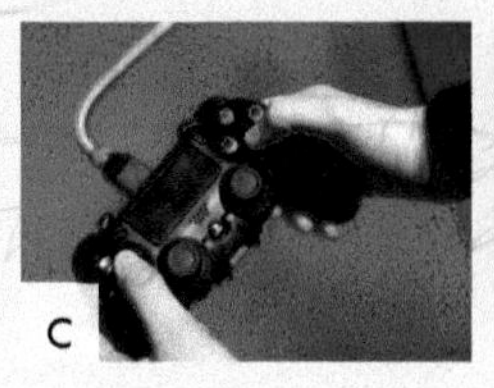
c

d

________ ________ ________ ________

WATCH

5 Watch part 2 and match.

1	a new tablet	cheap
2	a video game	ten dirhams
3	a coffee	two thousand dirhams

AFTER YOU WATCH

6 Write about you.

I buy ________ ________ once a ________ .
I pay by ________ .

REMEMBER

PART 3

7 Watch part 3. Say. Write.

a coffee a tablet fruit

1 Tom and Luca buy ________ . 2 Aiysha buys ________ .
3 Salem buys ________ .

MORE VOCABULARY: FOOD

8 Look. Match. Then write.

a

b

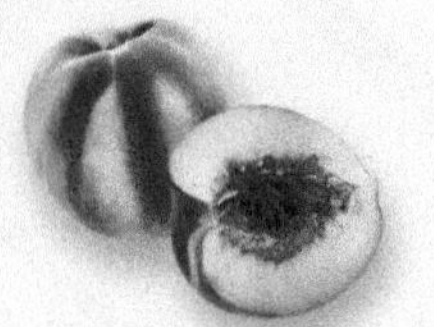
c

________ ________ ________

1	banana	a
2	peach	b
3	apple	c

ASK AND ANSWER

9 Ask and answer.

What's on your shopping list?

I buy ...

LANGUAGE FOCUS

VOCABULARY: MONEY

1 8.17 Listen and point. Then say.

euros
100 euros
one hundred euros

dollars
200 dollars
two hundred dollars

pounds
500 pounds
five hundred pounds

lira
1,000 lira
one thousand lira

dirhams
1,000,000 dirhams
one million dirhams

riyals
10,000 riyals
ten thousand riyals

2 8.18 Match. Then listen and check. Say.

1 120	forty thousand
2 355	seven million
3 760	one hundred and twenty
4 1,500	one thousand five hundred
5 40,000	three hundred and fifty-five
6 7,000,000	seven hundred and sixty

WRITING

3 8.19 Write. Then listen and check.

thousand five hundred
million ~~hundred~~
two thousand

NOTICE !
three hundred **and** fifty-five pounds
seven hundred **and** sixty dollars

1 six hundred (630) and thirty

2 ______________ (2,300) three hundred

3 five thousand ______________ (5,500)

4 two hundred ______________ (200,000)

5 four ______________ (4,000,000)

LISTENING FOR DETAIL

4 8.20 Listen and write. Then say.

Excuse me. How much is this English dictionary?
It's 220 lira.

1 How much is this smartphone? It's ___560___ dollars.

2 How much is this car? It's ________ dirhams.

3 How much is this bag? It's ________ riyals.

4 How much is this television? It's ________ lira.

5 How much is this house? It's ________ euros.

PRONUNCIATION FOR SPEAKING

5 8.21 Listen and say.

How much is this smartphone?
How much is this bag?
How much is this car?
How much is this television?
How much is this house?

SPEAKING

6 Student A: Look at page 201.

Student B: Look at page 204.

ACADEMIC LISTENING AND SPEAKING

PREPARING TO LISTEN

1 8.22 Match. Then listen and check.

1 How much money do you spend on books?
2 How often do you buy food?
3 Do you have a bank card?

I buy food once a day.
No, I don't.
I think I spend 200 lira on books in a month.

LISTENING FOR MAIN IDEAS

2 8.22 Listen again and circle.

Kemal
Mustafa

Kemal and Mustafa talk about ...

a clothes and shoes.
b video games.
c books.
d food and drink.
e restaurants.
f laptops.

LISTENING FOR KEY INFORMATION

3 8.22 Listen again, read and circle.

Student name Mustafa

1	How much money do you spend on books?	*200 lira*
2	How often do you buy books?	*once / twice* a month
3	How much money do you spend on tea and coffee in a month?	*350 / 300* lira
4	How often do you buy food?	*once a day*
5	How much money do you spend on clothes and shoes in a month?	*100 / 250* lira
6	Do you have a bank card?	*no*

CRITICAL THINKING: UNDERSTAND

4 8.23 Write the questions. Then listen and check.

do you spend on | How much money | How often | ~~do you spend~~ | do you buy

1 How much money *do you spend* on books?
2 How often ______ books?
3 ______ do you spend on tea and coffee in a month?
4 ______ do you buy food?
5 How much money ______ clothes and shoes in a month?
6 Do you have a bank card?

CRITICAL THINKING: APPLY

5 Write the questions.

1 How much money *do you spend on* (you / spend / do / on) your phone in a month?
2 How often ______ (you / buy / do) a new phone?
3 How much ______ (money / you / spend / do / on) coffee in a month?
4 How ______ (buy / often / do / you) coffee?
5 How ______ (money / you / spend / much / do / on) clothes in a month?
6 How ______ (buy / often / do / you) clothes?

PRONUNCIATION FOR LISTENING

6 8.24 Listen and say.

Do you buy coffee once a day?
Do you have a bank card?
How much money do you spend on clothes?
How often do you buy shoes?

SPEAKING TASK

7 Look at page 207.

ACADEMIC READING AND WRITING

PREPARING TO READ

1 8.25 Read and write. Then listen and check.

% percent | money | spend

1. Students spend ten ______________ of their money on clothes and shoes.
2. Some students spend a lot of ______________ on computers and smartphones.
3. They don't ______________ a lot of money on their health.

NOTICE !

Students spend a lot on computers.

Students pay a lot for computers.

2 Look at 1. Think about students in your country. Say *Yes* or *No*.

PREVIEWING

3 Look at 4. Read and circle.

This is about

a. the USA.
b. Turkey.
c. India.
d. Mexico.
e. Pakistan.

This is about

a. food people eat.
b. clothes and shoes people buy.
c. money people spend on things.

READING FOR KEY INFORMATION

4 8.26 Look and read. Then write the **countries**. Listen and check.

HOW DO WE SPEND OUR MONEY?

The World Bank studies how people around the world spend their money.

In ______________, people spend 32% of their money on food and drink. They spend 19% on their houses and 5% on clothes and shoes. They spend 1% on schools and universities.

People in ______________ spend 23% on food and drink and 8% on schools and universities. They spend 6% on clothes and shoes. They don't spend a lot of money on health.

In ______________, people spend 50% of their money on food and drink. They spend 5% on clothes and shoes and 2% on computers and smartphones.

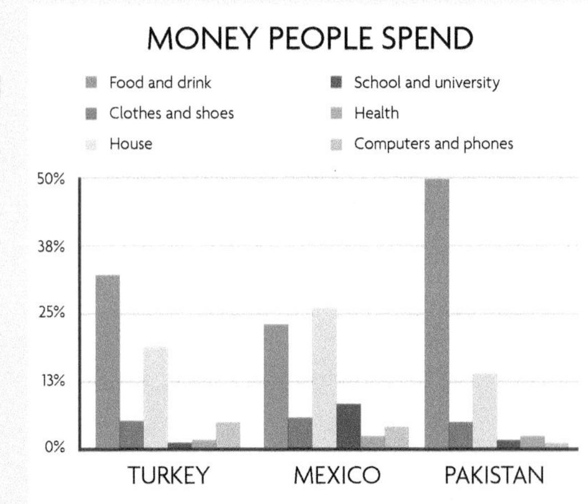

READING FOR KEY INFORMATION

5 Look at 4. Read again and circle *Yes* or *No*.

1 People in Turkey spend 32% on food and drink. Yes No
2 In Turkey, people spend 15% on clothes and shoes. Yes No
3 People in Mexico spend 18% on schools and universities. Yes No
4 In Mexico, people spend 6% on clothes and shoes. Yes No
5 In Pakistan, people spend 15% on food and drink. Yes No
6 People in Pakistan spend 2% on computers and smartphones. Yes No

ACADEMIC WRITING SKILLS

6 8.27 Write the letters. Listen and check.

1 h u ndr __ d
2 th __ __ s __ nd
3 m __ ll __ __ n
4 m __ nth
5 sh __ __ s
6 sp __ nd
7 p __ y
8 __ nt __ rn __ t
9 sm __ rtph __ n __
10 cl __ th __ s

CRITICAL THINKING: UNDERSTAND

7 Look. Write the numbers.

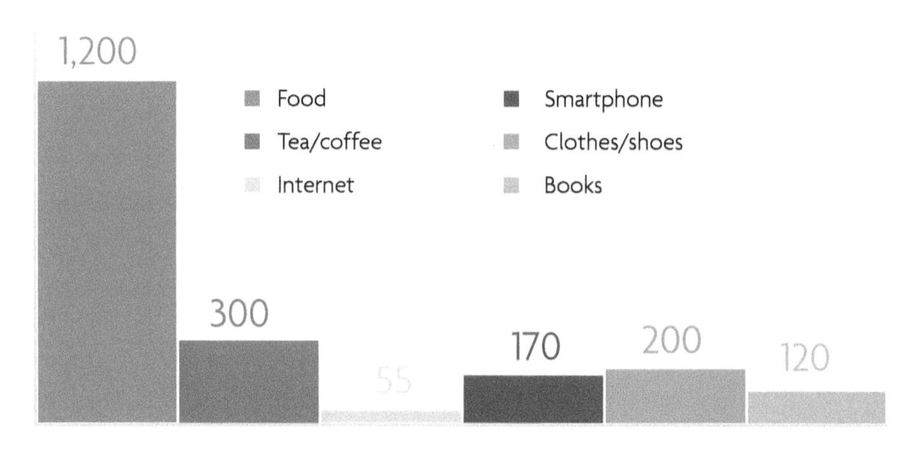

How much money do you spend on things?
I spend one thousand two hundred dirhams on food.
I spend ______________ dirhams on tea and coffee.
I pay ______________ dirhams for the internet and ______________ dirhams for my smartphone.
I spend ______________ dirhams on new clothes and shoes and ______________ dirhams on books for my classes.

CRITICAL THINKING: APPLY

8 Draw your spending for one month. Swap and talk.

MY SPENDING EVERY MONTH

WRITING

9 Read and write the sentences with *and*.

I spend one hundred dollars on shoes.

I spend two hundred dollars on clothes.

I spend one hundred dollars on shoes and two hundred dollars on clothes.

1 I spend twenty riyals on coffee.
I spend eighty riyals on food.

____

____

2 I spend one hundred lira on books.
I spend eighty lira on T-shirts.

____

____

WRITING TASK

10 Look at 8. Write.

How much money do you spend on things?
I spend ______________________________ on
______________________________ .
I spend ______________________________ on
______________________________ .
I pay ______________________________
for ______________________________ and
______________________________ .
I ______________________________
and ______________________________ .

11 Swap and check.

OBJECTIVES REVIEW

I can ...

understand big numbers and currencies.	☐
understand what people have and buy.	☐
ask and answer questions about shopping.	☐
talk about things I have and buy.	☐
read about how people spend money.	☐
read about what people have.	☐
write about how often I do things.	☐
write about how I spend my money.	☐

WORDLIST

bank card	newspaper
buy	once a week
buy clothes	pay by card
buy shoes	pay with cash
buy things on the internet	pounds
day	riyals
dirhams	smartphone
dollars	spend money
euros	T-shirt
go shopping	tablet
How much is ... ?	thousand
hundred	twice a week
laptop	video game
lira	watch
million	week
month	year

LEARNING OBJECTIVES

Listening	How often people do things How often people use technology
Speaking	Ask for and give opinions Talk about things and what they *can* and *can't* do
Reading	Technology Interesting facts with numbers
Writing	Write with *and* and *but* Write about what you *do* and *don't* do in English
Watch and remember	A video about technology and what it can do

TECHNOLOGY UNIT 9

UNLOCK YOUR KNOWLEDGE

Look and circle.

1 What is it?

a a computer　　b a car　　c a video game

2 I think it's

a big　　b small　　c interesting　　d good

e beautiful　　f cheap　　g expensive

LISTENING AND READING 1

VOCABULARY: COMPUTERS AND THE INTERNET

1 9.1 Listen and point. Then say.

a blog

an app

a website

GPS

a USB drive

a webinar

2 9.2 Match. Listen and check. Then say.

1	play	a blog	2	learn	English online
3	look at	apps	4	use	webinars
5	write	websites	6	need	a USB drive
7	buy	video games	8	watch	GPS

LISTENING FOR MAIN IDEAS

3 9.3 Listen and match.

1	Samir and Kemal	blogs
2	Yuna and Lucia	learning English

READING FOR DETAIL

4 9.3 Read and listen again. Then write *Yes* or *No* on page 167.

1 **Samir:** What's this?

Kemal: I usually learn English online. I look at English websites and I often watch webinars.

Samir: Oh, I never look at English websites, but I play video games in English.

Kemal: How often do you play?

Samir: I always play video games!

2 **Lucia:** What's this?

Yuna: It's my blog. I write a blog about new technology.

Lucia: I never read blogs. What's it about?

Yuna: How to use GPS on your phone.

Lucia: I sometimes use GPS. I want to read this!

1 Kemal learns English online. ____
2 Kemal watches webinars. ____
3 Samir plays video games. ____
4 Lucia reads blogs. ____
5 Lucia uses GPS. ____

GRAMMAR: FREQUENCY ADVERBS

5 9.4 Write. Listen and check. Then say.

never always

____ sometimes usually often ____

0% 100%

6 Read **4** again. Match sentences 1–5.

a always 3
b never ____
c often ____
d sometimes ____
e usually ____

7 9.5 Listen and read. Say.

I You We They	never sometimes usually often always	play	video games.
He She		plays	

WRITING

8 Write.

1 I always look at English websites.
(always / at / look)

2 We ____________________.
(apps / buy / usually)

3 He ____________________ drive.
(a / needs / often / USB)

4 They ____________________.
(a / blog / never / write)

SOUND AND SPELLING: *p*, *b*

9 9.6 Listen and say.

GPS app play laptop
USB blog tablet buy

SPEAKING

10 Student A: Look at page 202.
Student B: Look at page 205.

LISTENING AND READING 2

VOCABULARY: THINGS WE USE

1 9.7 Listen and point. Then say.

a smartwatch

a fridge

send messages

cook

go online

make calls

LISTENING FOR KEY INFORMATION

2 9.8 Listen and write *1* or *2*.

smart fridge ☐   smartwatch ☐

READING FOR DETAIL

3 9.8 Read and listen again. Then circle *Yes* or *No*.

www.technologynews.com/smartobjects

SMART OBJECTS

Home | About | Technology | Community

1 This smartwatch is small and cheap. It has a camera and it can take photographs. It can make calls and send messages, and it can go online and play video. It can't have apps, but it has GPS.

2 This smart fridge is big and expensive. It has a computer and it can send messages when your food is old. It can go online and it can buy food, but it can't cook food. It has a camera, but it can't take photographs.

1	The smartwatch has a camera.	(Yes)	No
2	The smartwatch takes photographs.	Yes	No
3	The smartwatch doesn't have apps.	Yes	No
4	The smart fridge has a camera.	Yes	No
5	The smart fridge takes photographs.	Yes	No
6	The smart fridge cooks food.	Yes	No

GRAMMAR: *CAN* AND *CAN'T*

4 9.9 Listen and read. Then say.

It	can	send messages.
	cannot	take photographs.
	has	a camera.

NOTICE !

It can't go online.
= It cannot go online.

5 9.10 Write. Then listen and check.

1 It ___can go online___ , (go online ✔)
but it ______________ . (buy apps ✗)

2 It ______________ , (play video ✔)
but it ______________ . (take photographs ✗)

3 It ______________ , (go online ✔)
but it ______________ . (send messages ✗)

4 It ______________ , (send messages ✔)
but it ______________ . (make calls ✗)

PRONUNCIATION FOR SPEAKING

6 9.11 Listen and say.

can ...	can't ...
It can take photographs.	It can't take photographs.
It can go online.	It can't cook food.

WRITING AND SPEAKING

7 Student A: Look at page 202.
Student B: Look at page 205.

LISTENING AND READING 3

VOCABULARY: PEOPLE

1 9.12 Listen and point. Then say.

a person

people

a man

men

a woman

women

a child

children

a child and an adult

a girl

a boy

PREPARING TO READ

2 9.13 Listen and match. Then say.

1	60 seconds	1 year
2	7 days	1 minute
3	365 days	1 million
4	1,000,000	1 billion
5	1,000,000,000	1 week

LISTENING FOR MAIN IDEAS

3 9.14 Listen and match.

1	China	video games
2	the USA	smartphones

SCANNING FOR KEY INFORMATION

4 9.14 Read and listen again. Then match.

INTERESTING FACTS ABOUT TECHNOLOGY

MOBILE PHONES

- In China, 780 million people buy smartphones every year, and 3 people buy a new smartphone every second.
- 749 million adults and 31 million children use smartphones.
- 561 million people use their smartphones every day, and 32 million people use their smartphones only every week.

VIDEO GAMES

- In the USA, people spend 25 billion dollars on video games every year.
- Every week, 74 million men and 74 million women play video games and 23 million boys and 20 million girls play video games.

1 780 million — people buy smartphones
2 31 million
3 25 billion
4 74 million
5 20 million

dollars on video games
people buy smartphones
men play video games
girls play video games
children use smartphones

GRAMMAR: FREQUENCY EXPRESSIONS 2

5 9.15 Listen and read. Then say.

People	buy	smartphones	every	second.
Men	play	video games		minute.
Women	play	video games		hour.
Children	use	smartphones		day.
				week.
				year.

WRITING

6 9.16 Write. Then listen and check.

1 People watch 133 million hours of video every day.
(133 million hours of video / every / People / day. / watch)

2 ______
(buy / month. / 58 million USB sticks / Adults / every)

3 ______
(People / year. / send / 4 million photos / every)

4 ______
(watch / 100 minutes of TV / A lot of children / day. / every)

5 ______
(minute. / every / People / 347 blogs / write)

SPEAKING

7 Look at page 208.

WATCH AND REMEMBER

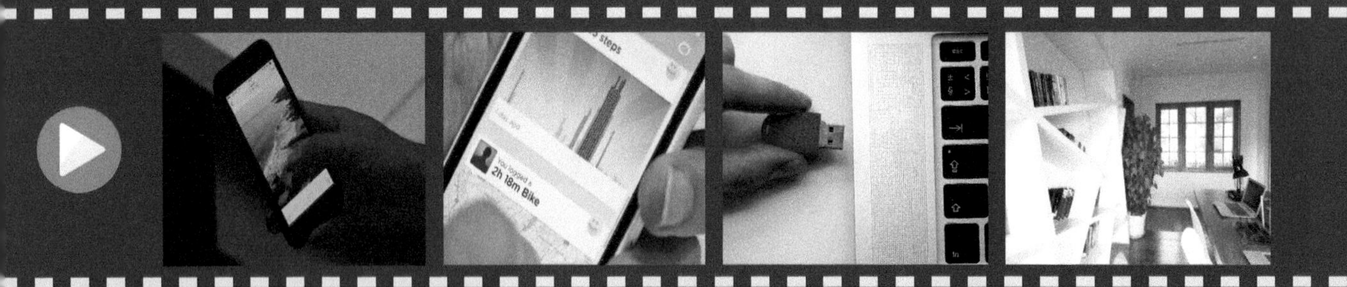

PART 1

BEFORE YOU WATCH

1 Look. Match.

a

b

c

____________ ____________ ____________

1	It can go online.	a
2	It can take photographs.	b
3	It can buy things.	c

2 9.17 Look at 1. Listen and check. Then write.

WATCH

3 Watch part 1 and (circle).

1. Mike has a shopping app. It can buy *clothes* / (*food*).
2. Sarah has a good app. It can download *books* / *the news*.
3. Paul has a nice app. It can *take photographs* / *play videos*.
4. Aliyah and her mother have an app. It can *call people* / *send emails*.
5. Sam has an app that's *good* / *not good* for you!

AFTER YOU WATCH

4 Read and write.

online help download app

Sarah: I have an ____________ for reading English newspapers ____________. It can ____________ the news. It can ____________ you learn new words.

PART 2

5 Look. Match. Then write.

GPS   a USB drive   a Wi-Fi router

a ______________

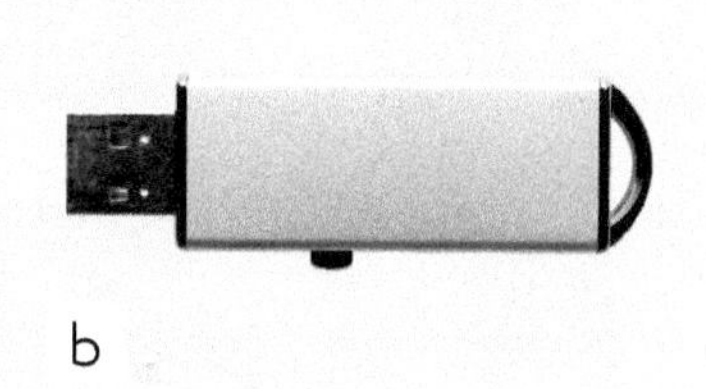
b ______________

c ______________

6 Watch part 2 and circle.

1 Sophie needs *GPS* / *a USB drive*.

2 She needs it for *work* / *photographs*.

3 She buys *one* / *two*.

7 Write about you.

laptop   tablet   smartphone   new   old

I have a ______________ . My ______________ is ______________ .

PART 3

8 Watch part 3. Say. Write.

1 Mike: His app can ______________ .

2 Paul: His app can ______________ .

3 Aliya: Her app can ______________ .

4 Sophie: Her computer can download ______________ .

9 Look. Match. Then write.

a ______________

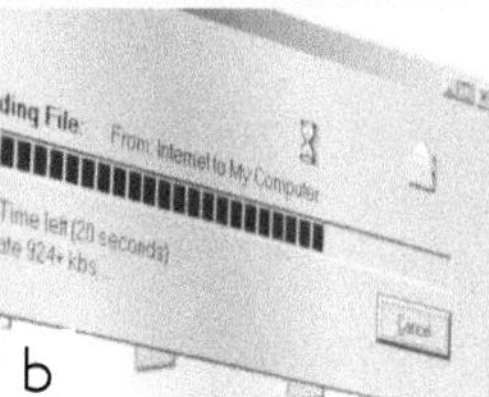

b ______________

c ______________

1 download a   2 save b   3 call c

10 Talk about your apps.

> The app I use a lot is ... It can ...

BEFORE YOU WATCH

WATCH

AFTER YOU WATCH

REMEMBER

MORE VOCABULARY: TECHNOLOGY

ASK AND ANSWER

LANGUAGE FOCUS

LISTENING FOR MAIN IDEAS

1 9.18 Listen and write *1*, *2* or *3*.

☐ 

☐ 

☐ 

LISTENING FOR DETAIL

2 9.18 Read and listen again. Then (circle) *Yes* or *No*.

Mia: What do you think of smart glasses?
Tomomi: I think they're great.
Mia: I think so too! They have GPS, I think.
Tomomi: Yes, and they can take photographs too. They're really good.
Mia: I agree.

Juan: I don't think this smartwatch is very good. What do you think?
Carlos: I disagree. I think it's very good. It can send messages and play video.
Juan: Yes, but your smartphone can send messages and play video! You don't need a smartwatch.
Carlos: You're right, but it's a beautiful watch.

Osman: I need a new app to study English. What do you think?
Ercan: Good idea! I think smartphone apps are cheap.
Osman: I don't think so. I think English apps are expensive.
Ercan: I disagree.

NOTICE !
I need a new app **to study** English.

1	Tomomi **and** Mia like smart glasses.	Yes	No
2	Juan **and** Carlos like smartwatches.	Yes	No
3	Osman **and** Ercan think English apps are cheap.	Yes	No

VOCABULARY: ASKING FOR AND GIVING OPINIONS

3 9.19 Listen and say.

Question and answer	✔	✗
What do you think of smart glasses? I think they're great. What do you think?	I think so too. I agree.	I don't think so. I disagree.

NOTICE !

I think so too.

I don't think so.

I disagree. = I don't agree.

4 9.20 Write. Listen and check.

1 What do you think of smartphones?
(do / smartphones? / think / What / of / you)

2 ______
(so / too. / I / think)

3 ______
(do / What / you / think?)

4 ______
(don't / I / so. / think)

5 ______
(do / smart fridges? / think / What / of / you)

5 9.21 Listen and say.

What do you think?

I think so too.

I agree.

What do you think of smartphones?

I don't think so.

I disagree.

6 Student A: Look at page 202.

Student B: Look at page 205.

ACADEMIC WRITING SKILLS

PRONUNCIATION FOR SPEAKING

SPEAKING

ACADEMIC LISTENING AND SPEAKING

PREPARING TO LISTEN

1 Read and write ✓ or ✗. Then talk.

How do you use the internet to study English?

- I read English websites. ☐
- I read English newspapers online. ☐
- I watch English TV online. ☐
- I use apps. ☐
- I play vocabulary games. ☐
- I play grammar games. ☐

LISTENING FOR MAIN IDEAS

2 9.22 Listen and circle.

Some people think the internet doesn't help you learn English.

1 Amalia *agrees / doesn't agree.*
2 Pilar *agrees / doesn't agree.*

LISTENING FOR KEY INFORMATION

3 9.23 Listen, read and circle.

Amalia

I agree. The internet doesn't help you learn English. I buy English *books / dictionaries* and read English newspapers.

Pilar

I don't think so. English books are very *old / expensive* and we don't have a lot of English newspapers in the shops.

OK, but there are a lot of English newspapers in *the library / the shops*. I go there every day and read for one hour.

I don't agree with you. I think it's boring. On the internet, I buy English *games / apps*. I also study with my smartphone. It's easy.

CRITICAL THINKING: UNDERSTAND

4 9.23 Look at 3. Write *A* for *Amalia* and *P* for *Pilar*. Then listen again and check.

1 There are newspapers in the library. [A]
2 It is easy to study on the smartphone. [P]
3 I study on my smartphone. [ ]
4 I read English newspapers. [ ]
5 There are a lot of English apps on the internet. [ ]
6 I buy English books. [ ]

CRITICAL THINKING: ANALYZE

5 Read the ideas. Write ✔ for ***I agree*** and ✗ for ***I don't agree***.

Some people think the internet helps you learn English.	**Some people think the internet doesn't help you learn English.**
I play word games online. I don't play word games in my notebook. [ ]	I play word games in my notebook. I don't need the internet for this. [ ]
It's easy to study on the internet. [ ]	I talk to my teacher in the classroom. I don't talk to my smartphone. [ ]
I read English websites. It's easy on your smartphone. [ ]	I buy a paper dictionary. I don't need an online dictionary. [ ]

PRONUNCIATION FOR LISTENING

6 9.24 Listen and say.

It's easy to study on the internet.

You don't need a smartphone for this.

I talk to my teacher in the classroom.

Students go to the library.

SPEAKING TASK

7 Look at 5. Discuss.

Some people think the internet doesn't help you learn English.

I agree.
I play word games in my notebook.

REMEMBER !

What do you think?

I agree.	I don't agree.
I think so too.	I don't think so.

ACADEMIC READING AND WRITING

PREPARING TO READ

1 Read and (circle) *Yes* or *No*. Then discuss.

In my country,

1	a lot of people use the internet.	Yes	No
2	the internet is cheap.	Yes	No
3	a lot of people have smartphones.	Yes	No
4	smartphones are expensive.	Yes	No

READING FOR MAIN IDEAS

2 Read. Then write ✔.

The text is about

- a how to use the internet and smartphones. ☐
- b how many people use the internet and smartphones. ☐
- c how much money people spend on the internet and smartphones. ☐

HOME | BLOG | ABOUT | ARCHIVES | SUBSCRIBE | SEARCH

The internet and smartphones

There are 7.4 billion people in the world. ___% of adults and children use the internet every day. A lot of people use the internet on their smartphones.

	Internet use	Smartphone use
Sweden	95%	63%
UAE	88%	74%
Turkey	46%	30%
Saudi Arabia	60%	73%
Mexico	51%	35%

In Sweden, ___% of men and women use the internet. They shop online and watch TV on their computers. 63% of people in Sweden use smartphones every day.

In the United Arab Emirates (UAE), ___% of the people use the internet. 74% of adults have smartphones with the internet.

SCANNING FOR KEY INFORMATION

3 9.25 Look at 2. Read and listen. Then write the numbers.

READING FOR DETAIL

4 Look at 2. Read and (circle) *Yes* or *No*.

1	46% of people in Turkey use the internet.	(Yes)	No
2	60% of people in Saudi Arabia have smartphones.	Yes	No
3	In Mexico, 35% of men and women have smartphones.	Yes	No
4	95% of people in Sweden don't use the internet.	Yes	No
5	In the UAE, 74% of adults use the internet.	Yes	No

ACADEMIC WRITING SKILLS

5 9.26 Write the letters. Listen and check.

1 w e bs __ t __ s
2 bl __ g
3 w __ b __ n __ rs
4 __ nl __ n __
5 USB dr __ v __
6 p __ __ pl __
7 __ d __ lts
8 ch __ ldr __ n

CRITICAL THINKING: ANALYZE

6 Read the sentences. Then circle and write ✔ or ✗.

Study Skills
Things you do on your computer in English

Student name: Li Wei

How often do you use a mobile phone?
I use a mobile phone every ____________
I never / sometimes / usually / often / always use a mobile phone to learn English.

I ...
read emails in English. ✔
write emails in English. ✗
read English websites.
write a blog in English.
watch webinars.
learn English online.
use Microsoft Word® in English.
use PowerPoint® in English.
read English eBooks.
watch English TV.

Li Wei

NOTICE !

I read English websites, but I don't write a blog.

I use a mobile phone every day. I usually use a mobile phone to learn English.
I read emails in English, but I don't write emails in English.
I read English websites, but I don't write a blog.
I watch webinars and I learn English online.
I use Microsoft Word® in English, but I don't use PowerPoint® in English.
I read English eBooks and I watch English TV.

ACADEMIC WRITING SKILLS

7 Read. Then write the sentences with *and* or *but*.

I listen to webinars **and** I learn English online.

I read English websites, **but** I do not write a blog.

1 I play games on my tablet. I watch TV on my smartphone.
I play games on my tablet and I watch TV on my smartphone.

2 I use the internet every day. I do not use GPS every day.

____

____

3 I have a USB drive. I do not have a smartwatch.

____

____

4 I buy new apps every week. I do not buy a new smartphone every week.

____

____

CRITICAL THINKING: UNDERSTAND

8 Read and write about yourself. Write ✔ or ✗.

Study Skills
Things you do on your computer in English

Student name: ____________
How often do you use a mobile phone?
I use a mobile phone ______________________
I *never* / *sometimes* / *usually* / *often* / *always* use a mobile phone to learn English.

I ...
read emails in English.
write emails in English.
read English websites.
write a blog in English.
watch webinars.
learn English online.
use Microsoft Word® in English.
use PowerPoint® in English.
read English eBooks.
watch English TV.

WRITING TASK

9 Look at 8. Write about yourself.

I ____________ a mobile phone ____________ .
I ____________ use ____________ to learn English.
I ______________________________ and
I ______________________________ .
I ______________________________ , but
I ______________________________ .
I ______________________________ and
______________________________ .

10 Swap and check.

OBJECTIVES REVIEW

I can ...

- understand how often people do things. ☐
- listen to people talk about how often they use technology. ☐
- ask for and give opinions. ☐
- talk about things and what they *can* and *can't* do. ☐
- read about technology. ☐
- read interesting facts with numbers. ☐
- write with *and* and *but*. ☐
- write about what I *do* and *don't* do in English. ☐

WORDLIST

adult	men
billion	minute
boy	need a USB drive
buy apps	people
child	person
children	play video games
cook	second
fridge	send messages
girl	smartwatch
go online	tablet
glasses	use GPS
hour	watch webinars
learn English online	woman
look at websites	women
make calls	write a blog
man	

LEARNING OBJECTIVES

Listening	Clothes and free time What people like and don't like doing
Speaking	Say what you like and don't like doing and wearing Ask and answer questions about free time, clothes and colours
Reading	Information about student clubs A student email
Writing	Write words with *-ing* Write an email about a student club
Watch and remember	A video about free time and clothes

FREE TIME AND FASHION UNIT 10

UNLOCK YOUR KNOWLEDGE

1 Look at the family in the photograph. What do they usually do in the evening?

a play video games　　b watch TV　　c go online
d read books　　e talk　　f go to restaurants
g eat at home

2 What do families in your country do in the evenings?

LISTENING AND READING 1

VOCABULARY: FREE TIME 1

1 10.1 Listen and point. Then say.

go for a walk

bake cakes

have a picnic

talk on the phone

go to the park

visit friends and family

do exercise

SOUND AND SPELLING: *o, a, i*

2 10.2 Listen and write ✔ or ✗. Listen again and check. Say.

1	go	✔	phone	✔	do	✗
2	walk	☐	bake	☐	talk	☐
3	visit	☐	family	☐	exercise	☐

USING VISUALS TO PREDICT THE CONTENT

3 10.3 Look at the photographs in 4 and circle. Listen and check.

1 In her free time, Emel
 a goes shopping. b goes online. c bakes cakes.

2 In his free time, Saif
 a visits friends and family. b talks on the phone. c plays video games.

4 10.3 Read and listen again. Write ***E*** for ***Emel*** and ***S*** for ***Saif***.

1 talks on the phone S
2 bakes cakes E
3 has a picnic ____
4 does exercise ____
5 goes shopping ____
6 goes for a walk ____
7 goes to the park ____
8 visits family ____

WHAT DO YOU DO IN YOUR FREE TIME?

EMEL FROM ISTANBUL

I visit my sister and her family on Saturday. We go to the park and have a picnic. I often bake cakes on Friday for our picnic. I also watch TV.

SAIF FROM DOHA

I do exercise at home every evening. I also talk on the phone and I watch TV. I often go shopping with my friends. I sometimes go for a walk on the beach.

5 10.3 Listen again and circle.

1 Emel visits her sister *on Friday* / *on Saturday*.
2 Emel bakes cakes *on Friday* / *on Saturday*.
3 Saif does exercise *at home* / *on the beach*.
4 Saif goes for a walk *at home* / *on the beach*.

6 10.4 Read and circle. Listen and check. Then write.

1 I often go ___for___ a walk. (to / for)
2 They usually do exercise ________ home. (on / at)
3 We go ________ the park every Friday. (to / at)
4 She always talks ________ the phone. (on / at)

7 10.5 Listen and say.

They go to the park on Monday.
She talks on the phone with her friends.
I have a picnic with my family.
We visit friends and family.
He goes for a walk.

8 Look at page 208.

READING FOR KEY INFORMATION

LISTENING FOR DETAIL

ACADEMIC WRITING SKILLS

PRONUNCIATION FOR SPEAKING

SPEAKING AND WRITING

LISTENING AND READING 2

VOCABULARY: FREE TIME REVIEW

1 10.6 Write. Then listen and check.

take watch ~~go~~ learn travel buy

1 ___go___ shopping
2 ________ TV
3 ________ to different countries
4 ________ photographs
5 ________ new clothes
6 ________ new languages

PREPARING TO LISTEN

2 10.7 Listen and point. Then say.

sleep draw chat online wait

LISTENING FOR MAIN IDEAS

3 10.8 Look and listen. Then circle.

Student Radio Home About Schedule Listen live

Listen to Student Radio on Tuesday at 4:30.
It's about
a university subjects. b free time. c clothes.

READING FOR DETAIL

4 10.9 Read and listen. Then write ✓ or ✗.

What do you like doing in your free time?

I like chatting to my friends online. I also like taking photographs and drawing. I don't like baking or cooking. And I don't like waiting for people!

Marta, History student

I don't like talking on the phone or chatting online. I like sleeping and watching TV. I also like travelling to different countries and learning new languages. I like going to restaurants, but I don't like going shopping!

Bilal, Chemistry student

1 Marta likes ...
chatting online. ☐
drawing. ☐
baking. ☒
waiting. ☐

2 Bilal likes ...
talking on the phone. ☐
sleeping. ☐
travelling. ☐
going shopping. ☐

NOTICE !

I like taking photographs and drawing.

I don't like talking on the phone or chatting online.

GRAMMAR: *LIKE + -ING*

5 10.10 Listen and read. Then say.

I You We They	like do not like	chatting. sleeping. writing. travelling.
He She	likes does not like	drawing. cooking.

NOTICE !

take – taking
write – writing
travel – travelling
chat – chatting

ACADEMIC WRITING SKILLS

6 10.11 Write the words with *-ing*. Then listen and check.

1 do d o ing
2 wait __ __ __ __ ing
3 write __ __ __ __ ing
4 travel __ __ __ __ __ __ __ ing
5 have __ __ __ ing
6 chat __ __ __ __ __ ing

7 10.12 Look and write. Then listen and check.

like likes do not like does not like

1 I like (✔) doing exercise at home.
2 You ________ (✗) chatting to your friends online.
3 She ________ (✔) baking cakes for her friends.
4 He ________ (✗) walking in the park.
5 We ________ (✗) waiting for our friends.
6 They ________ (✔) having a picnic on the beach.

SOUND AND SPELLING: *-ing*

8 10.13 Listen and say.

drawing watching walking taking having travelling

SPEAKING

9 Look at page 209.

LISTENING AND READING 3

VOCABULARY: CLOTHES

1 10.14 Listen and point. Then say.

a coat

a jacket

a dress

trousers

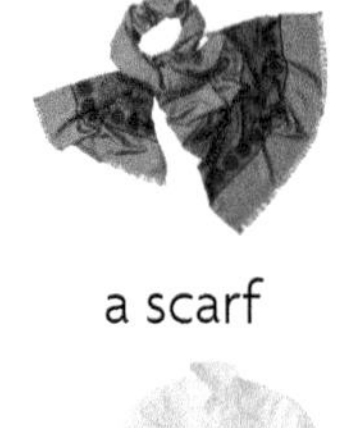

a scarf

a hat

a shirt

2 Look and match. Say.

NOTICE !

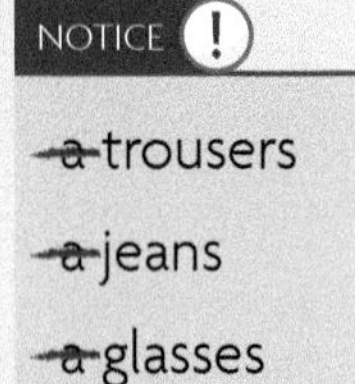

~~a~~ trousers
~~a~~ jeans
~~a~~ glasses

a

b

c

1 wear a coat and a scarf ☐
2 wear a T-shirt and jeans ☐
3 wear shoes ☐

LISTENING FOR MAIN IDEAS

3 10.15 Listen and tick ✔.

1 The women talk about
a buying shoes. ☐
b clothes from different countries. ☐
c Indian food. ☐

2 The men talk about
a people from Canada. ☐
b doing exercise. ☐
c winter clothes. ☐

READING FOR DETAIL

4 10.15 Read and listen again. Then (circle) *Yes* or *No*.

1
Maya: Look. This is a nice dress.
Zainab: It's a *sari*. It's from India.
Maya: I like wearing Indian clothes. I have a beautiful scarf from India. And what are these?
Zainab: These are trousers from Thailand. I don't like wearing trousers.

2 **Daniel:** What are these?
Greg: These are my winter shoes. I travel to Canada every winter holiday.
Daniel: Is it cold?
Greg: Yes, it is, but I like wearing winter clothes. I usually wear a warm coat, a shirt, trousers and a hat.

1	Maya likes the sari.	(Yes)	No
2	Maya likes wearing clothes from India.	Yes	No
3	Zainab likes wearing trousers.	Yes	No
4	Greg has winter shoes.	Yes	No
5	Greg travels to Canada every summer.	Yes	No

NOTICE !

I usually wear a warm coat, a shirt, trousers and a hat.

ACADEMIC WRITING SKILLS

5 10.16 Write the letters. Then listen and check. Say.

1 shi r t 2 ___ ___ othes 3 ___ ___ arf
4 ___ ___ ess 5 ___ ___ ousers 6 ja ___ ___ et

GRAMMAR: *THIS IS / THESE ARE*

6 10.17 Listen and read. Then say.

This is	a nice dress. a beautiful scarf.	These are	my shoes. his jeans.
What is this? Is this your hat?		What are these? Are these his shoes?	

7 10.18 Read and write. Then listen and check.

1 ___This is___ an expensive bag.
2 ______________ my new shoes.
3 ______________ his trousers?
4 ______________ a jacket from Mexico?
5 ______________ their shirts.
6 ______________ my new coat.

SPEAKING

8 Look at page 209.

WATCH AND REMEMBER

PART 1

BEFORE YOU WATCH

1 Look. Match.

a

b

c

______ ______ ______

1 go for a walk	a
2 bake a cake	b
3 have a picnic	c

2 10.19 Look at 1. Listen and check. Then write.

WATCH

3 Watch part 1 and circle.

1 Chris likes cooking with his *brother* / *son*.
2 They *go online* / *read a book* for help.
3 They *drive* / *walk* to buy the food.
4 Rashid, Talihah and Omar eat *in the park* / *at home*.

AFTER YOU WATCH

4 Read and write.

plays take talk drinking walk eating have

Rashid: We ______ a picnic. We like ______ fruit and ______ tea. We ______ and we ______. We ______ photographs of the family. Omar ______ in the park.

PART 2

BEFORE YOU WATCH

5 Look. Match. Then write.

a 

b 

c

d

1. a jacket — a
2. a shirt — b
3. a T-shirt — c
4. a shoe — d

WATCH

6 Watch part 2 and circle.

1. Peter *likes / doesn't like* blue and white shirts.
2. He *always / usually* wears a jacket at work.
3. He never wears *jeans / T-shirts*.

AFTER YOU WATCH

7 Write about you.

I like wearing ____________. I never wear ____________.

PART 3

REMEMBER

8 Watch part 3. Say. Write.

fruit shirts eggs tea milk

1. Chris and Robert buy ____________ and ____________.
2. Rashid, Talihah and Omar eat ____________ and drink ____________.
3. Peter wears ____________, ties, jackets and shoes.

MORE VOCABULARY: FOOD AND CLOTHES

9 Look. Then write.

tie biscuit egg

a 

b 

c 

ASK AND ANSWER

10 Ask and answer.

What do you do in your free time with your family?

LANGUAGE FOCUS

VOCABULARY: COLOURS

1 10.20 Listen and point. Then say.

red blue white

green black yellow

GRAMMAR: ORDER OF ADJECTIVES

NOTICE !

~~She has a black new jacket.~~

She has a new black jacket.

2 10.21 Listen and write. Then listen and check.

First day at school –

This is Li Na. She has a __________ __________ dress and a new black jacket. She also has a __________ __________ school bag and a very nice black hat.

Li Na from Shanghai

3 10.22 Circle. Listen and check. Then write.

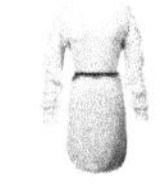

1 This is a ______________________________ dress.
(beautiful yellow / beautiful white / yellow beautiful)

2 These are ______________________________ trousers.
(blue new / black new / new blue)

3 This is an ______________________________ hat.
(green old / old green / old red)

LISTENING FOR KEY INFORMATION

4 10.23 Listen and circle.

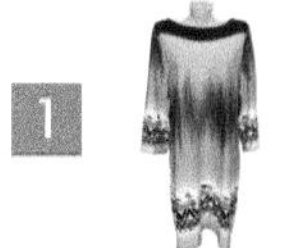

1 **Carla:** This is a beautiful *blue / green* dress.
Alia: It's my sister's favourite dress. But I sometimes wear it.

2 **Raul:** Are these your shoes?
Pedro: No. These are my brother's shoes. They are very *small / big*.

3 **Maria:** Is this your jacket?
Fabiola: No, it's Lara's jacket. My jacket is *red / yellow*.

GRAMMAR: POSSESSIVE 'S

5 10.24 Listen, read and say.

my sister	my brother	Lara
my sister's dress	my brother's shoes	Lara's jacket

6 10.25 Read and write. Listen and check.

1. This is ___my father's___ old hat. (my father)
2. ______________ new black dress is beautiful. (Yasemin)
3. ______________ new car is expensive. (Paulo)
4. These are ______________ white trousers. (Raj)

LISTENING AND WRITING

7 10.26 Listen and write. Then listen and check.

These are Akram's school clothes. Akram's trousers are __________ and his shirt is __________ . He has a __________ __________ school bag and __________ __________ shoes.

Akram from Uzbekistan

SOUND AND SPELLING: *s, sh*

8 10.27 Listen and say.

clothes	jeans	bags	my brother's
my teacher's	Mohammed's	school	students
dress	shirt	T-shirt	shop

SPEAKING AND WRITING

9 Look at page 209.

ACADEMIC LISTENING AND SPEAKING

PREPARING TO LISTEN

1 10.28 Read and match. Then listen and check.

1 What do you like doing in your free time?	I wear brown trousers and a shirt.
2 What do you like wearing at home?	It's blue.
3 What do you wear to university?	I like chatting to friends online.
4 What is your favourite colour?	At home, I like wearing jeans.

LISTENING FOR MAIN IDEAS

2 10.29 Listen and tick ✔.

This is about Murat's

- free time. ☐
- clothes. ☐
- studies. ☐
- favourite colours. ☐
- job. ☐

LISTENING FOR DETAIL

3 10.29 Listen again and circle *Yes* or *No*.

1 Murat likes having a picnic in the park.	Yes	No
2 He likes cooking good food.	Yes	No
3 At home, he likes wearing jeans and a T-shirt.	Yes	No
4 At university, he wears a black shirt.	Yes	No
5 His grandfather's jacket is old, but beautiful.	Yes	No
6 Murat's favourite colour is green.	Yes	No

CRITICAL THINKING: UNDERSTAND

4 10.29 Look at Rafet's notes. Listen again. Then write.

a shirt green going to restaurants jeans and a T-shirt ~~walking in the park~~

Student Survey: Free time and clothes

1 What do you like doing in your free time?
walking in the park

2 What do you like wearing at home?
____

3 What do you wear to university?
black trousers, black shoes and _______________

4 What is your favourite colour?
____

CRITICAL THINKING: CREATE

5 Write about you.

Student Survey: Free time and clothes

1 What do you like doing in your free time?
____

2 What do you like wearing at home?
____

3 What do you wear to university?
____

4 What is your favourite colour?
____

PRONUNCIATION FOR LISTENING

6 10.30 Listen and say.

1 What do you like doing in your free time?
2 What do you like wearing at home?
3 What do you wear to university?
4 What is your favourite colour?

SPEAKING TASK

7 Student A: Look at page 202.
Student B: Look at page 205.

ACADEMIC READING AND WRITING

USING VISUALS TO PREDICT CONTENT

1 Look at the photograph. Write ✔ or ✗.

1 The students meet in their free time. ☑
2 University students can join the club. ☐
3 The teachers help the students. ☐
4 The students like playing chess. ☐

READING FOR KEY INFORMATION

2 🔊 10.31 Read and listen. Answer the questions.

UNIVERSITY CLUB DAY!

When? Tuesday 20 September

What time? 9:00 – 12:30

Do you like …

reading interesting books? taking beautiful photographs? drawing? learning new languages? cooking or baking cakes? working on your computer? buying beautiful clothes?

Join our clubs!

Reading Club
(Room 12)

Photography Club
(Room 14)

Drawing Club
(Room 6)

Japanese Club
(Room 9)

Cooking and Baking Club
(Room 18)

Computer Club
(Room 21)

Fashion Club
(Room 25)

To join a student club, send an email to clubs@uni.ac.sa.

1 When is the Club Day? Tuesday 20 September

2 What time is the Club Day? ______

3 Is there a Drawing club? ______

4 Is there an English Club? ______

5 Where is the Computer Club? ______

6 Where is the Fashion Club? ______

ACADEMIC WRITING SKILLS

3 🔊 10.32 Write the letters. Then listen and check.

1 dr _a_ w _i_ ng
2 b __ k __ ng
3 c __ __ k __ ng
4 r __ __ d __ ng
5 f __ sh __ on
6 cl __ th __ s
7 l __ __ rn __ ng
8 fr __ __ t __ m __

READING FOR DETAIL

4 10.33 Read and listen to the email and (circle) *Yes* or *No*.

To: newstudents@camuni.ac.uk Reply Forward
From: Fiona.P@camuni.ac.uk
Subject: Japanese Club

To all new students,

Welcome to the Japanese Club!

What do we do?

We like reading Japanese books and watching Japanese TV. We also learn Japanese.

There are four Japanese students in our club. They are our teachers! We speak Japanese for one hour every week.

We like eating Japanese food. We go to a restaurant every month.

Where do we meet?

We meet in room 9 at 7:00 every Tuesday evening. All university students are welcome!

Regards,

Fiona P.

NOTICE !

Regards,
Fiona P.

1 This is an email to new students. (Yes) No
2 Students in the Japanese Club watch Japanese TV. Yes No
3 All students in the Japanese Club learn Japanese. Yes No
4 Students in the Japanese Club cook Japanese food. Yes No
5 Students in the Japanese Club meet every week. Yes No

CRITICAL THINKING: UNDERSTAND

5 Look at Fiona's notes. Read the email again. Then write.

What do we do?

read books, ________ TV, learn ________

four Japanese students – our ________ !

speak Japanese for ________ hour every ________

eat Japanese food, go to a ________ every ________

Where do we meet?

room ____ at 7:00 every ________ evening

ACADEMIC WRITING SKILLS

6 Look. Then write.

We like reading Japanese books and ~~we like~~ watching Japanese TV.

1 I like going to interesting places. I like taking beautiful photographs.

____

2 I like cooking interesting food. I like baking cakes.

____

3 I like computers. I like the internet.

____

CRITICAL THINKING: CREATE

7 Look at 2. Choose a club. Write.

What do we do? We ______________________________

____

Where do we meet? ______________________________

WRITING TASK

8 Look at 4 and 7. Write an email to new students at your university.

To: newstudents@camuni.ac.uk Reply Forward

From: ____________@camuni.ac.uk

Subject: ____________ Club

To all new students,

Welcome to the ____________ Club!

____

____

____

____

____

____

____

All university students are welcome!

____

____

9 Swap and check.

OBJECTIVES REVIEW

I can ...

- listen to students talk about their clothes and free time. ☐
- understand what people like and don't like doing. ☐
- say what I like and don't like doing and wearing. ☐
- ask and answer questions about free time, clothes and colours. ☐
- read information about student clubs. ☐
- read a student email. ☐
- write words with *-ing*. ☐
- write an email about a student club. ☐

WORDLIST

bake cakes	have a picnic
black	jacket
blue	red
chat online	scarf
coat	shirt
do exercise	sleep
draw	talk on the phone
dress	trousers
favourite	visit friends and family
go for a walk	wait
go to the park	wear
green	white
hat	yellow

PAIRWORK ACTIVITIES

UNIT 3, PAGE 59, EXERCISE 8

Student A

Ask and answer.

Your subjects:

English Maths

Chemistry

REMEMBER !

What subjects do you study?
I study ...

REMEMBER !

When is our ... class?
Our ... class is on Monday.
What time is our ... class?
It's at ...

UNIT 3, PAGE 67, EXERCISE 7

Student A

Say. Then write.

SCIENCE CLASS A140
University timetable

	Sunday	Monday	Tuesday	Wednesday	Thursday
MORNING					
8:00–9:30	________	Chemistry	________		Biology
10:00–11:30		English		Chemistry	
AFTERNOON					
1:00–2:30	________		________	English	

UNIT 4, PAGE 81, EXERCISE 10

Student A

Ask and answer.

Istanbul in Turkey

new?
cheap?
beautiful?
big?

REMEMBER !

Is ...?
Yes, it is.
No, it isn't.

UNIT 5, PAGE 99, EXERCISE 8

Student A

Look and write. Then ask and answer.

a nurse

REMEMBER !

She / He ...
Is she / he a ...?
No, she / he isn't.

He works ___at night___.
He starts work ________________.
He meets ________________.

UNIT 5, PAGE 103, EXERCISE 7

Student A

Ask and answer. Listen to Student B and write. Then check.

REMEMBER !

When is ...? In February.

winter holiday – in January

first day of university – ______________

When is the winter holiday?

Maths exam – ______________

IT exam – in March

English exam – in April

Chemistry exam – in May

Biology exam – ______________

summer holiday – in July

UNIT 7, PAGE 131, EXERCISE 8

Student A

REMEMBER !

I live near ... and ...
I don't live near ...

1 Look at the map and say where you live.

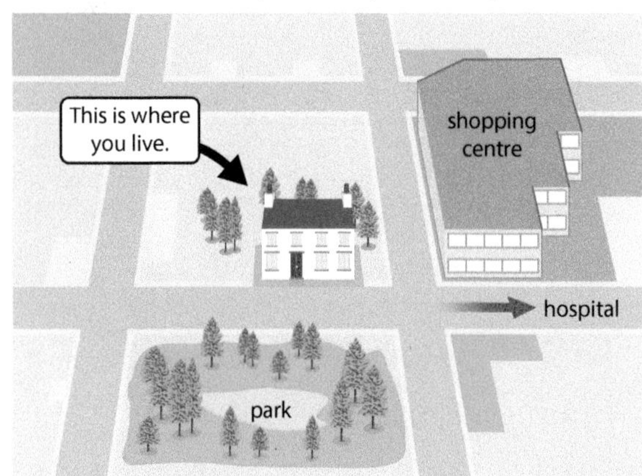

2 Listen to Student B and write.

______________ lives ______________
______________ and ______________.
______________ ______________ live
______________ ______________.

UNIT 7, PAGE 139, EXERCISE 6

Student A

Look at the map. Ask and answer.

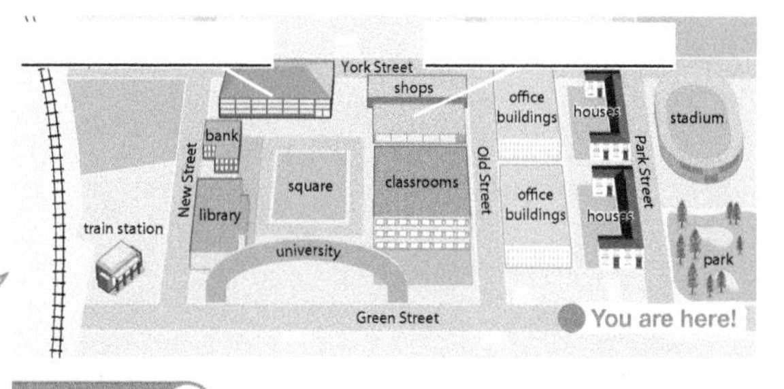

REMEMBER !

Excuse me.
I'm sorry. I don't understand.
Where's that?
Could you say that again please?
You're welcome.

Ask:

Where's the hotel?

Where's the restaurant?

UNIT 8, PAGE 157, EXERCISE 6

Student A

REMEMBER !

How much is this computer?
It's 500 dollars.

Ask and answer.

Ask about:

______________ ______________ ______________

Answer:

650 dollars 1,200 pounds 35,000 euros

UNIT 9, PAGE 167, EXERCISE 10

Student A

Ask and answer.

REMEMBER !

How often do you ...? Twice a year.
Never.
Once a week. Sometimes.

Ask student B about:

video games / apps / blogs

UNIT 9, PAGE 169, EXERCISE 7

Student A

Look and write. Then say.

REMEMBER !

It can ... It can't ...

Look and write. Then say.

cook
send messages
use Wi-Fi
take photographs
~~go online~~
play video games
use GPS

can ✓	can't ✗
go online	

UNIT 9, PAGE 175, EXERCISE 6

Student A

Read and write ✓ or ✗. Then talk to Student B.

Do you agree?

English grammar is easy. ☐
People don't need smart glasses. ☐
Video games aren't good for children. ☐
Business is an interesting subject. ☐

REMEMBER !

Do you agree? What do you think?
I agree. I don't think so.
I don't agree. I think so too.

UNIT 10, PAGE 195, EXERCISE 7

Student A

1 Ask and write.

Student Survey: Free time and clothes

1 What do you like doing in your free time?

____

2 What do you like wearing at home?

____

3 What do you wear to university?

____

4 What is your favourite colour?

5 Look at Student B. What colours are your friend's clothes?

____

2 Listen to Student B and answer the questions.

UNIT 3, PAGE 67, EXERCISE 7

Student B

Say. Then write.

REMEMBER !

When is our ... class?
Our ... class is on Monday.
What time is our ... class?
It's at ...

SCIENCE CLASS A140
University timetable

	Sunday	Monday	Tuesday	Wednesday	Thursday
MORNING					
8:00–9:30	IT	________	Business		Biology
10:00–11:30		________		________	
AFTERNOON					
1:00–2:30	Business		IT	________	

UNIT 3, PAGE 59, EXERCISE 8

Student B

Ask and answer.

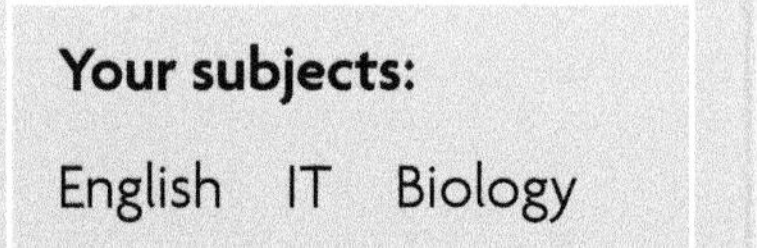

Your subjects:

English IT Biology

REMEMBER !

What subjects do you study?
I study ...

UNIT 4, PAGE 81, EXERCISE 10

Student B

Ask and answer.

New York in the USA

new?
cheap?
beautiful?
big?

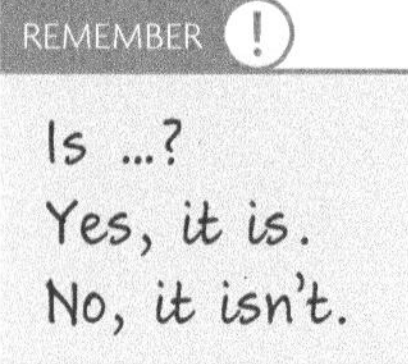
REMEMBER !

Is ...?
Yes, it is.
No, it isn't.

UNIT 5, PAGE 99, EXERCISE 8

Student B

Look and write. Then ask and answer.

a bank manager

REMEMBER !

She / He ...
Is she / he a ...?
No, she / he isn't.

She works *in the city*.
She starts work ________________.
She reads ________________.
She meets ________________.

UNIT 5, PAGE 103, EXERCISE 7

Student B

Ask and answer. Listen to Student A and write. Then check.

REMEMBER !

When is ...? In February.

When is the winter holiday?

winter holiday – in January

first day of university – in February

Maths exam – in March

IT exam – ______________

English exam – ______________

Chemistry exam – ______________

Biology exam – in May

summer holiday – ______________

UNIT 7, PAGE 131, EXERCISE 8

Student B

REMEMBER !

I live near ... and ...
I don't live near ...

1 Listen to student A and write.

__________ lives __________
__________ and __________.
__________ __________ live
__________ __________.

2 Look at the map and say where you live.

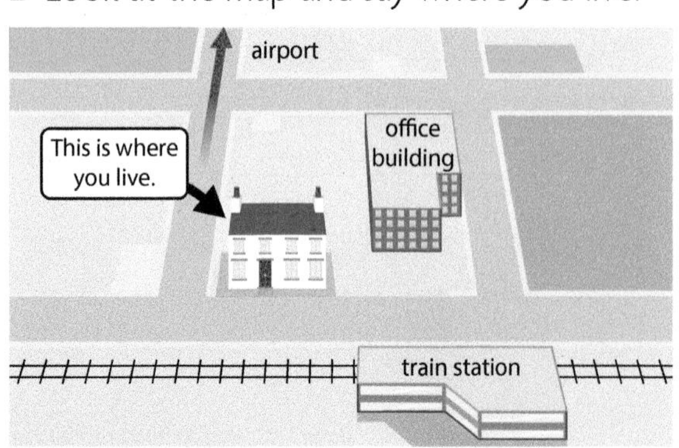

UNIT 7, PAGE 139, EXERCISE 6

Student B

Look at the map. Ask and answer.

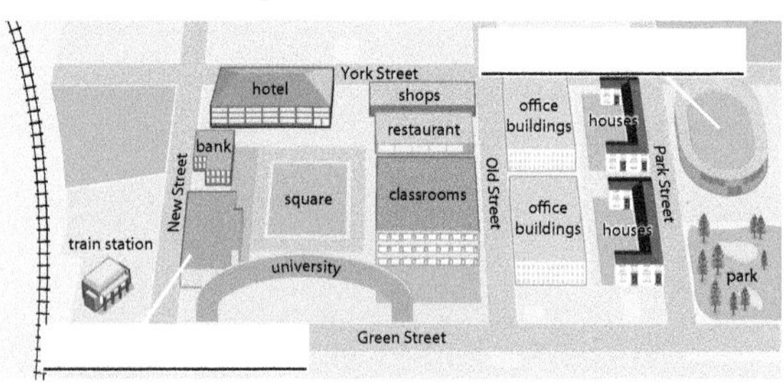

REMEMBER !

Excuse me.
I'm sorry. I don't understand.
Where's that?
Could you say that again please?
You're welcome.

Ask:

Where's the stadium?

Where's the library?

UNIT 8, PAGE 157, EXERCISE 6

Student B

REMEMBER !

How much is this computer?
It's 500 dollars.

Ask and answer.

Answer:

820 dollars 2,600 pounds 300,000 euros

Ask about:

__________ __________ __________

UNIT 9, PAGE 167, EXERCISE 10

Student B

Ask and answer.

REMEMBER !

How often do you …? Twice a year.
Never. Once a week.
Sometimes.

Ask student A about:

GPS / webinars / English online

UNIT 9, PAGE 169, EXERCISE 7

Student B

Look and write. Then say.

REMEMBER !

It can … It can't …

cook send messages use Wi-Fi
take photographs go online
play video games ~~use GPS~~

can ✓	can't ✗
use GPS	

UNIT 9, PAGE 175, EXERCISE 6

Student B

Read and write ✓ or ✗. Then talk to Student A.

Do you agree?

English vocabulary is difficult. ☐

Smartwatches are beautiful. ☐

People spend a lot of money on apps. ☐

Teachers have an easy job. ☐

REMEMBER !

Do you agree? What do you think?
I agree. I don't think so.
I don't agree. I think so too.

UNIT 10, PAGE 195, EXERCISE 7

Student B

1 Listen to Student A and answer the questions.

2 Ask and write.

Student Survey: Free time and clothes

1 What do you like doing in your free time?
____

2 What do you like wearing at home?
____

3 What do you wear to university?
____

4 What is your favourite colour?
____

5 Look at Student A. What colours are your friend's clothes?
____

UNIT 2, PAGE 41, EXERCISE 9

Write. Then ask and answer.

REMEMBER !

Who's this? This is my ...

1 mother
Name: ____________

2 father
Name: ____________

3 ____________
Name: ____________

4 ____________
Name: ____________

UNIT 4, PAGE 81, EXERCISE 10

Student C

Ask and answer.

Tokyo in Japan

old?	interesting?
small?	wet?

REMEMBER !

Is ...?
Yes, it is.
No, it isn't.

UNIT 5, PAGE 97, EXERCISE 9

Say. Listen and write the time.

REMEMBER !

I go to university at 7:00.
I start classes at 7:30.

Name: ____________

Time	
___	go to university
___	start classes
___	finish classes
___	go to the library
___	go home
___	meet friends

UNIT 6, PAGE 113, EXERCISE 7

Say what you eat and don't eat. Listen and write.

Name: ______________________

Yes ✓	No ✗

Name: ______________________

Yes ✓	No ✗

Name: ______________________

Yes ✓	No ✗

REMEMBER !

I eat ...
I don't eat ...

UNIT 8, PAGE 153, EXERCISE 8

Read and circle. Then say.

Al Wafa Shopping Centre

Please answer the questions.

How often do you go shopping?
twice a month once a month

How often do you buy clothes?
once a month twice a year

How often do you buy new shoes?
once a month twice a year

Where do you buy your clothes?
on the internet at the market
in the shopping centre

How often do you buy things on the internet?
once a week once a month

Do you pay by card or by cash?
by card by cash

Thank you!

REMEMBER !

100 = one hundred
1000 = one thousand
Once a day / week / month.

UNIT 8, PAGE 159, EXERCISE 7

Ask and answer. Listen and write.

	Name ________	Name ________	Name ________
1 How much money do you spend on your phone in a month?			
2 How often do you buy a new phone?			
3 How much money do you spend on coffee in a month?			
4 How often do you buy coffee?			
5 How much money do you spend on clothes in a month?			
6 How often do you buy clothes?			

UNIT 9, PAGE 171, EXERCISE 7

Read and circle. Then say.

REMEMBER !

I look at my mobile phone every hour.
I never watch TV on my mobile phone.

I look at my mobile phone every hour.

I never watch TV on my mobile phone.

How often do you ...?

look at your mobile phone?

a every second   b every minute   c every hour   d every day   e never

read messages on your mobile phone?

a every second   b every minute   c every hour   d every day   e never

play games on your mobile phone?

a every second   b every minute   c every hour   d every day   e never

send emails on your mobile phone?

a every second   b every minute   c every hour   d every day   e never

watch TV on your mobile phone?

a every second   b every minute   c every hour   d every day   e never

UNIT 10, PAGE 185, EXERCISE 8

1 Ask 3 students and write ✔ or ✗.

REMEMBER !

What do you do in your free time?
Do you ...?

	Student 1 Name: ______	Student 2 Name: ______	Student 3 Name: ______
do exercise			
go to the park			
go for a walk			
go shopping			
have picnics			
talk on the phone			

2 Say.

Mariam and Anwar do exercise at home. Samira doesn't do exercise at home.

UNIT 10, PAGE 187, EXERCISE 9

1 Read and write ✔ or ✗.

What do you like doing in your free time? Write ✔ or ✗.

• chatting online ☐	• reading blogs ☐	• cooking ☐
• going to the park ☐	• going to a restaurant ☐	• going shopping ☐
• walking on the beach ☐	• playing video games ☐	• taking photographs ☐
• watching TV ☐	• buying shoes ☐	• visiting friends and family ☐
• doing exercise ☐	• reading books ☐	

2 Say.

REMEMBER !

I like ... -ing. I don't like ... -ing

UNIT 10, PAGE 189, EXERCISE 8

Match. Ask and answer.

a  b  c

☐ ☐ ☐ ☐

☐ ☐ ☐ ☐

REMEMBER !

What is this?
What are these?
This is ...
These are ...

UNIT 10, PAGE 193, EXERCISE 9

1 Choose a photograph. Write the clothes and the colours.

Yeshey from Bhutan

Andrew from the UK

____

____

____

____

____

2 Say. Describe what the child in your photograph wears to school.

GLOSSARY

Vocabulary	Page number	In your language
UNIT 1		
book	30	
country	21	
dictionary	30	
email address	24	
family name	27	
first name	27	
India	26	
Japan	26	
library card	30	
Mexico	26	
mobile phone	30	
name	24	
notebook	30	
pen	30	
pencil	30	
phone number	24	
Saudi Arabia	26	
spell	22	
student	27	
student ID card	30	
teacher	27	
the United Kingdom (the UK)	26	
Turkey	26	
UNIT 2		
bag	44	
brother	40	
camera	44	
car	44	
computer	44	
Dr (doctor)	41	
family	40	
father	40	
grandfather	40	
grandmother	40	
mobile phone	44	
mother	40	
Mr	41	
Mrs	41	
sister	40	
television	44	

Vocabulary	Page number	In your language
UNIT 3		
Biology	58	
boring	62	
Business	58	
Chemistry	58	
day	60	
difficult	62	
easy	62	
English	58	
Friday	60	
History	58	
interesting	62	
IT	58	
Japanese	58	
Maths	58	
Monday	60	
o'clock	66	
room	60	
Saturday	60	
subject	58	
Sunday	60	
Thursday	60	
time	66	
Tuesday	60	
Wednesday	60	
UNIT 4		
beautiful	80	
big	76	
cheap	80	
city	86	
clean	80	
cold	76	
country	74	
dry	76	
expensive	80	
hot	76	
new	80	
old	80	
place	74	
small	76	
warm	76	
wet	76	

Vocabulary	Page number	In your language
UNIT 5		
April	102	
August	102	
bank manager	94	
December	102	
dentist	94	
exam	102	
February	102	
finish work / classes	96	
first day of university	102	
go home	96	
go to university	96	
go to the library	96	
go to work	96	
help people	98	
January	102	
July	102	
June	102	
March	102	
May	102	
meet friends	96	
meet people	98	
November	102	
nurse	94	
October	102	
photographer	94	
pilot	94	
police officer	94	
read emails	98	
September	102	
start work / classes	96	
summer holiday	102	
take photographs	98	
travel to different countries	98	
winter holiday	102	
work in the city	98	
write emails	98	
UNIT 6		
bread	112	
busy	120	
cheese	112	
coffee	112	
coffee with milk and sugar	116	

Vocabulary	Page number	In your language
drink	112	
drive to work	114	
eat	112	
fine	120	
fish	112	
fruit	112	
get up	114	
get up early	116	
go to bed	114	
go to bed late	116	
great	120	
green tea	116	
have breakfast	114	
have dinner	114	
have lunch	114	
healthy	124	
hungry	120	
juice	112	
meat	112	
not bad	120	
not well	120	
red meat	116	
rice	112	
tea	112	
tired	120	
vegetables	112	
walk to university	114	
water	112	
UNIT 7		
airport	130	
beach	130	
beautiful beaches	134	
between	138	
busy square	134	
factory	132	
famous stadium	134	
hospital	130	
hotel	132	
house	132	
interesting market	134	
near	138	
next to	138	
office building	130	
old street	134	
on the left	138	

Vocabulary	Page number	In your language
on the right	138	___
park	130	___
restaurant	132	___
shop	132	___
shopping centre	130	___
tall buildings	134	___
train station	130	___
You're welcome.	139	___
UNIT 8		
bank card	148	___
buy	150	___
buy clothes	152	___
buy shoes	152	___
buy things on the internet	152	___
cook	168	___
day	150	___
dirhams	154	___
dollars	154	___
euros	154	___
go shopping	152	___
go online	168	___
How much is ...?	157	___
hundred	156	___
laptop	148	___
lira	156	___
million	156	___
month	150	___
newspaper	148	___
once a week	150	___
pay by card	152	___
pay by cash	152	___
pounds	154	___
riyals	156	___
smartphone	148	___
spend money	152	___
T-shirt	148	___
tablet	148	___
thousand	156	___
twice a week	151	___
video game	148	___
watch	148	___
week	150	___
year	150	___

Vocabulary	Page number	In your language
UNIT 9		
adult	170	___
billion	170	___
boy	170	___
buy apps	166	___
child	170	___
children	170	___
cook	168	___
fridge	168	___
girl	170	___
glasses	168	___
go online	168	___
hour	171	___
learn English online	166	___
look at websites	166	___
make calls	168	___
man	170	___
men	170	___
minute	170	___
need a USB drive	166	___
people	170	___
person	170	___
play video games	166	___
second	170	___
send messages	168	___
smartwatch	168	___
use GPS	166	___
watch webinars	167	___
woman	170	___
women	170	___
write a blog	166	___
UNIT 10		
bake cakes	184	___
black	192	___
blue	192	___
chat online	186	___
coat	188	___
do exercise	184	___
draw	186	___
dress	188	___
favourite	192	___
go for a walk	184	___
go to the park	184	___

Vocabulary	Page number	In your language
green	192	
hat	188	
have a picnic	184	
jacket	188	
red	192	
scarf	188	
shirt	188	
sleep	186	
talk on the phone	184	
trousers	188	
visit friends and family	184	
wait	186	
wear	188	
white	192	
yellow	192	

Vocabulary notes

VIDEO AND AUDIO SCRIPTS

STARTER UNIT

0.14

He is 16.
He is 19.
She is 15.
She is 17.
She is 11.
He is 13.

0.16

radio
nine
palm
doctor
zero
taxi
queen
message
bus
four
salad
jeans

0.20

1

A: Two lemons, please.
B: Thank you.
I'm sorry.

2

A: Two salads, please
B: Thank you.
I'm sorry.

UNIT 1

1.2

A: Hi! I'm Khalifa. K – h – a – l – i – f – a
B: Hello. My name's Mariam.
M – a – r – i – a – m
C: Hello. My name's Rafael.
R – a – f – a – e – l
D: I'm Yasemin. Y – a – s – e – m – i – n

1.5

1 A: What's your phone number?
B: My number is 0774 566 212.
2 A: What's your phone number?
B: My number is 0774 902 154.
3 A: What's your number?
B: My phone number is 0714 332 503.

Unit 1 Meeting people
Part 1. My name's Saif.

Saif: Hello. My name's Saif. I'm from Saudi Arabia. This is my city, Riyadh. I'm a teacher.
Carlos: Hi. I'm Carlos. I'm from Mexico City, in Mexico. I'm a student.
Elaine: Hi. My name's Elaine. I'm from the UK. This is my city, London. I'm a teacher. Nice to meet you.

Part 2. He's in the library.

Narrator: He's Demir. He's from Ankara, in Turkey. He's a new student. He's in the university library. His first name is Demir – D E M I R. His family name is Topuz – T O P U Z.

Part 3. Remember.

Where is Saif from?
Where is Carlos from?
What's her job?
What's his family name?

1.20

1 A: Excuse me. Can I have your book, please?
B: No. I'm sorry.
2 A: Excuse me. Can I have your student ID card, please?
B: Here you are.
A: Thank you.
3 A: Excuse me. Can I have a dictionary, please?
B: Here you are.
A: Thank you.
4 A: Excuse me. Can I have a pencil, please?
B: No. I'm sorry.
5 A: Excuse me. Can I have your notebook, please?
B: Here you are.
A: Thank you.

1.21

A: Hello.

Gabriela: Hi. I need a student ID card.

A: Yes, of course. What's your first name?

Gabriela: My name's Gabriela.

A: What's your family name?

Gabriela: My family name is Lopez.

A: Errr ... how do you spell that?

Gabriela: L – o – p – e – z.

A: OK. And where are you from?

Gabriela: I'm from Mexico.

A: Aha and ... what's your phone number?

Gabriela: My phone number is 0832 556 436.

A: OK, 0832 556 436. And ... what's your email address?

Gabriela: My email address is alopez@myemail.com.

1.24

1 name	2 country	3 phone
4 email	5 book	6 pencil
7 pen	8 dictionary	

UNIT 2

2.3

A: Ahmed, who's this?

Ahmed: This is my mother, Rana.

A: Who's this?

Ahmed: This is my father, Yusuf.

A: And who's this?

Ahmed: This is my grandfather, Hasan.

A: Who's this?

Ahmed: This is my grandmother, Sara.

A: And who's this?

Ahmed: This is my sister, Sena.

A: Who's this?

Ahmed: This is my brother, Tariq.

2.5

1 This is Mrs Williams. She's my English teacher.

2 This is Dr Farrel. He's my doctor.

3 This is Mr Erkol. He's my teacher.

2.14

1 A: How many cameras do you have?
B: I have five cameras.

2 A: How many bags do you have?
B: I have eight bags.

3 A: How many cars do you have?
B: We have one car.

4 A: How many computers do you have?
B: We have six computers.

2.15

one	two	three
four	five	six
seven	eight	nine
ten		

2.17

1 A: How many cars do you have?
B: I have two cars.

2 A: How many cameras do you have?
B: I have three cameras.

3 A: How many televisions do you have?
B: I have four televisions.

4 A: How many bags do you have?
B: I have five bags.

5 A: How many computers do you have?
B: I have one computer.

Unit 2 People and things
Part 1. My family has three cars.

Hachiro: This is Japan. I'm Hachiro. I like books. This is my grandfather, my father and my brother. I have one brother. My brother is six years old. My grandfather is 71 years old. This is my grandmother. She's 66 years old. And this is my mother and my father. My mother and father have two cars. My grandfather has one car.

Part 2. I have one camera.

Sheila: My name is Sheila. My family name is Smith. I'm from the USA. I have one daughter. Her name is Anna. And I have one son. His name is David. They're at university. Look, I have one camera!

David: I'm David. I have one mobile phone.

Anna: I'm Anna and I'm a student. This is my computer. I have one computer here. And this is our house. We have one computer here ... and we have one television here. And I have one television here. We have two televisions – my television and a family television. This is my father, James. He has one mobile phone and he has one computer here. We have three computers – my computer, his computer and a family computer. And my mother has one bag! Her camera is in the bag!

Part 3. Remember

How many brothers does Hachiro have?

How many computers do the Smith family have?

How many televisions do the Smith family have?

2.20

eleven	twelve	thirteen
fourteen	fifteen	sixteen
seventeen	eighteen	nineteen

2.25

Ercan: Look, Taner. This is my teacher.

Taner: What's his name?

Ercan: His name's Mr Rosales. He's from Mexico.

Taner: How old is he?

Ercan: He's 40 years old.

Taner: Mmm.

Ercan: And this is my car. My car is a Nissan.

Taner: How old is your car?

Ercan: My car is twelve years old. My car is from Japan.

Taner: How many cars do you have?

Ercan: I have two cars. This is a Nissan and this is a Jaguar. The Jaguar is from the UK. My Jaguar is five years old.

2.28

1 sister	2 friend	3 brother
4 mother	5 father	6 eighteen
7 thirty-seven	8 fifty-five	

UNIT 3

3.2

1 English 2 teacher 3 Chemistry

3.3

1 **Yasemin:** Hi Nur.

Nur: Hi Yasemin.

Yasemin: Nur, what subjects do you study?

Nur: I study Maths, Business and IT. And you, Yasemin?

Yasemin: I study History, English and Japanese.

2 **Marco:** Hi Paul.

Paul: Hi Marco.

Marco: Paul, what subjects do you study?

Paul: I study English, Maths and IT. And you, Marco?

Marco: I study Biology, Chemistry and English.

3.7

1 **Student 1:** When is our Business class?

Student 2: On Thursday afternoon.

2 **Student 1:** When is our Chemistry class?

Student 2: On Wednesday morning.

3 **Student 1:** Where is our IT class?

Student 2: In room 24.

3.8

Student 1: When is our English class?

Student 2: On Sunday morning.

Student 1: Where is our English class?

Student 2: In room 11.
Student 1: When is our Biology class?
Student 2: On Thursday morning.
Student 1: Where is our Biology class?
Student 2: In room 17.
Student 1: When is our Maths class?
Student 2: On Tuesday afternoon.
Student 1: Where is our Maths class?
Student 2: In room 13.

3.12

1 **Tahir:** Rashid, what subjects do you study?
Rashid: I study Maths, English and Chemistry.
Tahir: Mm. What's Maths like?
Rashid: It's easy. It isn't difficult.

2 **A:** Toki, what subjects do you study?
Toki: I study Business and IT.
A: What's IT like?
Toki: It's interesting. It isn't boring.

3 **A:** Robert, what subjects do you study?
Robert: I study English.
A: What's English like?
Robert: It's difficult. It isn't easy.

Unit 3 University life
Part 1. I'm a student.

Mira: Hi, I'm Mira. I'm a student in Abu Dhabi, in the UAE. I study Business.
Faisal: Hello, my name is Faisal. I'm a student in Jeddah, in Saudi Arabia. I study IT. It's interesting!
Fathima: Hello. My name's Fathima. I'm from Muscat, in Oman. I study Japanese. It's difficult!
Emma: Hello. I'm Emma. I'm from Dublin, in Ireland. I study chemistry. It isn't easy.

Part 2. When's your class?

Narrator: When's your class?
Mira: My Business class is on Wednesday morning. My class is at eight o'clock.
Narrator: Where's your class?
Mira: It's in room 42.
Narrator: What floor is it on?
Mira: It's on the third floor.
Narrator: When's your class?
Faisal: My IT class is on Monday afternoon at three o'clock.
Narrator: Where's your class?
Faisal: It's in room 21.
Narrator: What floor is it on?
Faisal: It's on the fourth floor.
Narrator: When's your class?
Fathima: My Japanese class is on Tuesday morning.
Narrator: What time is your class?
Fathima: It's at nine o'clock.
Narrator: Where's the class?
Fathima: It's in room 82.
Narrator: What floor is it on?
Fathima: It's on the second floor.
Narrator: When's your class?
Emma: My chemistry class is on Friday afternoon.
Narrator: Where is it?
Emma: It's in room 18.
Narrator: What floor is it on?
Emma: It's on the first floor.
Teacher: Please look at your new Chemistry timetable. There are some changes this week. Your Chemistry classes are on Monday, Tuesday, Wednesday and Thursday. The class on Monday is in room 1. It isn't in room 8. It's easy. The class on Tuesday is not in room 12. It is in room 22. The class on Wednesday is not in room 23. It is in room 13. The class on Thursday in room 5 on the first floor is very interesting. Don't be late! Do you have any questions?

Part 3. Remember

What does Mira study?
What does Fathima study?
What does Faisal Study?
What does Emma study?

3.22

1 A: Good morning! What time is it?
B: It's 6:30.
A: Oh no, I'm late!
2 A: What time is our Maths class?
B: It's at three o'clock.
3 A: Oh, it's 9 o'clock! What time is our Chemistry class?
B: It's at 8:30! We're late!

3.23

1 A: When is your Business class?
B: It's on Monday at 9:30.
2 A: When is your IT class?
B: It's at 10 o'clock on Tuesday.
3 A: When is your English class?
B: It's on Friday at 1:30.
4 A: When is your Biology class?
B: It's at 3 o'clock on Thursday.

3.24

Sarah: Hi, Amal!
Amal: Hi, Sarah! Look, this is my new timetable.
Sarah: What subjects do you study?
Amal: I study IT, Business and Maths.
Sarah: I study Business too! It's interesting. When is your Business class?
Amal: It's on Tuesday afternoon at 1:30.
Sarah: Thursday afternoon?
Amal: No, Tuesday.
Sarah: And where is it?
Amal: It's in room 43.
Sarah: Err ... what's your Business class like, Amal?
Amal: Hmm ... it's interesting, but it isn't easy. When is your Business class?

UNIT 4

4.5

1 A: What's the UK like?
B: The UK is small. It's cold and wet.
2 A: What's Turkey like?
B: Turkey is big. It's warm and dry.
3 A: What's Japan like?
B: Japan is small. It's warm and wet.
4 A: What's India like?
B: India is big. It's hot and wet.

4.7

1 A: The Hagia Sophia is in Saudi Arabia.
B: No. It isn't in Saudi Arabia. It's in Turkey.
2 A: This pyramid is in the USA.
B: No. It isn't in the USA. It's in Sudan.
3 A: Tacos are from Brazil.
B: No. They aren't from Brazil. They're from Mexico.
4 A: Curry is from Canada.
B: No. It isn't from Canada. It's from India.

4.16

1 Dubai 2 London
3 Doha 4 Mexico City
5 Istanbul 6 Tokyo

Unit 4 Different countries
Part 1. Where's this?

Narrator: Hello Maryam. Nice to meet you.
Maryam: Nice to meet you too.
Narrator: Where are you from?
Maryam: This is Doha, in Qatar.
Narrator: What's it like in Doha?
Maryam: It's warm and dry.
Narrator: Who's this?
Maryam: This is my brother, Ali.
Narrator: And where's this?
Maryam: It's in Doha. It's the 'Pearl'.
Narrator: Is it new?

Maryam: Yes, it is. It's a new city. It's beautiful and clean ... and very expensive.

Narrator: Hi Antonio, where's this?

Antonio: This is Mexico City, in Mexico.

Narrator: Is it big?

Antonio: Yes, it is. It's very big. It's new! And it's old. This is the palace.

Narrator: And who's this?

Antonio: This is Mr Garcia. He's very busy.

Part 2: What's it like?

Narrator: Hello Mohammed.

Mohammed: Hi.

Narrator: Where are you from?

Mohammed: I'm from Muscat, in Oman.

Narrator: What's this?

Mohammed: It's the fort in Muscat. It's very old.

Narrator: Is Muscat old?

Mohammed: There are new places and there are old places. There are beautiful places too.

Narrator: What's this?

Mohammed: It's the palace. It's hot and dry in Oman.

Narrator: Hello Nicola. Where's this?

Nicola: It's London, in the UK.

Narrator: What's it like in London?

Nicola: It's wet and cold.

Narrator: And who's this?

Nicola: This is me!

Narrator: Hello Min-seo. Where are you from?

Min-seo: I'm from Seoul, in South Korea. This is the palace. And this is the fort.

Narrator: Is it cold in Seoul?

Min-seo: It's very cold in Seoul!

Part 3: Remember

What's the 'Pearl'?

Where is it hot and dry?

Where is it wet and cold?

Where is it very cold?

4.24

Natalia: I'm Natalia. Argentina is my country. It's big. It's hot and dry. My mother and father are from Buenos Aires. It's old and beautiful. It isn't expensive. La Boca is in Buenos Aires. It's interesting. It isn't old. Thank you. Any questions?

A: Is Buenos Aires cold?

Natalia: No, it isn't. It's warm.

B: Is Buenos Aires clean?

Natalia: Yes, it is.

4.27

1 country 2 city 3 beautiful
4 warm 5 interesting 6 small
7 cheap 8 expensive

UNIT 5

5.3

A: This is my sister Sena.

B: Is she a nurse?

A: No, she isn't. She's a dentist.

A: This is her husband, Atilla.

B: Is he a police officer?

A: Yes, he is. He's a police officer in Ankara.

B: Is this your brother?

A: No, it isn't. This is Joel. He's a friend from the USA.

B: Is he a pilot?

A: No, he isn't. He's a photographer. And this is his wife, Kate.

B: Is she a bank manager?

A: Yes, she is.

5.4

1 father 2 phone 3 coffee
4 photographer 5 friend

5.6

Valeria: My name is Valeria and I'm from Mexico. I study Business at Cambridge University. On Tuesdays, I go to university at 7:30. We start classes at 8 o'clock. We finish classes at 3 o'clock. At 3:30, I meet my friends. We go to the library. We go home at 6 o'clock. On Wednesdays, I work at a bank. I start work at 8:30. I finish work at 4:30. At 5 o'clock, I go to the library and study.

5.11

1 read 2 email 3 meet
4 people 5 countries

Unit 5 Work
Part 1. What are their jobs?

A: Who's this?
B: This is Neil.
A: Is he a pilot?
B: Yes, he is. He travels to different countries and he meets a lot of people.
A: What's it like?
B: It's interesting.
A: Who's this?
B: This is Aadab.
A: Is she a nurse?
B: No, she isn't. Her name is Dr Aadab Nazari. She's a doctor. She helps people.
A: What's it like?
B: It's difficult.
A: Who are they? Are they photographers?
B: Yes, they are. They take photographs of interesting people.
A: What's it like?
B: It's a nice job!
A: And who's he?
B: He's an actor. It's a very nice job!
A: Who's this?
B: He's a waiter. He's very busy this evening.
A: Who's he?
B: He's a driver. He meets interesting people.

Part 2. When does it start?

Narrator: Hello William. Where are you from?
William: I'm from the UK.
Narrator: Are you a doctor?
William: No, I'm not. I'm a dentist.
Narrator: When does your holiday start?
William: It starts in January.
Narrator: Where is it?
William: It's in Switzerland.
Narrator: Hi Saad. Where are you from?
Saad: I'm from Saudi Arabia.
Narrator: Are you a police officer?
Saad: No, I'm not. I work in an airport. I work in Riyadh.
Narrator: Where is your holiday?
Saad: It's in Jeddah.
Narrator: When does your holiday start?
Saad: It starts in June.
Narrator: Hi Safiya. Where are you from?
Safiya: I'm from Dammam, in Saudi Arabia.
Narrator: Where do you study?
Safiya: I study in London, in the UK.
Narrator: What do you study?
Safiya: I study Biology.
Narrator: When is the first day of university?
Safiya: It's in September.

Part 3. Remember

Look at Neil. What's his job?
Is Aadab a nurse?
When is the holiday for William?
When is the holiday for Saad?

5.22

1 April 2 August 3 October
4 February 5 September 6 November

5.23

A: This is my friend, Maitha.

B: Is she from Turkey?

A: No, she isn't. She's from Egypt. She's a manager. She works in the city, in Dubai.

B: Is it interesting?

A: Yes, it is. She starts work at 10 o'clock in the morning. She works on her computer. She reads and writes emails. In the afternoon, she meets bank managers. She finishes work at 7:30.

B: And who's this?

A: This is my friend, John. He's from the UK. He's a pilot. He works with people from different countries. He travels to interesting places. He starts work at different times. He works at night and in the morning. It isn't easy.

5.26

1 finish 2 start 3 study
4 work 5 student

UNIT 6

6.3

1 drink 2 fruit 3 bread

Unit 6 Food and health
Part 1. What do you eat?

Narrator: What's your name?

Gamze: My name's Gamze. I'm a student. I study History. I'm from Istanbul, in Turkey.

Narrator: When do you get up?

Gamze: I get up early. I get up at seven o'clock. And I have breakfast at seven thirty.

Narrator: What do you have for breakfast?

Gamze: I drink coffee. A lot of people in Turkey drink tea for breakfast, but I drink coffee. A lot of people in Turkey eat bread for breakfast. I don't eat bread. I eat salad with cheese and olives.

Narrator: Do you walk to university?

Gamze: No, I don't. I go to university by bus. But some people in Istanbul walk to university.

Narrator: What do you have for lunch?

Gamze: For lunch we eat bread and drink tea. Bread and tea are cheap. The name of this bread in Turkey is 'simit'. I have lunch with my friend Oya.

Narrator: What do people in Turkey have for dinner?

Gamze: A lot of people in Turkey eat meat for lunch or dinner. Some people in Istanbul have a big and expensive dinner. They eat meat for dinner too. I have dinner with Oya. For dinner we eat noodles. We're students, and noodles are cheap!

Narrator: When do you go to bed?

Gamze: I go to bed late. I'm a student!

Narrator: What's your name?

Kashif: I'm Kashif. I'm from Dubai. I'm a bank manager. I work there. It's an interesting job.

Narrator: When do you get up?

Kashif: I get up early and go to work. Dubai has a lot of markets.

Narrator: What do you eat?

Kashif: I eat a lot of fruit. It's good for you. And I eat a lot of vegetables. I eat some fish. But he eats a lot of fish! And I eat dates. People in the UAE eat a lot of dates. They're good for you. I'm hungry! Let's have lunch. We eat fish and vegetables for lunch.

Part 2: We eat a lot of fruit and vegetables.

Amy: My first name is Amy. Our family name is Brown. We're from the UK. I eat a lot of fruit and vegetables. I drink tea and we drink green tea. My grandfather drinks a lot of coffee with milk and sugar. It's not good for you. He goes to the market. He eats vegetables. And a lot of bread and cheese.

Part 3. Remember

What does Gamze eat for breakfast?

What does Kashif eat a lot of?

Where does the grandfather go?

6.18

Mark Jones: OK, so here's what I eat and drink. I drink a lot of coffee. I drink coffee for breakfast and lunch. I don't drink a lot of water. I drink some tea. I have tea in the evenings. I don't drink a lot of juice. I eat a lot of sugar. I have sugar in my coffee and tea. I eat some fruit and vegetables, but I don't eat a lot of fish. I eat a lot of red meat.

6.22

South Korea

For breakfast, they eat fruit and vegetables.

For lunch and dinner, they eat fish.

They get up early.

the USA

For breakfast, they eat sugar and bread.

For lunch and dinner, they eat red meat.

They get up late.

6.23

1	cheese	2	fruit	3	vegetables
4	meat	5	fish	6	sugar
7	bread	8	rice		

UNIT 7

7.18

Advik from India

Advik: I live near Chandni Chowk. It's a famous market in India. It's busy and old. There are a lot of small shops with books, mobile phones, cameras, and bags. There are a lot of cheap restaurants. Some restaurants are very old. Their food is great.

Rachel from Singapore

Rachel: I live near Orchard Road. It's a famous street in Singapore. It isn't very old. It's new and clean. There is a busy shopping centre. There are a lot of great shops from different countries. There are some tall buildings and new hotels. It's an interesting place.

Unit 7 Places

Part 1. There are a lot of interesting places.

Rashid: I live in the UAE. In Dubai there is a famous tall building. The name of the tall building is Burj al-Arab. And there are beaches and parks. There are a lot of shops and a big shopping centre. There are a lot of interesting fish in the shopping centre! There are beautiful, expensive hotels. There are a lot of fish in the hotel too! There's an airport. It's beautiful! This is the metro station in the airport. There are interesting metro stations. Some trains go over the bridge to the hotel. And there are good hospitals in the UAE too. We have a lot of things in the UAE!

Ji-woo: I live in Incheon in South Korea. There are a lot of tall office buildings and a big park in my city. I walk to work and I go over the bridge. I live near some beautiful beaches. And there's a big car factory in my city. There are a lot of new cars and some big boats!

Part 2. Where's Green Park?

A: Excuse me, where's Green Park?

B: It's on Old Street.

A: Where's that?

B: Go over the bridge. Turn right. Go straight on. Then turn left. There's City Park. Turn right. Turn left at Queen's Park. Queen's Park is big. Turn right. Turn left. Then turn right. Then turn left. There's Green Park.

A: I'm sorry. Could you say that again, please?

B: Of course! Go over the bridge. Turn right. Go straight on. Then turn left. There's City Park.

A: OK.

B: Turn right.
Turn left at Queen's Park.

A: Queen's Park?

B: Yes. Turn right. Turn left. Then turn right. Then turn left. There's Green Park. Green Park is beautiful and interesting.

A: Thank you very much.

B: You're welcome.

Part 3. Remember

What is famous in Dubai?

Where are the fish?

What is in the factory?

What's Green Park like?

7.22

1 restaurant	2 classrooms	3 library
4 train station	5 house	
6 office building	7 park	

UNIT 8

8.22

Kemal: How much money do you spend on books?

Mustafa: I think I spend 200 lira on books in a month.

Kemal: How often do you buy books?

Mustafa: I buy books twice a month.

Kemal: How much money do you spend on tea and coffee in a month?

Mustafa: I think I spend 300 lira on coffee in a month. I don't drink tea.

Kemal: How often do you buy food?

Mustafa: I buy food once a day. I have lunch at the university restaurant.

Kemal: How much money do you spend on clothes and shoes in a month?

Mustafa: 100 lira. I don't spend a lot of money on clothes.

Kemal: Do you have a bank card?

Mustafa: No, I don't.

Kemal: Thank you.

Unit 8 Spending
Part 1. What's on your shopping list?

Narrator: Hello Tom. What's on your shopping list?

Tom: I buy bread twice a week. I buy fruit, vegetables and meat once a week.

Narrator: What fruit do you buy?

Tom: I buy bananas. I eat a lot of bananas.

Narrator: How much are they?

Tom: I buy five bananas. They're one pound. I buy a newspaper once a day.

Narrator: Do you pay for the bananas and newspaper by cash?

Tom: Yes, I do.

Narrator: How much is a newspaper?

Tom: It's one pound.

Narrator: Hello Luca. Where are you from?
Luca: Hi! I'm from Italy.
Narrator: What's on your shopping list?
Luca: I buy fruit twice a week.
Narrator: How much is it?
Luca: A bag of apples is three euros.
Narrator: What fruit do you buy?
Luca: I buy a lot of apples.
Luca: And I buy some peaches.
Narrator: Hello Eric. What's on your shopping list?
Eric: I buy milk twice a week. I buy fruit and vegetables once a week. I buy some food on the internet. And I buy some food at the market.
Narrator: How much are the apples?
Eric: The apples are six dollars for three bags.
Narrator: Do you buy a newspaper?
Eric: No, I don't. I read the newspaper on my tablet.

Part 2. How many tablets do you have?

Narrator: Hello Aiysha. How many tablets do you have?
Aiysha: I have one tablet. I buy a new tablet once a year.
Narrator: How much is it?
Aiysha: It's two thousand dirhams.
Narrator: Do you pay by bank card or by cash?
Aiysha: I pay by card.
Narrator: Hi Adam. Is this your laptop?
Adam: Yes, it is. I work in a clothes shop.
Narrator: How many laptops do you have?
Adam: I have one laptop. I buy a new laptop once a year.
Narrator: And how many clothes do you have?
Adam: I have a lot of clothes! I buy new clothes once a month.
Narrator: Hello Zhou.
Zhou: Hi.
Narrator: How many computers do you have?
Zhou: I have one computer.
Narrator: And how many video games do you have?
Zhou: I have one hundred video games.
Narrator: How often do you buy video games?
Zhou: I buy one twice a month.
Narrator: Are they expensive?
Zhou: No, they're not. They're cheap.
Narrator: Hi Salem. How much is a coffee?
Salem: It's ten dirhams.
Narrator: Do pay by cash or bank card?
Salem: I pay by card.

Part 3. Remember

Look at Tom. What's on his shopping list?
Look at Luca. What's on his shopping list?
Look at Aiysha. What does she buy?
Look at Salem. What does he buy?

8.27

1	hundred	**2**	thousand	**3**	million
4	month	**5**	shoes	**6**	spend
7	pay	**8**	internet	**9**	smartphone
10	clothes				

UNIT 9

9.22

Teacher: So, this week in our Study Skills class the topic is the internet and English. *Some people think the internet doesn't help you learn English.* Yes, Amalia ... what do you think?
Amalia: I agree. The internet doesn't help you learn English. I buy English books and read English newspapers.
Pilar: I don't think so. English books are very expensive and we don't have a lot of English newspapers in the shops.

Teacher: So, this week in our Study Skills class the topic is the internet and English. *Some people think the internet doesn't help you learn English.* Yes, Amalia ... what do you think?

Amalia: I agree. The internet doesn't help you learn English. I buy English books and read English newspapers.

Pilar: I don't think so. English books are very expensive and we don't have a lot of English newspapers in the shops.

Amalia: OK, but there are a lot of English newspapers in the library. I go there every day and read for one hour.

Teacher: Good idea! What do you think Pilar?

Pilar: I don't agree with you. I think it's boring. On the internet, I buy English apps. I also study with my smartphone. It's easy.

Unit 9 Technology
Part 1. Do you have any good apps?

Narrator: Hi Mike, where are you from?

Mike: I'm from London, in the UK.

Narrator: Do you have any apps on your smartphone?

Mike: Yes, I do.

Narrator: What app do you like?

Mike: I like this app. It can buy food.

Narrator: Are you hungry?

Mike: Yes, I am!

Narrator: Hello Sarah, who's this?

Sarah: This is my brother, Paul.

Narrator: Where are you and your brother from?

Sarah: We're from Paris, in France.

Narrator: Do you have any good apps on your smartphone?

Sarah: Yes, I do. I have an app for reading English newspapers online. It can download the news. It can help you learn new words.

Narrator: Paul, do you have any good apps?

Paul: This is a nice app. It can take photographs and it can save the photographs.

Narrator: Hello Aliyah. Where are you from?

Aliyah: I'm from New York, in the USA.

Narrator: Who's on your phone?

Aliyah: This is my mother.

Narrator: Where's your mother?

Aliyah: She's in the USA too. She's in Chicago. Do you have family or friends in a different city? This app can help you. It can call your family and friends. My mum has it too.

Aliyah: Hi mom!

Mother: Hi Aliyah!

Narrator: Good morning, Sam.

Sam: Good morning!

Narrator: Where are you from?

Sam: I'm from London, in the UK.

Narrator: Do you have any good apps on your smartphone?

Sam: Yes, I do. Buy this app! It's good for you!

Part 2. Do you have a USB drive?

Shop assistant: Good morning.

Sophie: Good morning. Excuse me, do you have a USB drive? I need a big one.

Shop assistant: Yes, we have a lot of USB drives. Here you are.

Sophie: Is it good?

Shop assistant: Yes. It's very big. It can save a lot of photographs or a lot of work.

Sophie: I need it for my work. How much is it?

Shop assistant: It's three pounds.

Sophie: Two USB drives, please.

Shop assistant: That's six pounds.

Sophie: Can I pay by card?

Shop assistant: Of course.

Sophie: I'm sorry. How do you use the USB drive?

Shop assistant: Do you have a laptop?

Sophie: Yes. Here you are.

Shop assistant: Look.

Sophie: Thank you!

Let's go home and start work!

I have a lot of work! I can save my work on my new USB drive.

And I have a lot of emails to read! My computer can download emails but it can't read emails!

Part 3. Remember

What can this app do?

What can this app do?

What can this app do?

What can the computer do?

9.26

1	websites	2	blog	3	webinars
4	online	5	USB drive	6	people
7	adults	8	children		

UNIT 10

10.8

Presenter: Welcome to student radio. We study a lot, but we also need some free time. What do you like doing in your free time?

10.9

Presenter: Welcome to student radio. We study a lot, but we also need some free time. What do you like doing in your free time?

Marta – History student

Marta: I like chatting to my friends online. I also like taking photographs and drawing. I don't like baking or cooking. And I don't like waiting for people!

Bilal – Chemistry student

Bilal: I don't like talking on the phone or chatting online. I like sleeping and watching TV. I also like travelling to different countries and learning new languages. I like going to restaurants, but I don't like going shopping!

10.16

1	shirt	2	clothes	3	scarf
4	dress	5	trousers	6	jacket

10.29

Rafet: Hi Murat. Thank you for your help with this survey. So, what do you like doing in your free time?

Murat: In my free time, I like walking in the park. I also like going to restaurants and eating good food. But I don't like cooking.

Rafet: And what do you like wearing at home?

Murat: At home, I like wearing jeans and a T-shirt.

Rafet: What do you wear to university?

Murat: At university, I wear black trousers, black shoes and a white shirt. I also like wearing my grandfather's brown jacket. It's very old, but it's beautiful.

Rafet: What is your favourite colour?

Murat: It's green. It's also my father's favourite colour.

Unit 10 Free time and fashion
Part 1. What do you like doing in your free time?

Chris: I like cooking interesting food with my son, Robert. We don't bake cakes. Cakes are difficult! We bake biscuits. Biscuits are easy! We go online with the tablet to look at different things to make. Then we walk to the shop to buy the food. We like going for a walk. We buy milk and eggs.

Let's start. We use the tablet. Here are the eggs. Here's the milk. I like talking and baking with my son. Here are the biscuits!

Narrator: Hi Rashid.

Rashid: Hi. This is my wife Talihah and my son Omar.

Narrator: What do you like doing in your free time?

Rashid: We have a picnic. We like eating fruit and drinking tea. We walk, and we talk and we take photographs of the family. Omar plays in the park.

Part 2. Do you like buying new clothes?

Narrator: Hello Peter. Do you like buying new clothes?

Peter: Yes, I do. I like wearing nice clothes at work.

Narrator: What do you wear at work?

Peter: I wear nice shirts. My favourite colours are blue and white. And I wear a nice tie. I like blue ties and red ties.

Narrator: Do you wear a jacket?

Peter: Yes, I usually wear a jacket at work. I like black or blue jackets.

Narrator: What shoes do you like?

Peter: I always wear black shoes.

Narrator: Do you wear T-shirts?

Peter: No, I never wear T-shirts.

Narrator: You look very nice with your white shirt, your blue tie and your blue jacket.

Peter: Thank you!

Part 3. Remember

What do Chris and Robert buy?

What do Rashid, Talihah and Omar eat and drink in the park?

What does Peter wear?

10.32

1 drawing **2** baking **3** cooking
4 reading **5** fashion **6** clothes
7 learning **8** free time

ACKNOWLEDGEMENTS

Author acknowledgements

First of all, I would like to thank Fran Disken for inviting me to write for *Unlock* in 2010. Million thanks goes to the amazing editors of this book: Claire Croal, Angela Page, Jenny Farmer and Monika Schmitt. The biggest thank you goes to my husband, Robert Ryan, for his endless support and encouragement.

Publisher acknowledgments

The publishers are extremely grateful to the following people for reviewing this course during its development. The course had benefited hugely from your insightful comments and feedback.

Ashwaq Al-Jahlan, Princess Noura University, Saudi Arabia; Peggy Alptekin; Dr. Wafa Aws, Dar Al Uloom, Saudi Arabia; Anil Bayir, Izmir University, Turkey; Patrick Boylan, King Abdulaziz University, Saudi Arabia; Pauline Chahine, Qatar Armed Forces, Qatar; Esengul Hademir, Atilim University, Turkey; Dr Anwar Jamal, Kuwait University, Kuwait; Megan Putney, Dhofar University, Oman; Tracy Quayat, Princess Noura Univeristy, Saudi Arabia; Katherine Rick, Lincoln College, Saudi Arabia; Hussein Saeed, Jubail Industrial College, Saudi Arabia

TCR): Gisela Matta/Image Bank Film: Signature/Getty Images; p. 46 (TCL): HeroImagesFootage/Creatas Video/Getty Images; p. 46 (TR): The Lighthouse Film Co, Inc./The Lighthouse Film Company/Getty Images; p. 46 (photo a): absolut_100/iStock/Getty Images Plus/Getty Images; p. 46 (photo b): Vladimir Godnik/Getty Images; p. 46 (photo c): SolStock/E+/Getty Images; p. 47 (photo a): Coast-to-Coast/iStock Editorial/Getty Images Plus/Getty Images; p. 47 (photo b): Neil Godwin/T3 Magazine/Future/Getty Images; p. 47 (photo c): Daniel Hurst Photography/Photographer's Choice/Getty Images; p. 49 (T): Jutta Klee/Canopy/Getty Images; p. 49 (BC): Elena Eliachevitch/Moment/Getty Images; p. 49 (B): DreamPictures/Vanessa Gavalya/Blend Images/Getty Images; p. 50 (BG): Klaus Vedfelt/DigitalVision/Getty Images; p. 50 (gradutes): Barry Austin PhotographyIconica/Getty Images; p. 52 (sibling): meaghanbrowning/RooM/Getty Images; p. 52 (friends): Morsa Images/DigitalVision/Getty Images; p. 52 (Yolanda): Ghislain & Marie David de Lossy/Cultura/Getty Images; p. 52 (Asma, Khadijah): Svetlana Zibnitskaya/ArabianEye/Getty Images; p. 52 (Melis): Peathegee Inc/Blend Images/Getty Images; p. 52 (Sou), p. 174 (TL), p. 186 (sleep): Indeed/Getty Images; p. 52 (Minato): ULTRA.F/DigitalVision/Getty Images; pp. 56–57: Thomas Imo/Photothek/Getty Images; p. 58 (Maths), p. 59 (Maths): Jeffrey Coolidge/The Image Bank/Getty Images; p. 58 (Chemistry), p. 59 (Chemistry): Halfdark/Getty Images; p. 58 (Biology), p. 59 (Biology): Philip Dowell/Dorling Kindersley/Getty Images; p. 58 (History), p. 59 (History): Alfredo Maiquez/Lonely Planet Images/Getty Images; p. 58 (IT), p. 59 (IT): Chris Parsons/Stone/Getty Images; p. 58 (Business), p. 59 (Business): GeorgiMironi/iStock/Getty Images Plus/Getty Images; p. 58 (Japanese), p. 59 (Japanese): lantapix/iStock/Getty Images Plus/Getty Images; p. 58 (Nur): RoBeDeRo/E+/Getty Images; p. 58 (Yasemin): Pavliha/iStock/Getty Images Plus/Getty Images; p. 58 (Paul), p. 83 (photo d), p. 96 (friends), p. 203 (R): Sam Edwards/Caiaimage/Getty Images; p. 58 (Marco): DRB Images, LLC/iStock/Getty Images Plus/Getty Images; p. 62 (boring): OnTheWind/iStock/Getty Images Plus/Getty Images; p. 62 (interesting): PeopleImages/DigitalVision/Getty Images; p. 62 (easy): Andrzej Tokarski/iStock/Getty Images Plus/Getty Images; p. 62 (difficult): Maxiphoto/E+/Getty Images; p. 62 (B), p. 115 (T): Ababsolutum/E+/Getty images; p. 62 (CR), p. 168 (CL): Tom Merton/Caiaimage/Getty Images; p. 64 (TL): typhoonski/Creatas Video+/Getty Images Plus/Getty Images; p. 64 (TCL): abdul7amid/Creatas Video/Getty Images; p. 64 (TCR): eastlight/Vetta/Getty Images; p. 64 (TR): Frank Perl/Image Bank Film: Signature/Getty Images; p. 64 (photo a): Flashpop/Iconica/Getty Images; p. 64 (photo b): welcomia/iStock/Getty Images Plus/Getty Images; p. 64 (photo c): GentleAssassin/iStock/Getty Images Plus/Getty Images; p. 65: Tatabrada/iStock/Getty Images Plus/Getty Images; p. 67: Cultura RM Exclusive/Clarissa Leahy/Cultura Exclusive/Getty Images; p. 68, p. 69, p. 130 (Steve), p. 174 (TC): Hill Street Studios/Blend Images/Getty Images; p. 70 (TL): SISKA GREMMELPREZ/Stringer/AFP/Getty Images; p. 70 (TC): Frikota/iStock/Getty Images Plus/Getty Images; p. 70 (TR): GUSTOIMAGES/IIT BOMBAY/SPL/Science Photo Library/Getty Images; p. 71: Arabian Eye FZ LLC/ArabianEye/Getty Images; pp. 74–75: Torsakarin/iStock/Getty Images Plus/Getty Images; p. 76 (hot), p. 77 (parasol): Mario Ramadan/EyeEm/Getty Images; p. 76 (warm), p. 77 (cloud): SilviaMilanova/RooM/Getty Images; p. 76 (cold): Winslow Productions/Getty Images; p. 76 (wet), p. 77 (rainy): Martin Barraud/Caiaimage/Getty Images; p. 76 (dry), p. 77 (dry): Ron Nickel/Perspectives/Getty Images; p. 76 (Canada): Javier Encinas/Moment/Getty Images; p. 76 (Singapore): photography by spintheday/Moment Open/Getty Images; p. 78 (photo a, soup): imagenavi/Getty Images; p. 78 (photo b): mshch/iStock/Getty Images Plus/Getty Images; p. 78 (photo c): Stephen Studd/Photographer's Choice/Getty Images; p. 78 (photo d): Alex Robinson/AWL Images Ltd/AWL Images/Getty Images; p. 78 (photo e): Jeff Vinnick/NHLI/Getty Images; p. 78 (CL): Patrick Foto/Moment/Getty Images; p. 78 (photo 2.1): beyhanyazar/iStock/Getty Images Plus/Getty Images; p. 78 (photo 2.2): AGF/Universal Images Group/Getty Images; p. 78 (photo 2.3): AdShooter/E+/Getty Images; p. 78 (photo 2.4), p. 79 (curry): MIB Pictures/UpperCut Images/Getty Images; p. 79 (Big Ben): joe daniel price/Moment/Getty Images; p. 79 (students): Pavliha/E+/Getty Images; p. 79 (football player): NurPhoto/Getty Images; p. 79 (Shard), p. 206 (Shard): Richard Newstead/Moment/Getty Images; p. 79 (Manhattan), p. 206 (Manhattan): Ninoslav Vrana/Photographer's Choice/Getty Images; p. 80 (new): Nadine Rupp/Getty Images News/Getty Images; p. 80 (old): Ruy Barbosa Pinto/Moment/Getty Images; p. 80 (expensive): gerenme/E+/Getty Images; p. 80 (cheap), p. 112 (man eating): Image Source/Getty Images; p. 80 (beautiful): Richard Cummins/Lonely Planet Images/Getty Images; p. 80 (clean), p. 186 (wait): PeopleImages.com/DigitalVision/Getty Images; p. 80 (Doha): Ian Cumming/Perspectives/Getty Images; p. 80 (Seoul): Baron Reznik (www.reznik.net)/Moment Open/Getty Images; p. 80 (Landon): NurPhoto/NurPhoto/Getty Images; p. 81 (TL), p. 89: Iain Masterton/arabianEye/Getty Images; p. 81 (CL): Clara Rose/First Light/Getty Images; p. 81 (BL): Tuul and Bruno Morandi/The Image Bank/Getty Images; p. 82 (TL): Gavin Hellier/Image Bank Film/Getty Images; p. 82 (TCL): Gallo Images/AVANTGARDE GESELLSCHAFT FUR KOMMUNIKATION MBH/Image Bank Film/Getty Images; p. 82 (TCR): Roy JAMES Shakespeare/Photodisc/Getty Images; p. 82 (TR), p. 136 (TCR): Multi-bits/Image Bank Film/Getty Images; p. 82 (photo b): Walter Bibikow/Photolibrary/Getty Images; p. 82 (photo c): Simon Carter/Photolibrary/Getty Images; p. 82 (photo d): Stanislav Krasilnikov/TASS/Getty Images; p. 83 (photo a): MarianVejcik/iStock/Getty Images Plus/Getty Images; p. 83 (photo b): Nirian/iStock/Getty Images Plus/Getty Images; p. 83 (photo c): bjdlzx/iStock/Getty Images Plus/Getty Images; p. 84 (TL): J Carrier/Getty Images News/Getty Images; p. 84 (TC): Darrell Gulin/DigitalVision/Getty Images; p. 84 (TR): Marla Rutherford/The Image Bank/Getty Images; p. 84 (C): David De Lossy/DigitalVision/Getty Images; p. 84 (B): Eric Lafforgue/ArabianEye/Getty Images; p. 85 (New Delhi): Panoramic Images/Getty Images; p. 85 (food): Eriko Koga/The Image Bank/Getty Images; p. 85 (srabanti): Kelvin Murray/Taxi/Getty images; p. 85 (Kerala): DEA/V. DEGRANDI/De Agostini/Getty Images; p. 85 (sari): Kunal_Sarkar/iStock/Getty Images Plus/Getty Images; p. 85 (Sashem): Neleman/WIN-Initiative/Getty Images; p. 86: Hiroshi Higuchi/Photographer's Choice/Getty Images; p. 88 (TL): Shina Teo/EyeEm/Getty Images; p. 88 (TR): Garry Black/All Canada Photos/Getty Images; pp. 92–93: Menno Boermans/Getty Images; p. 94 (policeman): ullstein bild/ullstein bild/Getty Images; p. 94 (photographer): UpperCut Images/UpperCut Images/Getty Images; p. 94 (dentist): Echo/Cultura/Getty Images; p. 94 (manager): Jose Luis Pelaez/Iconica/Getty Images; p. 96 (work): Jon Feingersh Photography Inc/Blend Images/Getty Images Plus/Getty Images; p. 96 (university): Tomas Rodriguez/Corbis/Getty Images; p. 96 (library): thelinke/iStock/Getty Images Plus/Getty Images; p. 96 (home): Creatas/Getty Images Plus/Getty Images; p. 96 (work start): JAG IMAGES/DigitalVision/Getty Images; p. 96 (work finish): GeorgeRudy/iStock/Getty Images Plus/Getty Images; p. 96 (girl): Jupiterimages/Photolibrary/Getty Images; p. 97 (TL): Peter Dazeley/Iconica/Getty Images; p. 98 (photographs): Lane Oatey/Blue Jean Images/Collection Mix: Subjects/Getty Images; p. 98 (tablet): Kritchanut/iStock/Getty Images Plus/Getty Images; p. 98 (laptop): Muthardman/iStock/Getty Images Plus/Getty Images; p. 98 (help people): DragonImages/iStock/Getty Images Plus/Getty Images; p. 98 (meet people): Robert Daly/OJO Images/Getty Images; p. 98 (businessman): Geri Lavrov/Photographer's Choice/Getty Images; p. 98 (photo 3.1): Jon Feingersh/Blend Images/Getty Images Plus/Getty Images; p. 98 (photo 3.2): ramzihachicho/iStock/Getty Images Plus/Getty Images; p. 98 (photo 3.3): sozaijiten/Datacraft/Getty Images; p. 99 (T): Reza Estakhrian/Stone/Getty Images; p. 99 (BL): Adam Crowley/Blend Images/Getty Images; p. 99 (BR): Xavierarnau/iStock/Getty Images Plus/Getty Images; p. 100 (TL): cautionfilm/Creatas Video/Getty Images; p. 100 (TCL): Ascent Xmedia/one80: Signature/Getty Images; p. 100 (TCR), p. 154 (TCR), p. 172 (TL, TCL): Sky News/Film Image Partner/Sky News/Getty Images; p. 100 (TR): Discovery FootageSource/Getty Images; p. 100 (photo a, photo c): Tetra Images/Getty Images; p. 100 (photo b): Terry Vine/Blend Images/Getty Images; p. 100 (photo d): Rob Brimson/Taxi/Getty Images; p. 101 (TL), p. 168 (BR): Bloomberg/Getty Images; p. 101 (TC): JW LTD/Stone/Getty images; p. 101 (TR): David Levingstone/The Image Bank/Getty Images; p. 101 (BL): wrangel/iStock Editorial/Getty Images Plus/Getty Images; p. 101 (BC): Karan Kapoor/The Image Bank/Getty Images; p. 102 (photo b): Maria Wachala/Moment Open/Getty Images; p. 102 (photo c): Ken Gillespie/Design Pics/First Light/Getty Images; p. 102 (photo d): Jon Boyes/Canopy/Getty Images; p. 104 (pilot): Blend Images - Dan Bannister/Brand X Pictures/Getty Images; p. 105 (teacher): erkan523/iStock/Getty Images Plus/Getty Images; p. 105 (photographer): Dave Fleetham/Perspectives/Getty Images; p. 105 (pilot): Siri Stafford/The Image Bank/Getty Images; p. 106 (photo a): crispyicon/DigitalVision Vectors/Getty Images; p. 106 (photo b): Dacian_G/iStock/Getty Images Plus/Getty Images; p. 106 (computers): Yellow Dog Productions/DigitalVision/Getty Images; p. 107: triloks/E+/Getty Images; pp. 110–111: Loop Images/Martin Berry/Passage/Getty Images; p. 112 (drink): Hill Creek Pictures/UpperCut Images/Getty Images; p. 112 (espresso): Adrian Burke/Photodisc/Getty Images; p. 112 (black tea): hayatikayhan/iStock/Getty Images Plus/Getty Images; p. 112 (water): George Coppock/Photolibrary/Getty Images; p. 112 (juice), p. 116 (tea): Andrew Unangst/Photographer's Choice/Getty Images; p. 112 (bread loaf): Laszlo Balogh/EyeEm/Getty Images; p. 112 (cheese slice): yevgenromanenko/iStock/Getty Images Plus/Getty Images; p. 112 (rice), p. 113: Alex Ortega/EyeEm/Getty Images; p. 112 (fish): Veronica Garbutt/Lonely Planet Images/Getty Images; p. 112 (vegetables): Will Heap/Dorling Kindersley/Getty Images; p. 112 (meat): John Shipes/StockFood Creative/Getty Images; p. 112 (Naomi): Cultura RM Exclusive/Luc Beziat/Cultura Exclusive/Getty Images; p. 112 (Vinood): Steve Debenport/E+/Getty Images; p. 112 (cooked bream): Laurence Mouton/Canopy/Getty Images; p. 112 (bread): Lew Robertson/Photolibrary/Getty Images; p. 112 (capsicum): Iryna Rieber/EyeEm/Getty Images; p. 112 (tea): Deepak Swarna/EyeEm/Getty Images; p. 112 (cheese): BOULAY Jacques/hemis.fr/hemis.fr/Getty Images; p. 112 (steak): The Picture Pantry/Alloy/Getty Images; p. 112 (coffee): Fabian Krause/EyeEm/Getty Images; p. 114 (get up): Blasius Erlinger/Stone/Getty Images; p. 114 (go to bed): AndreyPopov/iStock/Getty Images Plus/Getty Images; p. 114 (breakfast): Wavebreakmedia Ltd/Wavebreak Media/Getty Images Plus/Getty Images; p. 114 (lunch): Alistair Berg/DigitalVision/Getty Images; p. 114 (dinner): Klaus Vedfelt/Taxi/Getty Images; p. 114 (drive): PhotoAlto/Odilon Dimier/PhotoAlto Agency RF Collections/Getty Images; p. 114 (walk): Livia Corona/The Image Bank/Getty Images; p. 114 (friends): Ann Hermes/The Christian Science Monitor/Getty Images; p. 115 (B):

Stewart Sutton/Iconica/Getty Images; p. 116 (get up): Lambert/Archive Photos/Getty Images; p. 116 (go to bed): PhotoAlto/Antoine Arraou/Brand X Pictures/Getty Images; p. 116 (green tea): Nick Purser/Ikon Images/Getty Images; p. 116 (fruits): boschettophotography/E+/Getty Images; p. 116 (meat): Jacky Lam/EyeEm/Getty Images; p. 116 (coffee): daneger/E+/Getty Images; p. 116 (dish), p. 119 (noodles): DigiPub/Moment/Getty Images; p. 117: Gallo Images-David Malan/DigitalVision/Getty Images; p. 118 (TL): zgr_pro/Creatas Video+/Getty Images Plus/Getty Images; p. 118 (TCL): Gary John Norman/Image Bank Film: Signature/Getty Images; p. 118 (TCR): Richard Wiese/Image Bank Film/Getty Images; p. 118 (TR): ER Productions Ltd/Iconica Video: Signature/Getty Images; p. 118 (photo a): tashka2000/iStock/Getty Images Plus/Getty Images; p. 118 (photo b): Leland Bobbe/Image Source/Getty Images; p. 118 (photo c): Scott R Barbour/The Image Bank/Getty Images; p. 119 (photo a): skodonnell/iStock/Getty Images Plus/Getty Images; p. 119 (photo b): kemie/E+/Getty Images; p. 119 (photo c): encrier/iStock/Getty Images Plus/Getty Images; p. 119 (olives): Image Source/DigitalVision/Getty Images; p. 119 (dates): bhofack2/iStock/Getty Images Plus/Getty Images; p. 120 (healthy): Mark Webster/Cultura/Getty Images; p. 120 (tired): DRB Images, LLC/E+/Getty Images; p. 120 (hungry): Anthony Bradshaw/Photographer's Choice/Getty Images; p. 120 (great): franckreporter/E+/Getty Images; p. 120 (busy): Steve Cole/The Image Bank/Getty Images; p. 120 (unwell): Chris Ryan/OJO Images/Getty Images; p. 120 (photo 2.1): elenaleonova/E+/Getty Images; p. 120 (photo 2.2): Eric Audras/PhotoAlto Agency RF Collections/Getty Images; p. 120 (photo 2.3): Ben Pipe Photography/Cultura/Getty Images; p. 120 (photo 2.4): Eric Chuang/Photolibrary/Getty Images; p. 120 (photo 2.6): Yuri_Arcurs/E+/Getty Images; p. 121 (TL): Antonio_Diaz/iStock/Getty Images Plus/Getty Images; p. 121 (TR): 0kzenon/iStock/Getty Images Plus/Getty Imgaes; p. 121 (CL): Creatas Images/Creatas/Getty Images Plus/Getty Images; p. 121 (CR): Kentaroo Tryman/Maskot/Getty Images; p. 122 (photo a): aluxum/E+/Getty Images; p. 122 (photo b): Peter Hince/Photographer's Choice/Getty Images; p. 122 (photo c): Junos/Getty Images; p. 122 (CR): Richard Ellgen/iStock/Getty Images Plus/Getty Images; p. 124 (fruits): Nicolas Balcazar/EyeEm/Getty Images; p. 124 (fries): Holger Leue/Lonely Planet Images/Getty Images; p. 124 (breakfast): Topic Images Inc./Getty Images; p. 124 (muffin): Robert Simon/iStock/Getty Images Plus/Getty Images; pp. 128–129: Saadetalkan/iStock/Getty Images Plus/Getty Images; p. 130 (hospital), p. 131 (hospital): Marje Cannon/E+/Getty Images; p. 130 (beach), p. 131 (beach): Stéphanie Weber/EyeEm/Getty Images; p. 130 (station), p. 131 (station): Buena Vista Images/The Image Bank/Getty Images; p. 130 (mall), p. 131 (mall): Oktay Ortakcioglu/E+/Getty Images; p. 130 (park), p. 131 (park): Carol Polich Photo Workshops/Lonely Planet Images/Getty Images; p. 130 (airport), p. 131 (airport): Ugurhan Betin/E+/Getty Images; p. 130 (building), p. 131 (building): Howard Kingsnorth/Stone/Getty Images; p. 130 (Tokyo): Hiroshi Higuchi/Photolibrary/Getty Images; p. 130 (Jeddah): KARIM SAHIB/AFP/Getty Images; p. 130 (New York): Benjamin Howell/E+/Getty Images; p. 130 (Asma): Katarina Premfors/arabianEye/Getty Imgaes; p. 132 (restaurant): Mint Images/Mint Images RF/Getty Images; p. 132 (factory): ideeone/E+/Getty Images; p. 132 (hotel): FrancescoCorticchia/iStock/Getty Images Plus/Getty Images; p. 132 (shop): baona/iStock/Getty Images Plus/Getty Images; p. 132 (house): Roy Mehta/DigitalVision/Getty Images; p. 132 (wheel): Mieneke Andeweg-van Rijn/Moment/Getty Images; p. 132 (racecourse): Dan Istitene/Getty Images Sport/Getty Images; p. 132 (beach 1): John Harper/Moment/Getty Images; p. 132 (beach 2): Olaf Protze/LightRocket/Getty Images; p. 132 (beach 3): Marka/Universal Images Group/Getty Images; p. 132 (university 1): Kokkai Ng/Moment/Getty Images; p. 132 (university 2): Chris Hepburn/The Image Bank/Getty Images; p. 132 (university 3): Choul Jib Lee/Moment/Getty Images; p. 134 (street): adam smigielski/iStock/Getty Images Plus/Getty Images; p. 134 (market): Gavin Hellier/AWL Images/Getty Images; p. 134 (square): Image by Stefan Reiß/Moment/Getty Images; p. 134 (stadium): John Peters/Manchester United/Getty Images; p. 134 (building): Allan Baxter/Photolibrary/Getty Images; p. 134 (Ali): Peter Muller/Cultura/Getty Images; p. 134 (photo a): Douglas Pearson/The Image Bank/Getty Images; p. 134 (photo c): shomos uddin/Moment Open/Getty Images; p. 134 (Carmen): Alix Minde/PhotoAlto Agency RF Collections/Getty Images; p. 134 (photo d): marchello74/iStock/Getty Images Plus/Getty Images; p. 134 (photo e): Christophe Launay/Aurora/Getty Images; p. 134 (photo f): Roger de la Harpe/Gallo Images/Getty Images; p. 135 (Rome): James Emmerson/robertharding/Getty Images; p. 135 (street): Starcevic/iStock Unreleased/Getty Images; p. 136 (TL), p. 154 (TR), p. 190 (TCL): gmutlu/Creatas Video/Getty Images; p. 136 (TCL): Geoff Tompkinson/Iconica Video/Getty Images; p. 136 (TR): simonkr/Creatas Video/Getty Images; p. 136 (office): Patrick Eckersley/arabianEye/Getty Images; p. 136 (mall): Ali Al Mubarak/arabianEye/Getty Images; p. 136 (lobby): Gary John Norman/Iconica/Getty Images; p. 136 (factory), p. 166 (CR): Monty Rakusen/Cultura/Getty Images; p. 137 (right arrow): Kanoke_46/iStock/Getty Images Plus/Getty Images; p. 137 (left arrow): aitzpurua/iStock/Getty Images Plus/Getty Images; p. 137 (straight arrow): Willy Lamers/EyeEm/Getty Images; p. 137 (photo a): gaspr13/iStock/Getty Images Plus/Getty Images; p. 137 (photo b): Buena Vista Images/Photodisc/Getty Images; p. 137 (photo c): Kenneth Wiedemann/iStock Editorial/Getty Images Plus/Getty Images; p. 139 (T): T.T./Taxi/Getty Images; p. 139 (B): Kathrin Ziegler/Taxi/Getty Images; p. 140 (Advik): elkor/E+/Getty Images; p. 140 (market): Richard I'Anson/Lonely Planet Images/Getty Images; p. 140 (Rachel), p. 148 (B): BJI/Blue Jean Images/Getty Images; p. 140 (Orchard road): Xavier Loh/Moment/Getty Images; p. 142 (T): Craig Auckland/Passage/Getty Images; p. 142 (C): jax10289/iStock/Getty Images Plus; p. 142 (B): Allan Baxter/Photolibrary; pp. 146–147: R. Hackenberg/Corbis Documentary/Getty Images; p. 148 (smartphone): MacFormat Magazine/Future/Getty Images; p. 148 (game): pagadesign/iStock/Getty Images Plus/Getty Images; p. 148 (newspaper): Steve Gorton/Dorling Kindersley/Getty Images; p. 148 (laptop): zentilia/iStock/Getty Images Plus/Getty Images; p. 148 (watch): Dorling Kindersley/Getty Images; p. 148 (t-shirt), p. 192 (t-shirt): Gary Alvis/E+/Getty Images; p. 148 (tablet), p. 201 (tablet), p. 204 (tablet): Oleksiy Mark/iStock/Getty Images Plus/Getty Images; p. 149 (watch): t_kimura/E+/Getty Images; p. 149 (smartphone): Tom Smith/EyeEm/Getty Images; p. 149 (t-shirt): DAJ/Getty Images; p. 149 (man): Daniel Grill/Getty Images; p. 149 (laptop): Howard Kingsnorth/The Image Bank/Getty Images; p. 150 (L): Dave and Les Jacobs/Blend Images/Getty Images; p. 151 (camera), p. 201 (camera), p. 204 (camera): studiocasper/E+/Getty Images; p. 151 (laptop), p. 201 (laptop), p. 204 (laptop): PC Gamer Magazine/Future/Getty Images; p. 151 (coffee): Creative Crop/DigitalVision/Getty Images; p. 152 (shopping), p. 176 (BL): Betsie Van Der Meer/Taxi/Getty Images; p. 152 (clothes): Aaron Chong/Canopy/Getty Images; p. 152 (online shopping): AndreyPopov/iStock/Getty Images Plus/Getty Images; p. 152 (money): Joos Mind/The Image Bank/Getty Images; p. 152 (cash): Radius Images/Getty Images Plus/Getty Images; p. 152 (card): ViewStock/Getty Images; p. 152 (two men): Robert E Daemmrich/The Image Bank/Getty Images; p. 154 (TL): halbergman/Creatas Video/Getty Images; p. 154 (TCL): Mark Andersen/Photolibrary Video/Getty Images; p. 154 (photo a), p. 156 (USD): ©US Mint; p. 154 (photo b), p. 156 (AED): ©Central Bank of U.A.E.; p. 154 (photo c), p. 156 (EUR): © p. 154 (photo d), p. 156 (GBP): ©The Royal Mint; p. 155 (photo 5.a): Justin Sullivan/Getty Images News/Getty Images; p. 155 (photo 5.b): Nick David/Taxi/Getty Images; p. 155 (photo 5.c): Chesnot/Getty Images Entertainment/Getty Images; p. 155 (photo 5.d): Jacques LOIC/Photononstop/Getty Images; p. 155 (photo 9.a): Jon Boyes/Photographer's Choice RF/Getty Images; p. 155 (photo 9.b): milanfoto/E+/Getty Images; p. 155 (photo 9.c): Foodcollection RF/Getty Images; p. 156 (EUR): ©European Central Bank; p. 156 (SAR): ©BanknoteWorld.com; p. 156 (TRY): ©Central Bank of the Republic of Turkey; p. 157 (smartphone): Andrew Burton/Getty Images News/Getty Images; p. 157 (car): Sjo/iStock Unreleased/Getty Images; p. 157 (bag): Krisztian Bocsi/Bloomberg/Getty Images; p. 157 (television): 97/E+/Getty Images; p. 157 (house): PM Images/Getty Images; p. 158: JackF/iStock/Getty Images Plus/Getty images; pp. 164–165: Pictorial Parade/Archive Photos/Getty Images; p. 166 (TL): scyther5/iStock/Getty Images Plus/Getty Images; p. 166 (TC): Daniel Grizelj/Stone/Getty Images; p. 166 (TR): Henrik5000/E+/Getty Images; p. 166 (C): Brian Jackson/iStock/Getty Images Plus/Getty Images; p. 168 (TL), p. 174 (smartwatch), p. 184 (talking): Yuri_Arcurs/DigitalVision/Getty Images; p. 168 (TC): Ljupco/iStock/Getty Images Plus/Getty Images; p. 168 (C): KeremYucel/iStock/Getty Images Plus/Getty Images; p. 168 (CR): kizilkayaphotos/iStock/Getty Images Plus/Getty Images; p. 168 (BL): T3 Magazine/Future/Getty Images; p. 169: Images By Tang Ming Tung/DigitalVision/Getty Images; p. 170 (person): MrsWilkins/iStock/Getty Images Plus/Getty Images; p. 170 (people): Chris Ratcliffe/Getty Images News/Getty Images; p. 170 (man): petekarici/iStock/Getty Images Plus/Getty Images; p. 170 (men): georgeclerk/E+/Getty Images; p. 170 (woman): Nigel Pavitt/AWL Images/Getty Images; p. 170 (child): baobao ou/Moment/Getty Images; p. 170 (children): xPACIFICA/Iconica/Getty Images; p. 170 (girl): Thomas Fricke/Perspectives/Getty Images; p. 170 (boy): Andrew Rich/E+/Getty Images; p. 171: Yongyuan Dai/E+/Getty Images; p. 172 (TCR): uzhursky/Creatas Video+/Getty Images Plus/Getty Images; p. 172 (TR): gong hangxu/Creatas Video/Getty Images; p. 172 (photo a): hocus-focus/E+/Getty Images; p. 172 (photo b): Ridofranz/iStock/Getty Images Plus/Getty Images; p. 172 (photo c), p. 173 (GPS): Bet_Noire/iStock/Getty Images Plus/Getty Images; p. 173 (router): farakos/iStock/Getty Images Plus/Getty Images; p. 173 (call): Kathleen Finlay/Cultura/Getty Images; p. 173 (download): spxChrome/E+/Getty Images; p. 173 (save): ArtemSam/iStock/Getty Images Plus/Getty Images; p. 174 (CL): JGI/Jamie Grill/Blend Images/Getty Images; p. 174 (CR): Frank Egel/STOCK4B/Getty Images; p. 174 (smart glasses): ANDRZEJ WOJCICKI/Science Photo Library/Getty Images; p. 174 (TR): Yasin Emir Akbas/iStock/Getty Images Plus/Getty Images; p. 176 (T): cigdemhizal/iStock/Getty Images Plus/Getty Images; p. 176 (BR): Phillip Suddick/Taxi/Getty Images; p. 178: Tim Robberts/Taxi/Getty Images; p. 179: Jade/Blend Images/Getty Images; p. 184 (walk): xavierarnau/E+/Getty Images; p. 184 (cakes): Opus/Getty Images; p. 184 (picnic): dolgachov/iStock/Getty Images Plus/Getty Images; p. 184 (exercise): Oliver Rossi/The Image Bank/Getty Images; p. 184 (park): FredFroese/iStock/Getty Images Plus/Getty Images; p. 184 (visit): Ariel Skelley/Photographer's Choice/Getty

Images; p. 185 (L): Ezra Bailey/Iconica/Getty Images; p. 186 (online): Sally Anscombe/Moment/Getty Images; p. 186 (BR): Catherine Yeulet/iStock/Getty Images Plus/Getty Images; p. 188 (coat): Don Nichols/E+/Getty Images; p. 188 (jacket): skodonnell/E+/Getty Images; p. 188 (dress): iprachenko/iStock/Getty Images Plus/Getty Images; p. 188 (shirt): clu/E+/Getty Images; p. 188 (scarf): onurerdemphotography/iStock/Getty Images Plus/Getty Images; p. 188 (hat): GoodLifeStudio/iStock/Getty Images Plus/Getty Images; p. 188 (trousers): bonetta/iStock/Getty Images Plus/Getty Images; p. 188 (photo a): Plume Creative/DigitalVision/Getty Images; p. 188 (photo b): Topic Images/Getty Images; p. 188 (photo c): ML Harris/The Image Bank/Getty Images; p. 188 (sari), p. 189: Greg Elms/Lonely Planet Images/Getty Images; p. 190 (TL): ReeldealHD Ltd./Verve+/Getty Images; p. 190 (TCR, TR): Ilya2k/Creatas Video+/Getty Images Plus/Getty Images; p. 190 (photo a): MattJeacock/Stockbyte/Getty Images; p. 190 (photo c): Tim Graham/Getty Images News/Getty Images; p. 191 (shirt): pepifoto/iStock/Getty Images Plus/Getty Images; p. 191 (jacket): the-lightwriter/iStock/Getty Images Plus/Getty Images; p. 191 (shoe): Vincenzo Lombardo/Photographer's Choice RF/Getty Images; p. 191 (t-shirt): FlamingPumpkin/E+/Getty Images; p. 191 (tie): Photoevent/E+/Getty Images; p. 191 (egg): germi_p/iStock/Getty Images Plus; p. 191 (cookie): Bruno Crescia Photography Inc/First Light/Getty Images; p. 192 (white dress): Grape_vein/iStock/Getty Images Plus/Getty Images; p. 192 (trousers): praethip/iStock/Getty Images Plus/Getty Images; p. 192 (hat): Stefano Oppo/Stockbyte/Getty Images; p. 192 (sneakers): BeylaBalla/iStock/Getty Images Plus/Getty Images; p. 192 (shoes): Sorapop/iStock/Getty Images Plus/Getty Images; p. 192 (blue dress), p. 193 (blue dress): lypnyk2/iStock/Getty Images Plus/Getty Images; p. 192 (boots), p. 193 (boots): c-photo/iStock/Getty Images Plus/Getty Images; p. 192 (jacket), p. 193 (jacket): gopfaster/iStock/Getty Images Plus/Getty Images; p. 193 (sister): Thomas Barwick/Iconica/Getty Images; p. 193 (brother): Mike Harrington/Stone/Getty Images; p. 193 (Lara): Riitta Supperi/Folio Images/Folio Images/Getty Images; p. 193 (BL): Jay Blakesberg/UpperCut Images/Getty Images; p. 193 (BR): Alistair Berg/Iconica/Getty Images; p. 194: Dave and Les Jacobs/Kolostock/Blend Images/Getty Images; p. 196: Valery Matytsin/TASS/Getty Images; p. 200 (L): Richard Desmarais/Design Pics/Perspectives/Getty Images; p. 200 (R): David Sacks/Stone/Getty Images; p. 201 (house), p. 204 (house): L Alfonse/Photolibrary/Getty Images; p. 201 (car), p. 204 (car): Vladimiroquai/iStock/Getty Images Plus/Getty Images; p. 202: adventtr/iStock/Getty Images Plus/Getty Images; p. 203 (L): Alexander Spatari/Moment/Getty Images; p. 206 (Tokyo): Maremagnum/Photolibrary/Getty Images; p. 206 (pilaf): VadimZakirov/iStock/Getty Images Plus/Getty Images; p. 206 (samosas): highviews/iStock/Getty Images Plus/Getty Images; p. 209 (photo a): Valery Moiseev/Hemera/Getty Images Plus/Getty Images; p. 209 (photo b): Inti St Clair/Blend Images/Getty Images; p. 209 (photo c): Hoxton/Tom Merton/Hoxton/Getty Images; p. 209 (women's shoes): adisa/iStock/Getty Images Plus/Getty Images; p. 209 (coat): DonNichols/E+/Getty Images; p. 209 (shirt): gofotograf/iStock/Getty Images Plus/Getty Images; p. 209 (sandals): indigolotos/iStock/Getty Images Plus/Getty Images; p. 209 (scarf): Angela Coppola/Dorling Kindersley/Getty Images; p. 209 (men's shoes): TPopova/iStock/Getty Images Plus/Getty Images; p. 209 (bag): Stramyk/iStock/Getty Images Plus/Getty Images; p. 209 (jacket): Hugh Threlfall/Photolibrary/Getty Images; p. 209 (yeshey): Katie Garrod/AWL Images/Getty Images; p. 209 (andrew): Helen Rushbrook/Moment Open/Getty Images.

Cover Photography by David Kirkland/Perspectives/Getty Images.

Illustrations by Oxford Designers & Illustrators: pp. 12, 17, 18, 42, 66, 131, 132, 138, 143, 201, 204.

Accompanying videos by Getty Images.

Corpus
Development of this publication has made use of the Cambridge English Corpus (CEC). The CEC is a multi-billion word computer database of contemporary spoken and written English. It includes British English, American English, and other varieties of English. It also includes the Cambridge Learner Corpus, developed in collaboration with the University of Cambridge ESOL Examinations. Cambridge University Press has built up the CEC to provide evidence about language use that helps to produce better language teaching materials

Typeset by emc design ltd

EXTRA HANDWRITING NOTES

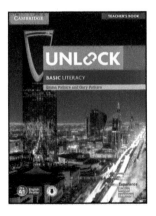

UNLOCK LEVELS 1–4

BUILD ON YOUR STUDENTS' SUCCESS

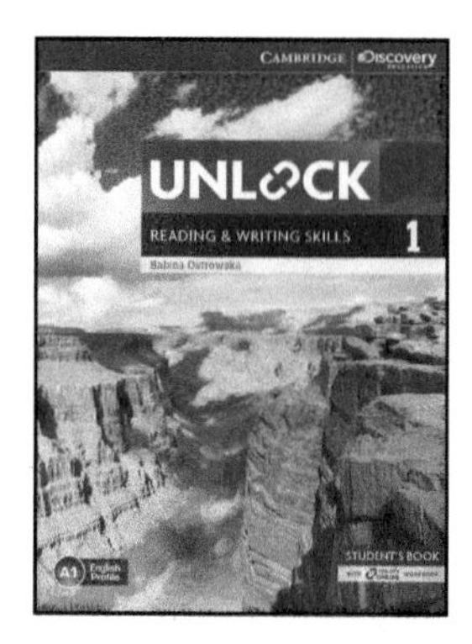

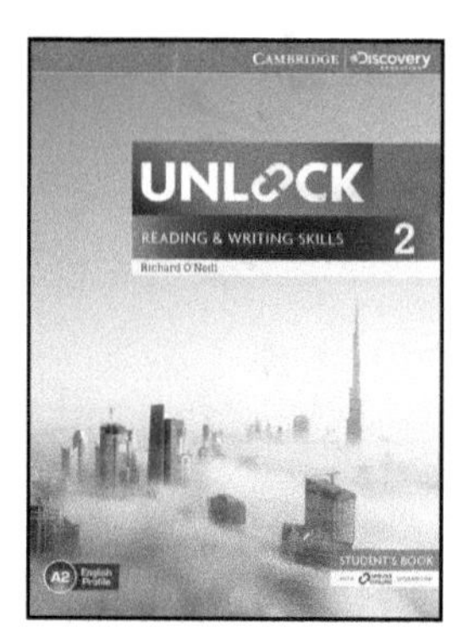

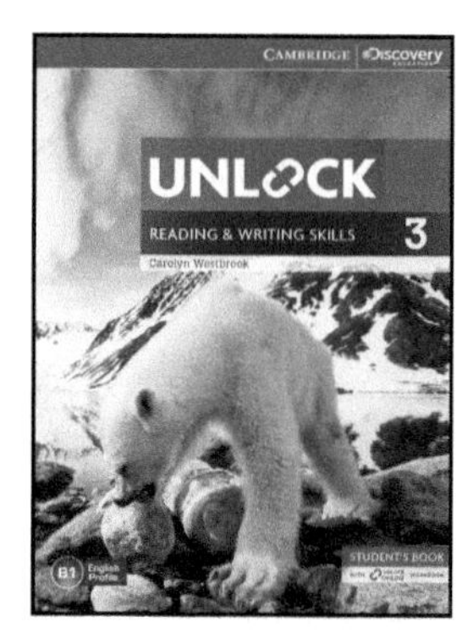

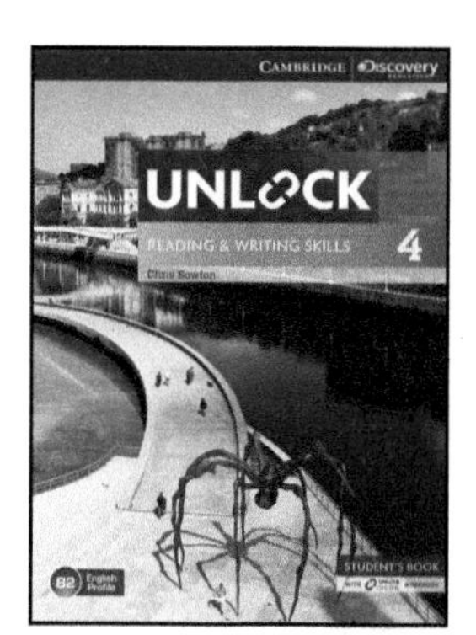

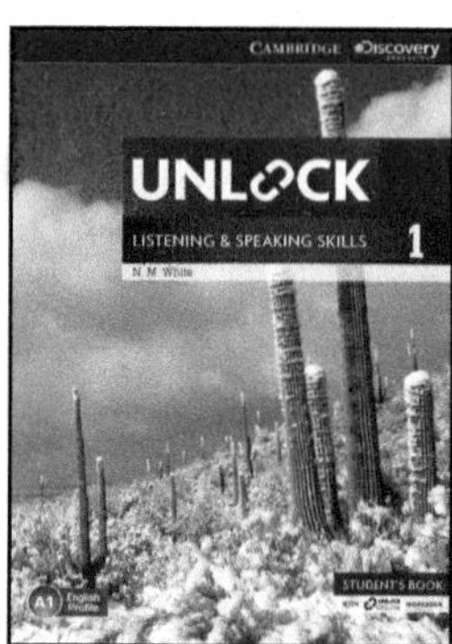

> *Unlock is the best textbook I have ever taught with. It contains a variety of topics that provide students with a wide range of vocabulary. Students are totally involved, which guarantees effective learning. Unlock helps to encourage and empower the students' critical thinking.*
>
> **Salima Al-Hadithi, Institute of Applied Technology, UAE**

Unlock Reading & Writing Skills	**Level 1**	**Level 2**	**Level 3**	**Level 4**
Student's Book with Online Workbook	978-1-107-61399-7	978-1-107-61400-0	978-1-107-61526-7	978-1-107-61525-0
Student's ebook with Online Workbook	978-1-107-65066-4	978-1-107-64409-0	978-1-107-63757-3	978-1-107-67139-3
Teacher's Book with DVD	978-1-107-61401-7	978-1-107-61403-1	978-1-107-61404-8	978-1-107-61409-3
Presentation Plus DVD-ROM	978-1-107-63800-6	978-1-107-65605-5	978-1-107-67624-4	978-1-107-68245-0
Unlock Listening & Speaking Skills	**Level 1**	**Level 2**	**Level 3**	**Level 4**
Student's Book with Online Workbook	978-1-107-67810-1	978-1-107-68232-0	978-1-107-68728-8	978-1-107-63461-9
Student's ebook with Online Workbook	978-1-107-67008-2	978-1-107-63562-3	978-1-107-67610-7	978-1-107-63710-8
Teacher's Book with DVD	978-1-107-66211-7	978-1-107-64280-5	978-1-107-68154-5	978-1-107-65052-7
Presentation Plus DVD-ROM	978-1-107-66424-1	978-1-107-69582-5	978-1-107-63543-2	978-1-107-64381-9